Norten Dablemont with his first bass (1927)

Ridge-Runner

From the Big Piney River, To the Battle of the Bulge

by

Norten Dablemont
As told to Larry Dablemont

**Lightnin'
Ridge Books**

Box 22
Bolivar • MO 65613
417-777-5227

Ridge-Runner

From the Big Piney to the Battle of the Bulge
The life story of the littlest paratrooper

Revised 2nd Edition
Copyright 2000 by Larry Dablemont

Published by
Lightnin' Ridge Publishing

Layout and Design
Dorothy R. Loges

ISBN: 0-9673975-3-7
Library of Congress Control Number: 00-093498

Table of Contents

Introduction...

Norten Dablemont is my uncle and this is his story. I first remember him when I was a small boy and he would come by our place in Southern Missouri on his way back from some lake or river where he had been guiding fishermen. He'd show me the big fish he had caught and give me whatever change he had in his pocket and call me a washout. Because Uncle Norten called me that, I was proud to be one.

When Norten was around, there was excitement and laughter and everyone was enjoying themselves. There was never a dull moment. You never sat around when he was there because he couldn't sit still and still can't. He'd get a softball game going in January. If there weren't enough participants to play softball, it would be a horseshoe pitching contest or a wiffle ball game.

He gave me my first fishing lures when I was just starting to fish the Big Piney and told me someday he would take me fishing with him. My mother said that would happen over her dead body. She good naturedly ran him off everytime he started talking about all the things he could teach me. Mom didn't fear anything more than Uncle Norten. Folks would say how I much I was like him and you could see her shudder.

Eventually, I got to go fishing with my uncle, and got to know him very well. We've spent a lot of years together fishing and hunting and guiding others and my mom still objects! But I never knew anyone who loved the outdoors more, nor have I ever known an outdoorsman as good at what he does.

There is no one anywhere who has spent more time on the rivers of the Ozarks than Norten. He has floated all of them, every mile of each and every one, and most of them over and over and over. He made his first trip as a guide about 1934, and he's still guiding at the time of this revised second printing, at the age of 82. That's about seventy years of guiding fishermen. When I fish a river with him, even today, I never paddle. He insists on doing all that, and enjoys catching more fish from the back of the boat than I can catch from the front.

We spent more than a year, between hunting and fishing trips, sitting in my office putting down these recollections and I've tried to put it down as he related it, or as close as possible. There was enough for two or three books, but I've tried to hit the main spots and cover it all as best as possible. Norten says that in twenty years or so we'll do another one with hunting and fishing stories yet to happen.

I always wished everyone could have had the opportunity to fish with my uncle and get to know him as I have. With this book, you are about to do just that!

Larry Dablemont

Foreward

It was December of 1944. Our trip to Paris for rest and relaxation had been cut short for some reason and we had been hurried to a place known as Bastogne, Belgium. I had never heard of it. Probably just another place to sit and wait, like Holland had been in the few days I had been there. Most of us were green recruits just arriving and now they were sending us somewhere important for some reason. There were more than 11,000 of us... Screamin' Eagles... the 101st Airborne.

The pine woods around us looked something like the woods back home. It was peaceful and quiet, and I thought about the flowing waters of the Big Piney River where I had spent my boyhood, hoping I'd see it again. Home seemed so far away. Somewhere along the banks of that beautiful Ozark river Pop was probably stretching furs and Mom was perhaps scolding my youngest brother for bringing chickens into the house. And there were most likely flocks of mallards peacefully dropping out of the skies into the old Mill Pond Eddy on cupped wings.

And suddenly there was the sound of incoming artillery shells, the first I had ever heard, a horrible sound I would soon hear way too much of. It hit not too far away and the forest began to tear apart as more explosions followed. I heard the screams of wounded and dying men, and officers yelling commands. We dug into the ground as we had never dug before and we were scared to death. None of us knew what was coming.

We were about to confront a massive German offensive in a bloody conflict which came to be known as the Battle of the Bulge, the biggest and costliest battle of World War II. They would soon call us the Battered Bastards of Bastogne.

Norten Dablemont

That's me at the Lone Star Mill with Pop's dog, Jack
and an old ridge-runner 'coon. Furbearers provided a
great percentage of our winter income.

Chapter 1
October of '23

I was born when the Big Piney River was at it's prettiest, during the peak of the fall foliage in October of 1923. Folks said the colors were prime then, the river full and flowing and the air crisp just after a heavy frost. I don't remember a thing about it but I remember everything that has happened since. Maybe not just exactly, but pretty close. I couldn't have picked a better place to have been born...nor a better time. When I was about four years old, Pop took me down to the river and baited a willow pole with a minnow and let me hold it. A bass darn near pulled me in. Pop helped me land it and right then I knew what was important in life and what wasn't.

There's a great deal of history on the Big Piney River which flows through the Ozarks of Southern Missouri. I started out at one of the more historic sites along the river, the old Lone Star Mill about five miles west of Houston, Missouri. That mill was old when I was born but Mom and Pop lived there and my dad was the operator. He never had many jobs because he was too darned cantankerous to work for anyone else very long. Pop had a hard time getting along with himself at times, let alone anyone else. He was an outdoorsman, the best I ever knew, and he taught me everything I ever learned that was worth knowing. I thought he was the greatest man who ever lived and the smartest. Pop thought so too but I don't think anyone else did.

Anyway, he operated that old Lone Star Mill, which provided electricity to the town of Houston at night, and if that mill didn't run they didn't have a movie nor lights at the local hotel. I guess at one time, long before I came along, the old mill was a grist mill for grinding flour, but when I was a kid it generated electricity. A huge wheel sat like a merry-go-round inside a forebay and the dam held back water in the river, backing it up during the day for a couple of miles,

1

October of '23

forming a big, long, quiet body of water we called the Mill Pond Eddy. By sunset there was enough water backed up to run that big wheel and Dad would open the forebay to let it run through. We lived in the looming two story mill-house just above it and the whole place creaked and rumbled and shook while the folks in Houston watched the movie. We lived pretty good when I was small because of the meager income Pop had from that job. Of course the river helped Pop make even more money. During the later years of my boyhood we guided fishermen on that Mill Pond eddy and got to where we'd take city folks all the way down the river on all-day float trips for a dollar-and-a-half per day. That included the wooden johnboat and a ride back. My brothers and I didn't ride back though, we would turn that old johnboat around and paddle it back up the river five or six miles to the old mill and wait until the next city folks came for a float trip. Pop made those wooden john-boats and the sassafras paddles to power them and he sold them quite often, to fishermen and giggers and trotliners and trappers mostly. They brought big money back then, about six dollars per boat, and that included the paddles.

But you've got to understand what a different time it was, three-quarters of a century ago. If a whole family made ten dollars per week that was very good money. Lots of men worked for a dollar a day in the rural Ozarks and when the depression came along nobody in his right mind would have turned down that kind of money, or any money at all for that matter. But Pop had lots of ways to make money, and me and my three brothers and my older sister made him a lot more money in our lives than we cost him. Heck, that's the way it had to be or you starved. But I'm getting ahead of myself.

Besides the money we made guiding float fishermen and selling johnboats, we caught catfish on trotlines in the spring, summer and fall, then gigged rough fish in the winter and took everything to town and sold it. Fish usually brought about five cents a pound or you could trade them

2

for something you didn't have, like eggs or milk. And at night during the summer in the 1930's we caught bullfrogs, which were thick along the river. We used miner's carbide lamps and caught them by hand. Sometimes in two or three hours I'd have a whole burlap bag full of frogs and we sold them to a seafood company out of St. Louis.

In the winter Pop ran a trapline on the river and when I was small, he set a single-season record for an individual trapper with the F.C. Taylor Fur Company in St. Louis. The St. Louis Globe-Democrat newspaper did a full page story about Pop and his dog and his trapping exploits in 1927 when I was only four years old.

3

Only four or five years later I began learning to set traps and deadfalls and I'm sure I was the youngest fur trapper the Big Piney ever saw. So you begin to get the idea. The Big Piney river was to be our livelihood and it was constant work. But I'll tell you this, I thought I was the luckiest kid in the whole world. I loved every second and every minute of it. Times were hard but times were great and that river was heaven to me.

It would have been wonderful to have stayed at the Lone Star Mill forever but it wasn't to be. The old wheel which generated electricity stopped every now and then and things went dark uptown until Dad could climb down in there and pull out the log or whatever it was that had stopped it. One evening when everything stopped, Dad put on his carbide lamp and got down to find out what had gone wrong. He reached down and felt solid flesh instead of the wood which normally caused the wheel to jam. And then in the clear water, with the light of his miner's lamp, he could see the white reflection of a man's leg caught in it.

Pop really got upset and he went to town to get the sheriff. I guess they canceled the motion picture that night and went to the coal oil lamps everywhere else. It was the next day before the sheriff and some of his help got out there to try to find out what they could about what Pop had already decided was a drowning victim or a murder victim. Knowing Pop, I doubt if he slept a wink that night.

The leg he had felt and caught a glimpse of turned out to be a big eel, as big as any I've ever heard of in the Piney, one about twenty pounds in size, six inches in diameter and several feet long. But it didn't matter, folks in Houston were tired of having electricity interrupted and they were talking about a new way of getting it from somewhere else. And that was the end of Pop's job, about the only one he ever had I suppose. I didn't know that we'd be back there to live someday but at five or six years of age, I was upset about leaving. We moved everything to an old house down river about eight or ten miles, back close to where my mother

4

was born. It was a house with a good wood cook stove and a board floor and plenty of room until Pop got some big notion of walling off the north side of it for chickens. The old Hinkle place, they called it. Between the chickens and Dad's trapline, we were going to do all right there. And then I found out I was going to have to go to school. Life went from good to bad in a hurry.

Our family in 1924 - Mom and Zodie
and me and Pop

Great Grandfather Pierre Dableaumonte surrounded by Pop's family - his mom and dad standing. Pop is the small boy in the foreground

Chapter 2
The Beginnings

Mom was born on the Big Piney and spent all her childhood there, the daughter of a hard-scrabble farmer who, like most every one else along the river, did whatever he could to make a living. There were ten kids in her family and ten in my dad's family. Pop was the son of a Frenchman who came to the United States as a teenager. His name was Victor and I've heard from some members of the family that he was running from the law for some reason or another but the most commonly accepted theory is that he was fleeing religious persecution. His mother was a devout Catholic and was trying to force him into the priesthood. I don't think he would have made much of a priest! I remember my grandfather fairly well and he and I didn't get along. He and Pop got along even less.

I learned from Pop that the name Dablemont (pronounced with a long a like cable or table) was shortened from the spelling--Dableaumonte', which meant "dweller of the mountains" in French. Victor's wife, my dad's mother, was the descendant of a French-Canadian trapper named Mallerie who had married a Cree Indian woman, or who's mother was a Cree Indian woman, I don't know for sure which way it was.

Anyway, you can see some of the Indian ancestry in my two youngest brothers, who looked and acted like Indians much of their younger lives. All that French and Indian ancestry made life tough for Pop. He was hot-headed and emotional and impulsive, nearly irrational at times and fairly eccentric. But he was a gifted man and meant for a life in the outdoors. He loved his mother, who babied him, and hated his father whom he often spoke of as a devil. From what I understand the old man beat Dad unmercifully and worked him like a slave. They lived down on the lower part of the river near Edgar Springs, Missouri on a big river-bottom farm.

The Beginnings

Somehow Victor eventually lost his farm to a bank but Pop had left by then. He got tired of the work and when World War I broke out Victor told his son he wanted him to go over and fight for "my countree"...France. Pop was 17 and he wasn't about to leave the Big Piney and fight for France. To escape the inevitable beating he packed up what he thought he would need to survive and headed for the Big Piney where he could live in caves and no one would ever find him.

No one could, either. He knew the river like no one did. He had an old johnboat and his dog and a .22 rifle with ammunition, and he paddled well up the river and just disappeared. About that time he was drafted and he learned about it when he went back to visit his mother in secret. Convinced that it was something his dad had arranged, Pop really did become a fugitive then....an outlaw of some sorts with the government trying to find him.

He kept traveling upriver and spent more than a year in the woods hiding out not far from the Harris farm where my mother was growing up.

He approached that farm when he became ill one winter and they took him in and nursed him back to health. I think he probably had the flu which killed millions of people in 1917 and 1918. I've heard that more soldiers were killed by the flu during that time than in combat. Most every family lost a member or a friend to that awful disease back in that time.

Pop told the Harris family his name was Billy Wilcox. George Washington Harris, known simply as G.W., took a liking to Pop and let him work around his farm on occasion. He had more daughters than sons and when it was plain that his daughter Tollie had also taken a liking to the young man, G.W. Harris eventually got to the bottom of his true identity and convinced him that he couldn't run from the law forever.

The government would forgive any draft-dodgers who would come in and join up and that's what Pop did. He

Pop as a young man before the war about 1915

wound up putting in his time at the end of the war, but didn't see any combat. He shoed horses instead and in doing so learned a great deal that would help him later in life. But he also was kicked in the stomach by a horse, which caused him some problems as he grew older.

When he came back to the Ozarks he married Tollie Harris and within a year my older sister Izora, nicknamed "Zodie", was born. That's when Pop moved from the Harris farm to the Lone Star Mill. For Mom, it was a rough life. In the first five years of marriage she had three children, and lost the second one at a year and a half of age. I was the third, born just after the death of her second child, named Dimple. My brother Farrel was born in 1927, four years after me, and brother Vaughn was born in 1929. The baby of the family was Bryce, born in 1934.

As hard as things were on Mom, life on the river was heaven for Pop. He had everything he could ask for there at the old mill... a job which required very little attention, a little bit of a wage to supplement what he made from the river, and a roof over his head. For a young man that had spent much of his life living in the woods in caves and bluff shelters along the river, just about any type of house was a luxury. He actually saved up money in those first few years at the mill and kept it buried in a can near our home. We needed a lot of things we didn't have but Pop kept saving everything he could just in case he or Mom got sick and had to go to a doctor. When word came that Houston had found an alternative electrical source and they were going to close the Lone Star Mill, it hit dad hard.

I was five years old and about to turn six when we moved and my brother Farrel was just a toddler. As I've already said, our new home was down river, on a ridge just above a low-water crossing known then and now as Sand Shoals, several miles north of Houston. The old house was called the Hinkle Place. It had a board floor, a fireplace and an old wood cookstove. Pop walled off the north end of that house, almost half of it, and ordered some baby chickens.

He made the north end of the house into a chicken house and Mom was to make money selling eggs and chickens while he trapped and sold fish and hewed railroad-ties.

Pop was supposedly the best railroad-tie cutter in the country and back in that day just before the depression hit, he could hack out six or eight of them in a day. They'd cut them from the big oaks on the blufftops above the river and float them downstream in great long rafts that sometimes stretched for miles. It was hard work and dangerous. Lots of railroad-tie hewers had big scars on their legs and feet, or toes missing, or walked with limps from a broad-axe glancing off the tie and cutting their ankles and feet. But a man who was good with a broad-axe was assured of making enough money to live on because the railroads needed the ties.

Surprisingly, I can remember the days at the Hinkle place very well. My bed was made of feed sacks sewn together and filled with oak leaves. It wasn't a bad place to sleep when you had new oak leaves but when they dried up and fell to pieces it wasn't a very good mattress. And we had bedbugs. I think they came from pine trees, where they lived underneath pine bark and came into houses with the pine wood used to build furniture. Dad and mom had a bed with a real mattress and dad would set each leg of that handmade bed in a baking soda can, in which he kept an inch or so of coal oil so the bedbugs couldn't crawl up the legs.

But I remember how we constantly had to take those old mattresses out and turn them over and air them out and kill the bedbugs collecting on the underside. Through most of my boyhood, bedbugs were something we coped with. But there were other nuisances, like roaches and flies and ants and wasps.

I can't emphasize enough how hard life was back then in comparison to modern days. We heated that old house with wood we cut and during the winter when Dad might be off for days running a trapline. My sister and I had to

11

The Beginnings

collect wood and do work that kids today wouldn't even consider. Keep in mind that I was five and Zodie was eight. There was one particular winter stretch when it got so cold it was dangerous. Country people back then would never forget it because the temperature one night in January dropped down past 20 degrees below zero. It was a sudden cold front that caught Pop on the river and he nearly froze to death before he got back home.

He came in shaking with hypothermia and I found an old stack of oak fence posts and brought them to the house to burn. Of course they were too long to fit in the fireplace. I stuck them up the chimney, as many as I could get in there, and built one heck of a fire. But the chimney caught on fire because of it and the flames spread to the shake shingle roof. Pop climbed up on the roof with an old blanket, and luckily we were able to get it out before it caused major damage.

Pop raised hell with me because of that, as he so often did. He never hit us kids or beat us as his dad had him, but he sure knew how to make you wish he'd just give you a good licking and just quit rantin' and ravin'.

"That's it," he would say, "...cause nothin' but pain and problems. ..you're just like them damn Harrises! Tollie, I wish you'd come and look what this good-for-nothing Harris kid of yours has done now!"

For years, every time Dad got mad at me, he'd call me a good-for-nothing $#%&*@#%$ Harris. I'm sure you wouldn't care to hear the descriptive language that preceded it. That didn't bother me...I liked the Harris family, my Grandpa G.W. and Grandma Amanda. G.W. was said to be the son of a civil war Colonel by the name of Greenberry Harris who fought for the Confederacy. He was captured and hanged by Yankees at Pilot Knob, Missouri after a big battle there. And I heard in later years that Grandma Amanda was a great niece of a Yankee General by the name of William Tecumseh Sherman, but folks kind of kept that quiet.

Anyway, Grandma and Grandpa Harris were the salt of

the earth. And Mom's brother, Uncle Johnny Harris, would let me take his old double-barrel shotgun out squirrel hunting when I was only eight or nine years old. No one else could have used that old shotgun and shoot up his hard-to-come-by shotgun shells, but I could...and I could even take his old squirrel dog along. But Pop didn't get along with anybody back then, let alone his in-laws. Heck, he didn't even get along with his own family.

They would have liked him better if he hadn't constantly shown them up with his superior ability in almost every outdoor category. Pop could do anything, make things with his hands and meager tools, catch fish and trap fur, butcher hogs or cattle, raise all kinds of garden goods with very little effort, and shoot a gun like no one else.

My mother's two sisters, Letha and Lenny, married two brothers named Ben and Ansel Williams, and they never lived far from us when I was a kid. I remember how Dad would get around the Williams brothers and Uncle Johnny or other of Mom's brothers and make fun of their shooting. He could take his old single-shot .22 Stevens rifle and shoot seed balls off the highest sycamore limbs while the rest of the clan were just trying to hit the tree. And then of course he'd rub it in. He'd point out that if he couldn't shoot any better than they could he'd just stick with a shotgun so he'd have a better chance.

But my mother's family loved me. Whenever there was a family get-together amongst the Harris family, Pop would never go. So I'd usually sneak off and join them, because for one thing I got lots of attention, and for another there was great food there. No one ever got enough to eat back then as I remember. A Decoration-Day celebration or the annual Fourth of July picnic or an occasional family get-together for a wedding or funeral was the only time I got to eat pie or cake and I absolutely loved pie and cake. I'd eat so much I'd be sick for two days. We just scraped by at home with most of our meals from the river--- fish or squirrels or ducks and even an occasional possum or raccoon or muskrat. There

Pop was a great outdoorsman and his hunting skills insured that we would never go hungry.

was a chicken for supper every now and then when one would die and we did have eggs every morning for breakfast. Unfortunately there wasn't much of a market for either and we seldom sold any. I remember that my mother, the angel that she was, wasn't a very good cook. But then she didn't have much to work with either. There were almost no deer or turkey back then and very few coyotes. But there were rabbits and quail everywhere. In the summer Pop would call up bobwhites and shoot their heads off with .22. In the fall when the birds would covey up, you tried to get a shot at them with a shotgun, on the ground, so you could get five or six with one shell if possible.

Remember that back then there were bunches of quail and no bird dogs or bird hunters. We had little effect on them. And we helped them survive by shooting hawks, trapping foxes and even trapping owls. Pop was sure that owls would be after our chickens so he cut the top out of a tall oak and cut the limbs back so he could set a steel trap on top of the sawed off trunk, twenty feet up off the ground. He caught two or three great-horned owls that way and that old tree, with the top missing, still stands today where the old Hinkle place was. Again, that doesn't set well with today's way of thinking but we were trying to survive and hawks and owls brought a 50-cent bounty back then after the depression ended.

It's amazing how few rabbits we have in the Ozarks today but back then they were abundant. It was fun to hunt rabbits but we weren't out there blazing away at running cottontails. Shotgun shells cost too much. You crept along watching for sitting rabbits and shot them in the head with a .22 rifle so the meat would be good. When there was an inch or so of snow you could find them easier. Farrel and I would hunt them when we got older by finding fresh tracks in the snow. One of us would stand on a stump waiting with the rifle while the other one followed the tracks, baying like a hound. I know that sounds silly but it worked.

As long as you could follow those tracks in the snow and make that rabbit hear you, he would circle just as if it were a beagle after him. Since Farrel was younger, I talked him into being the beagle more often so I could do more shooting. And I always thought he had a good voice for it. But his legs were longer than mine so he sometimes pressed the rabbits a little too close and made them run a bigger circle. Oh well, you couldn't ask for everything!

Farrel was a kid who survived things that seemed unsurvivable. He was badly burned as a small child, and it took him a long time to recover from that. And then a rabbit hunt nearly cost him his life one winter in the mid-30's. There was a heavy snow on and the weather was warming. He was all bundled up and had on a heavy pair of lined galoshes which made his feet hot. I don't know where he got boots like that. Seems like when we were young I never had anything but old shoes which we would wrap up in burlap bags, then tie on the burlap with binding twine. But Farrel came across those boots somehow and after chasing rabbits for awhile his feet were sweating. He decided he'd cool them off so he took off the boots and washed his feet in the snow. A few days later he began to run a high fever and Mom went for the doctor in Houston.

Old Doc Wommack came to the old house and shook his head when he examined my little brother. He had double pneumonia, something that most people didn't live through in that day and time. But that old country doctor came in and spent two nights doctoring Farrel there in our place, and pulled him through. And he probably got paid the next summer in catfish and garden produce!

We caught lots of rabbits in the winter in home-made rabbit traps, which were boxes about three feet long and six or eight inches wide and high. They were set in rabbit runs in thickets and high grass, and looked just like a hollow log. The open end had a lid which was tripped by a trigger inside. If you had some kind of bait to put inside it helped, but most anything which would attract a rabbit was something I'd eat before I got it to the trap.

I learned that you didn't eat rabbits after February because they were pregnant by then and we didn't eat them in the fall until after the first couple of good frosts because of the scare of tularemia, or 'rabbit fever' which rabbits carried. But there were lots of diseases to worry mothers back then... rabies for example, for which there was no vaccine that we knew of. Then there was the dreaded 'lock-jaw' which is known today as 'tetanus'. I saw someone with tetanus back when I was a boy but I don't remember much about it. Folks talked about people who died from "lock-jaw" and I remember how scary it sounded. But if stepping on rusty nails or getting cut on the foot by an old piece of tin, or getting punctured and cut and scraped by rusty, dirty objects would have given you lock-jaw, I should have had it a dozen times or more.

I remember once while we were living at the Hinkle place when Pop was repairing something or taking out a wall or whatever and he threw some old boards out in the yard. Well of course we had outdoor johns back then and I had to visit ours in the middle of the night. I should have taken a kerosene lamp with me, but I didn't. I jumped off the porch right on one of those old boards with a rusty nail sticking up out of it and put that nail right through my foot. And then while I was jumping around crying and yelling for help I got on another one with my other foot.

Dad came out and pulled them out and it hurt like thunder. He said it was just like me to do something like that. "Damn Harris kid...", he said. Then he bound up both feet with dirty rags soaked in kerosene and in a day or so I was hobbling around just fine. And nobody who ever knew me ever suggested I ever had lock-jaw!

Even when I was young, I always
liked girls who had shoes.

Chapter 3

A No - Account Harris

Things didn't go real well at the old Hinkle place. Dad worked so hard on his trapline it actually began to affect his health. He had been kicked in the stomach by a horse when he was shoeing horses in the army and he had lots of problems because of it. Later in life doctors at the Veteran's hospital in St. Louis said the blow had partially paralyzed his stomach and it didn't work right.

I think he may have had blood sugar problems as well because after a few hours of work he would get the shakes and have to sit down and rest quite a while. And traplines were hard work, especially when you went at it like Pop did. During those years of my boyhood he made much of his income from those two or three months of trapping. But in the late 1920's the price of fur began to decline, as Pop's health did. I know he suffered from exposure at times, being outdoors so much. In fact, sometimes in the winter he slept outdoors on the river much more often than he was home.

And the chickens just weren't making us the kind of money Pop thought they would when he turned over half the house to them. In the spring of 1930 he obtained, through a trade of some kind or another, eight or ten glass eggs which were suppose to cause the old chickens to lay more eggs in different nests. And early in the summer, he noticed that three or four of them were gone. You know who he thought got them... good ol' Norten, the kid who had a knack for goofing up no matter how hard he tried. I denied it with a great deal of fervor. But on occasion I had denied with a great deal of fervor other things I had actually done so Dad didn't believe for a minute I was innocent.

"Listen to this no-account Harris so-and-so kid, Tollie," he said, "he don't know where those eggs have disappeared to. It ain't enough that he drags my ax out in the woods and can't find it... it ain't enough that he cuts my sawhorses in

A No - Account Harris

two... now this damn kid has made off with half my glass eggs and he can't remember what he's done with 'em."

Well that really hurt of course. I didn't mind him calling me a no-account Harris if it was for something I really did but I hadn't touched those eggs. I figured Farrel did it. I got blamed for everything he did too. But I just idolized Pop and I knew if he said I was a no-account damn Harris I must indeed be one.

Then a few days later I was down in the woods below the house when I came across a big blacksnake wrapped completely around a six- or eight-inch hickory tree, and he was dead. There was a hole in his body with broken glass protruding from the wound. And there were a couple of other lumps in him the size of eggs. I found Pop and told him I had found his egg thief. And sure enough he cut open the snake to retrieve two of his glass eggs unbroken. The third one had been broken by that snake, squeezing his body around that tree.

Pop was absolutely amazed. "I will be damned," he said as he shook his head in disbelief. "If I hadn't seen it, I never woulda thought such a thing."

And then he looked at me and for a moment I thought sure he was about to accuse me of cramming those eggs into the blacksnake. But he didn't. He said he should have believed me and maybe I didn't have so much Harris in me as he first thought. It was looking more like I was a Dablemont, after all. I didn't get too excited about it though. The first darn thing that went wrong... he'd be cussing me again for causing it. And generally he'd be right and I'd blame Farrel or Zodie.

I don't know why I had such a penchant for getting in trouble but I was fascinated by everything, and wanted to do everything Pop did. Take for instance the time I saw him sharpen his axe with a file and make a little pile of shavings. He showed me and Zodie how you could light those metal shavings with a match and they'd burn in a bright, sparkling white flash. I was so fascinated with that I couldn't

20

wait to try it myself. So when Pop was away I found his file
and filed away about a quarter-inch of his axe blade just to
have shavings to light. I heard him out there the next morning trying to figure out what had happened to his axe. And
as smart as Pop was he never figured everything out, thank
goodness. Usually he did though. There was the time when he
took a good butcher knife and turned it into a hacksaw by
filing notches in the blade. He used it to cut nails off and
it really worked. I couldn't wait to try that for myself so I
got a regular kitchen butter knife and filed notches in the
blade just like Pop had done. But I didn't have any nails
to practice on. Then I found the one on the backside of the
back door which held on a large wooden spool as a door
handle. Those big spools which held sewing thread made
good door handles, all you had to do was drive a spike nail
through the hole and into the door.

My knife-turned-hacksaw worked well enough to cut
that nail almost through, and then I had to quit 'cause Pop
came home. It didn't break completely off until the middle
of the night when Pop had to go to the outhouse real bad
and the nail snapped. He couldn't get the door open with
the handle broke off and I heard him down there cussin'
and rantin' and ravin', and I heard my name mixed in with
it. I knew he wouldn't climb up there in the loft to whomp
me in the middle of the night but I was out of the house
before it got daylight the next day and didn't come in until
dark.

When it came to a real situation though, I was Pop's
right-hand man. Like that time we found a bee tree about
150 yards from Ben Williams place along the old road that
passed there. Honey trees were about the greatest thing that
could happen to an Ozark backwoods family because you
couldn't afford much sugar. We would tap the river maples
in the spring and fall, and you'd boil down five gallons of
the thin watery sap to get a pint of syrup. But honey was
thick and heavy and sweet and there was lots of it for less

work.

Pop knew how to find the bee trees like no one else could. He developed a way of tracking bees back toward their hives. He'd take an old bucket or container and put fruit and corn-cobs and watermelon rinds in it and then urinate in it. I don't know how he learned about that but brother it did attract bees. And he'd sprinkle flower on the bees that came there so he could see them better when they'd leave. I'd follow one as far as I could, then he'd take up that position and watch the next flight and so on and so forth until we figured out where the hive was. Then in July or August we'd cut the bee tree and Dad would get the honey.

He never would cut a bee tree after mid-August because he said the bees had to have time to build a new hive and make new honey so they could survive the winter. If you cut honey trees in the fall you destroyed the bees and they wouldn't be there next year. In ways like that, Dad was a true conservationist. He didn't know about the word itself, because it wasn't used in the thirties, but he knew about conservation. And our family took what was needed but no one wasted anything. If you went hunting you never killed anything just for sport. You hunted for food and when you cleaned game you utilized almost everything. We cooked the heads of rabbits and squirrels with the rest of the meat, we cleaned the gizzards on ducks...heck if it was edible, we ate it. We even kept the feathers from wild ducks to make pillows.

Anyway Pop looked at a bee tree as a real treasure. He'd put on heavy clothes and a home-made screen-wire head cover and not get stung much. And we'd fill a big tub with the combs and separate the honey and put it into jars to use during the winter. When Pop discovered that bee tree not more than a good stone's throw from uncle Ben's place, it was more than just a treasure, it was a challenge. There was going to be some high adventure in it.

He went to work and wrapped the iron wheels of an old cart we used around the place in burlap, to make it quiet and leave no tracks on the road.

Of course I think if Pop had told Uncle Ben he had found the bee tree on his place Uncle Ben would have told him he could have it. But Ben and Ansel Williams were his competitors, married to Mom's sisters as they were. They weren't actually well off but they had a sawmill and they lived a little better than we did so the last thing Dad wanted to do was share that honey with them.

And so there we were at two o'clock in the morning one hot August night, pulling that old cart a mile and a half up that old rocky road with a cross cut saw and all the paraphernalia needed to bring back that honey. When the tree came down it fell the wrong direction and went right across the road. But at least it busted open and it didn't take much work to get the combs out into a big wash tub. It was more honey than I ever remember seeing in one tree.

Pop got stung some that night but in the high excitement and drama of the heist he didn't pay much attention to it. To help with the details, Zodie and Farrel came with us that night and we should have left Farrel at home. He was only about four or five years old, and days later when Uncle Ben and Aunt Letha stopped by, all he wanted to do was talk about the "syrup tree" we had cut down.

Heck, Uncle Ben knew what had happened. He had to go up there the next day and get that tree out of the wagon road! But he never brought it up and that's just one more thing that made Pop mad.. all of 'em assuming that he went up there and cut that bee tree in the middle of the night and took all the honey without one shred of proof. That was the Williamses and the Harrises for you... always looking down their noses at Pop. He was sure of it and nobody was going to change his mind.

With all the problems we had, Pop began to think of moving and he found an ad in a magazine where some old codger in Louisiana was wanting to hire a family to pick green beans and peanuts on his place, 'cause he was sick and couldn't do it himself. He had a home to live in, big enough for a big family, and he would pay Mom to cook for him and keep the place clean. The guy was in pretty bad shape, he had cancer or something in his leg and could barely get around.

Well Pop saw this as a great opportunity and he took some money he received from the government as an allotment for war veterans and bought a five-year-old Model T Ford for a hundred dollars. We sold some of the chickens and gave away the others and headed for Louisiana early in the summer of 1930. It took three days to get there as I remember. We bought groceries as we went and fixed meals along the way. And we camped along the roadside at night. Of course those were just winding old gravel roads down through west Arkansas and you didn't see many people. The one big adventure on that trip took place down south of Ft. Smith when a wasp got in the car and Pop went to swatting at it and ran off the road down a pretty good sized ditch. Over the years Pop ran off the road several times and many of those times were because a bee or a wasp got in the car.

That mishap caused us a busted tire and Pop got out the tire pump and the repair kit and fixed it. Back in those days you figured on repairing tires as you went, on any long trip. You didn't just stop and have it done somewhere. Towns were quite aways apart and there weren't any stations or stores out in the middle of nowhere.

I had a great time on that trip because most of Arkansas looked much like southern Missouri with even more beautiful high mountains in places. But when we got down into Louisiana it wasn't anything like home. The old man we were to live with and work for wasn't real friendly and the house was damp and moldy and old, though it was bigger and better than anything we had ever lived in before.

The fall passed away quickly, with Dad and I picking beans and exploring the bayous around us when we could get away. Pop tried to do some fishing but we never caught anything we recognized. But you didn't have to recognize a fish to eat it! I saw some alligators four or five feet long and they said they were even bigger ones around so I didn't do much swimming or wading like we did back home.

There was a local school I was suppose to go to, but I didn't much care for it. I had never seen black people before, nor Mexicans. There were both at the school and I got along fine with the black kids but not the Mexicans. And there were too many of them to fight so after a couple of days I told Pop I wasn't going back. That suited him fine. I was good at picking beans because I was short so there'd be more money for the family.

In that day blacks and whites didn't associate much and I didn't understand why. There was a black family near us and we got to know them. They had kids about my age and I was fascinated with them. They seemed just as poor as us and they grew some of the best watermelons I ever tasted. One thing you should remember about me... I love watermelons and cantaloupes and always have. A family who raised watermelons were naturally going to be my friends. Pop and I went there on occasion and ate watermelon with those black folks and we got along great. Pop liked them even more when some of the local white people suggested it wasn't proper for us to go visit them. He always felt like an underdog himself I guess and when that happened he began to really identify with them.

Pop wasn't racist and neither am I. I've known lots of black people in my life... worked with them, got along with them fine. Of course I've met black people I didn't care for but it wasn't because of who they were, it was because of how they were. I've met plenty of white people I didn't care for either. Again, it didn't have anything to do with their color. I'm tired of hearing about racism. The great majority of black and white people don't hate one another. Television and the movies makes it seem that way but it isn't. Not with those of us who are just common people trying to get along in this world day by day the best we can. The television cameras and the politicians never focus on those of us, black and white, who are working together and helping each other whenever we can.

To some extent, blacks and whites are afraid of one another. But fear isn't hatred and most of the problems between black and white people isn't racism. Sometimes the two peoples don't have much in common and that's the biggest hurdle to overcome. We are so different in how we live and the things we like. I like country music and fishing and most of the black men I worked with in the city when I got older liked the city and dancing and whatever kind of music that was they listened to. But we got along by finding a few things we liked together, like baseball. We played baseball together after work and cork ball and bottle cap ball and we got along great. And there in Louisiana I became friends with the first black people I ever knew because we liked watermelon so much, and we were all so poor.

I had another friend in Louisiana. His name was Eldon Slayton and he was four or five years older than me. I think he liked my sister Zodie a lot more than me and he hung around us a lot because of her. He took me out and showed me the bayous and cypress groves and alligators and in the late winter, I think it was December of 1930, he became a hero to our family and saved my little brother's life.

Pop was bored and decided to take us all to a movie. We didn't see many movies back then and so there was some excitement about that. On the way, we stopped to get some gas in the old Model T. It was dark and for some reason Dad had an old kerosene lantern in the back where Eldon and I and my brother were sitting. Farrel was almost four years old at the time and he stayed in the seat to watch the attendant put gas in the tank. The old Ford had the tank under the front seat and you leaned the seat forward to get to it. When the fumes came up out of that tank the kerosene lantern ignited a flash fire and the attendant got scared and jerked the nozzle out without shutting it off. He sprayed Farrel's left side and immediately my brother was on fire. Pop didn't even know it, he grabbed an old blanket and covered the fire inside the car, smothering everything out quickly. Eldon and I grabbed Farrel and pulled him out and the two of us rolled him on the ground to put out his burning clothes. We saved his life but we weren't fast enough to prevent a horrible burn on his left side from just below his arm down to his hip. He was screaming and crying with pain and a man from across the street saw what had happened and took him into his home. He called a doctor and the doctor wanted to take him to a hospital but there were none anywhere close. The doctor dressed the burn and sent Pop to a drug store where he bought burn medicine and they dressed the burn with that ointment for days. The burn had to be kept saturated with that ointment and it cost a dollar per bottle. That was an awful lot of money and much of what Pop had saved that summer went into burn ointment.

Farrel says today he can't remember much about it but I can. He cried and moaned and suffered for two months without getting out of bed. Mom gave almost all of her time to doctoring him with medicines and clean dressings and ointments for weeks. But by February he was doing better and learning to walk again. Whenever it was apparent Farrel was going to survive, Pop loaded the Model T with everything we had and we said good-bye to Louisiana. We were all sick of it by then and there was no work left and Pop was running out of money.

And I could remember how pretty the Ozark hills were and how clear and clean the Big Piney was. There were catfish and craw-dads and coons and cousins back in those hills at home. No darned alligators and no swamps!

But it was going to be awhile before I got to see those Ozark hills again and wade the clear waters of the Big Piney. We drove right past them on our way to St. Louis where Pop's sisters lived. And they lived pretty well too, despite the depression, because their husbands had jobs. Aunt Julia's husband, Doc Moore, was sick or hurt or something

27

and Pop was going to St. Louis to take his place at Howell Packing Company working in the boiler room. Zodie and I lived with Aunt Julia and Pop and Mom and Farrel and Vaughn lived with Aunt Bertha, a few blocks away. It was a great situation for Mom because she had some help doctoring Farrel, who still wasn't getting around very well, and his burn took some attention. The little guy was hurting awfully bad, and while we were in St. Louis, he got lots of attention, and improved a lot.

There wasn't much to do in St. Louis and I think Zodie and I were about to drive Aunt Julia crazy. Relatives moving in always seems like a good idea until they've been there for a few days. But there was one thing I remember. Uncle Doc had a radio, the first one I ever heard. We listened to a program every evening called "Tony Caboose" or something like that and it was fascinating to me. We'd all sit around and listen and laugh at the program and then Uncle Doc would turn it off before a new program began. I would have liked to have heard more but my uncle was concerned about not using any more electricity than he could afford. Can you imagine that. The fascination everyone had at that time with radios and the programs they provided, but they selected one or two things to listen to, and turned it off because they were aware it cost a few pennies to operate it.

Another thing I remember about St. Louis is that all of us kids got measles and mumps as the winter ended. But I'd rather have had either or both than to have had to go to school. That was awful. My aunt made me wear knee pants and long socks and I felt like an idiot. I only went for a month and I just couldn't learn anything. It was hard to concentrate, hard to sit still, and though I didn't know it of course (and neither did anyone else back then), I had a learning disability and something teachers nowadays know as ADHD. Pop always said I was dumb as a sackful of rocks and I was beginning to figure he was right. It must be all that darn Harris blood in me!

Pop had learned himself to read... or taught himself,

whichever. Anyway he could read and write pretty good without much schooling. Mom was very educated, all the way through the eighth grade. She had even done some country school-teaching for awhile before she started having kids. Because Farrel couldn't do much but lay around, Mom read to him a lot and he was already learning to read. And Zodie took to school and learning like a frog takes to swamp-water. If Zodie and Farrel would have had the opportunity to go on to college as kids today can do, there's no telling what they could have been... maybe teachers or doctors. Probably not lawyers or politicians, as most Dablemont's are probably too honest for that kind of work, even Zodie and Farrel. I was hoping the Good Lord had something in mind for me that didn't require reading or writing or arithmetic.

Pop sold the old Model T in St. Louis for 25 dollars and that made it look like we were going to be in St. Louis for quite some time. But we were only there about 3 or 4 months. Getting along with his relatives was harder than Pop thought it was going to be and in the spring of 1931 he went back to the Ozarks and hired Elmer Smith, an old friend who owned a truck, to come to St. Louis and move us all back home. It cost him ten dollars... a lot of money for those days. But Elmer couldn't do it for much less, it would take two days and gas was six cents a gallon. If I had had any money, I would have chipped in. I was homesick for the Big Piney, and couldn't wait to wade in it's cool clean waters once again.

My sister, Zodie, and I collected pine knots for
Pop to use on gigging trips. In, 1931, she nearly
killed me with one.

Chapter 4

Coming Back to the Ozarks

Ben and Ansel Williams, Pop's brothers-in-law, had an old house down close to the Piney which they had been using as sort of a storage barn for this and that. It was too rickety for most folks to live in but just right for Pop. He agreed to pay them two dollars a month rent but they didn't get much of his money. Pop had a plan... we'd live there awhile and he and I would build us a log cabin down in the Williams hollow not far from the Bell Rock Eddy where the fishing was good and the fur was plentiful.

Elmer Smith's old ton-and-a-half truck was big enough to haul quite a load and Aunt Julia and Aunt Bertha gave us some old furniture and clothes and what-all to take back. It took us a whole day and part of the night to get there, a trip you can make today in about two-and-a-half hours. Zodie and I rode in the back with all the furniture and it was a long, rough ride.

When we pulled off the main gravel road down onto uncle Ben's road, I looked up over the top of the truck rack and an electric line or a telephone line caught me by the chin and peeled me right off that truck. It stunned me for awhile but I got back up and caught up with the truck. I couldn't figure out what had happened. After all, I had never seen a wire stretched across a road before. As I remember it the old road down to the house was too rough for the truck. I think we moved most everything down there with a horse and wagon a day or so later.

That spring Pop taught me how to use an axe and we cleared sprouts and built rail fences and began to put in a small garden. I finally figured out what God had made me for, it was cutting sprouts. I absolutely loved using that axe. Uncle Johnny Harris brought his old horse and plow over after we had cleaned out the rocks and stumps as best we could, and we planted ourselves a garden, fenced in against the free ranging hogs and wild creatures with barriers of

31

brush and rocks and poles and rails. It didn't look like much but it was a garden. We planted watermelon and banana mushmelons and cantaloupes, as well as corn and potatoes and beans and tobacco. I couldn't wait to get my hands on another watermelon.

Pop and I built a dam on the creek that ran by the garden toward the Piney and we backed up quite a pool of water to use for irrigation. Pop and Zodie and I hauled hundreds of buckets of water from the creek that summer because it was the first summer of the awful drought that hit in the thirties. The temperature soared above 100 degrees much of the time and there was a haze in the air on occasion. I remember seeing the sun turn red and fade under the clouds of dust coming out of Oklahoma at various times over the next two or three summers. What little rain we had was muddy.

To fight the drought, we hauled water to our garden almost daily but we didn't just pour it out on the dry ground. Pop had built boxes out of slabs from Ben Williams sawmill and put them up on legs over the garden plants, with small holes drilled in the bottom of each box. When you poured a bucket of water in each box it seeped out slowly and had the maximum effect.

Overall, and by today's standards, the garden was a failure, but we produced a little and there was enough food to get us through most of the winter. Mom canned what she could and we sacked the potatoes and buried them in boxes of sawdust to preserve them. We grew lots of peanuts in that garden, and they did well...as did a patch of tobacco which Dad planted.

We had a tobacco patch about every year because it made us a little money. A plug of tobacco could be sold for a nickel, and Grandma Harris was one of our best customers. She didn't want anyone to know it much, but she loved chewing tobacco. Pop would start his tobacco patch in February, cleaning off the brush, making a high stack of whatever he could find to burn, and leaving a big ash pile. He said the ash and the burning made the ground good for tobacco. Then after the burning was done we'd mix ash into the ground and try to get rid of all or any roots. Pop bought tobacco seed in town for a nickel, and it was tiny, you just spread it sparingly, and left it.

I remember Pop saying that tobacco had to go to hell and back before it would make anything...seems like it came up in mid-April, and looked something like real small cabbage. About three weeks later, in May, Pop would dig up the best plants, which were only about three inches high, and place them in rows about eighteen inches apart. He usually had about three good rows. Then we just worked to keep grass and weeds out of them and they grew fast, up to my waist in height by July, hip high to Pop. The leaves would be about eighteen inches wide and ten inches long, maybe 25 good leaves to a plant.

The bottom leaves were too small, just trash leaves... we didn't use them for chewing tobacco, just pulled them off when they got gray and brittle and Pop would crush them up and use them for his pipe. But the higher leaves began to turn brown and hang down in the heat of the late summer, and then Pop would cut off the entire plant at the ground and hang the whole plant in the loft of the cabin or the shed. The plants would cure in two or three weeks and he would take them down and cut the leaves off the stalk, sprinkle the leaves with water to make them moist, and then cut out the stems.

Dad got sawmill slabs, planed smooth and about three feet long, ten or twelve inches wide, then drilled a hole in each corner. Through those four holes he put old bolts. Then he would begin to stack leaves between the boards, and every three or four layers he would add a mixture of water and licorice and brown sugar and honey or molasses.

When the stack of leaves came up to four or five inches in height, he would add that top board, tighten it snug, but not too tight. Every day, I'd go out there and make a couple of turns on the bolts to tighten them more. In a week or more, I would have that tightened down to about three-quarters of an inch thick. By then it was all melted together and solid. It would be dried but gummy just like today's plugs of tobacco. Then Dad would measure out squares of it, each about three or four inches, and cut it up with a pole ax blade, which he would place on the tobacco, then hit with hammer. We wrapped them in some cellophane paper which had been used for something else and a store in town was throwing it away. It sold well at a nickel a plug because storebought tobacco cost three times that and wasn't as fresh. I think selling it was against federal law, but we didn't know it.

I never did taste the stuff, but Grandma loved it. Dad said if any of us kids used it he would break our necks. Pop did smoke a little, and chewed some, but the stuff we raised was too strong for a rolled cigarette. He was different than most men in that day....he eventually quit smoking altogether, I think mostly because it took money he didn't have.

About that time, Pop built a wooden johnboat from lumber the Williams brothers sawed for him, and a neighbor by the name of Archie Hicks hauled it down to the river with a horse and wagon. We set trotlines and caught catfish to eat and sold a few, though times were too hard to get much money from them. It was hard to get the fish to town without them spoiling in the heat. Pop would walk to town every couple of weeks, probably five or six miles. He'd get on his way at first light and come back in the cool of the evening. He'd buy the bare necessities in town, supplies we just had to have, and sell a catfish for about anything he could get.

Most of the time no one else in the family went to town. Maybe it was better that way. There in the hills above the river, we didn't hear about the suffering going on around the nation. And where I was, the word depression didn't have much impact. The drought and the heat darn sure did because it was making it unlikely that I was going to spend the summer eating watermelon and mushmelon like I had

34

been counting on.

I kept busy. I was up before dawn every morning and worked until dark. But it wasn't much like work to me. I enjoyed it. I loved using that axe and it was my job to keep the garden watered, to work on those fences, to cut cookwood for Mom, to keep the wood-box filled, to keep a full bucket of water in the house from the spring and to watch for anything that might get in that garden, from rabbits to free-ranging hogs. I ran into the house every time I saw a young rabbit and grabbed the rifle. But if I fired a shell, I knew I'd better have a rabbit to clean and eat for supper or breakfast. I think .22 shells were a nickel per box and I darn well had better not waste any and let Pop find out about it.

When September came and the river became clear we really got excited about gigging. A gig was a three- or four-pronged spear mounted on a long handle anywhere from 12 to 16 feet long because you were gigging fish in 15 feet of water at times. Pop used the blacksmithing knowledge he gained in the army to make gigs out of old farm tools and he used a straightened wagon rim to attach a basket holder at the mid-point of the johnboat. The wire basket was also something he made and it held burning pine knots out over the water to illuminate the river beneath us. You could gig fish during the day of course but it was much easier at night. All you really needed was pine knots and pine stumps and there were plenty of them up on the Big Piney bluff tops.

Years before, loggers had cut all the big pines along the river ridge tops because they were easy to get to. They left stumps and limbs and parts of the treetops which weathered there for years. When the sapwood had rotted away, the heartwood was left and it was full of resin. That resin-filled pine burned bright and long, if not real hot, and it was perfect for gigging. Zodie and I went along that fall on gigging trips and I would paddle the boat while Zodie kept the pine-knot fire going in the basket. The back half of the 16-foot boat was kept filled with pine knots. And Pop, in the front of the boat, kept his half filled with the fish he gigged, big redhorse up to 12 or 14 pounds and yellow suckers and hogmollies... and the black suckers which were only found in the spring branches.

We could have fish to eat all winter by gigging and Pop would sell some, a dozen or so at a time, cleaned and scored, for a quarter or whatever he could get. Suckers have a great number of fine thread-like bones and scoring them was the only way you could eat them without getting bones in your throat. You'd gut and scale the fish, then take a sharp knife and cut through the meat to the back bone, with vertical cuts about an eighth- or a quarter-inch apart, all the way down the body. That was 'scoring'. You did it on both sides and the backbone held the fish together while the fine bones were cut up. When a sucker was scored properly you never noticed the bones.

Of greatest importance to a gigger was the supply of resin-filled pine knots and stumps. Zodie and I were in charge of cutting that supply on bluff-tops up and down the river. You had to use a cross-cut saw and you had to keep turpentine on the blade when you cut them. Otherwise the resin would bind up the saw-blade so bad you couldn't get it to cut. There was so much pine slash on those bluff tops we would cut what we needed, toss it off to the base of the bluff, stack it all up and leave it there. Then we knew where the pine knot and   stump supplies were when we were gigging along the river, upstream or down, on a cold winter night. You just stopped and loaded up some new fuel when you needed it and you could find it at the base of each bluff.

In late September of that year Pop and Zodie and I headed upriver in the old johnboat one afternoon to the bluff overlooking the Mud-hole Eddy, a mile or so from the house. Dad put us out there and paddled on up the river a little ways to look for fur sign. Zodie and I climbed up on the bluff and began to cut pine limbs and knots and stumps. We found one really big stump and worked for a half hour to cut it off at the base with the crosscut saw. Then I used

Pop was awfully good with a gig and we sold fish he took. Zodie and I played a big part in his success.

my axe to split it into four pieces. Finally we had enough to stack up down by the river so I went down underneath the bluff, which receded back beneath the overhang by six or eight feet. Zodie would throw down a dozen or so pieces, then holler for me to go get them. She'd wait while I went out and picked up what she had thrown down and I'd stack them neatly against the bluff.

We had a big pile of knots and resin-filled pine chunks when Zodie yelled out she was throwing the big pieces down. "Don't let one of these hit you," I remember her say. "It'd kill you for sure."

Well it just happened that there was a big tree growing up that bluff and Zodie bounced one of those big pine chunks off that tree. It glanced off and came back toward me, down next to the bluff, hitting me on the top of the head. I remember feeling it hit me and there was a bright flash of light with an explosion in my head. That's all I remembered for awhile. Zodie ran up the river screaming for Pop, sure that I was dead. He found me beneath the bluff, unconscious and covered with blood.

Thankfully, I didn't weigh much back then and he carried me up to the closest homeplace a mile or so above the river, which belonged to Archie Hicks. I was beginning to come around a little and then I would pass out again. I had a full, thick head of hair, and after they washed the wound as best they could, they shaved my hair off and washed the wound with turpentine. I don't know, of course, but Pop always insisted that the skull was broken in that one spot and you could see my brain. He said it was down in there quite aways and not very big but it was good to know that I had one!

They bandaged my head with clean rags and sheets and Dad carried me home. I didn't come around much until the next day and I was terribly weak for days and days, perhaps from loss of blood. It was about two weeks before I could get up and get around again. Doctors told me later that I apparently had survived a minor skull fracture somehow with apparently no lasting affect.

Even with the depression, Christmas was always a great time. Pop made a little money out of his furs and dug up the can of money in the middle of the night to buy Christmas presents. Pop always went out and cut a little scraggly cedar tree, and we would decorate it with strings of popcorn. And Pop would make little candles out of possum fat and cotton string wicks, which he would attach to the tree. He bought some cap pistols and coconuts and socks and some fruit and candy. Mom would let us play with the cap pistols until we had shot up all the caps, then gather them up while we were doing something else and hide them until the next Christmas. We always figured we lost them somewhere, and then there they were under the tree again the next year, with a new roll or two of caps.

I was only eight years old in the winter of 1931, but I helped the family get by, using a small axe which Dad had nearly ground away in years of sharpening. I'd go over to the Leonard Halley place and cut sprouts most of the day for a gallon of milk taken from his old cow. Until then I hadn't had much milk and I was awfully small. I probably didn't weigh much more than 50 pounds when I was ten years old. But I think I started to grow a little and get stronger when I started drinking that milk. The rest of the family liked the cream. Mom would whip it and add salt to it and make wheat-short bread for breakfast to eat with that whipped cream.

I hated that bread made from wheat-shorts and I don't think it had much food value. Wheat-shorts were the hulls and husks of wheat. It had some wheat grain in it but not much. People bought it to feed to hogs back then but during the depression there were a lot of Ozark families who used it to make a flat, heavy bread. I could stomach that bread if we had a young rabbit to go with it, or a squirrel or some bullfrogs. I remember eating a bullfrog for breakfast lots of times back then, until it got too cold.

At the close of the winter in 1932, probably in late February, we started the cabin down the creek closer yet to the river. Pop said it was speculators land, whatever that was. It wasn't. It actually belonged to an old man by the name of John Bell but it was so remote and far away from anyone and anything that he didn't find out we had built it for years. Bell was an old, heavy-set man who owned more than 200 acres along the river and rented it out to other farmers on shares. The spot Pop picked out was in the corner of that land right next to the remains of the old homeplace where Mom had been born and raised. It was down at the end of that old rough and rugged wagon road, close to the river in the middle of nowhere.

There were hewn logs left in the walls of the old Harris cabin. We used some, and the rest I would chop up over the years for firewood. And on the hill above it was a stand of small oak trees, most of them six to eight inches in diameter. Pop and Zodie and I were going to make our cabin out of them.

We started by building a clay "foundation", which had to be built up so that water would run around it and not over it. That was going to be the floor of the cabin and we'd keep fresh sawdust over it. Lots of families in the hills lived on dirt or sawdust floors in that day. Sawdust wasn't bad to walk on when you were barefoot anyway. If you changed it every week or so it stayed clean and fresh and smelled good too. And we had a good supply of sawdust at the Williams sawmill not far away.

We cut those oak trees off with a cross-cut saw and an axe and we stripped limbs and cut them to just the right length. The main part of the cabin would be about ten feet by fourteen feet and a kitchen area of about eight feet by ten feet. We had an attic built from small poles laid across the top of the cabin where a ceiling would normally be. That attic would mostly be for storing things like garden pro-duce, but we could also make a bed or two up there and sleep there. After we moved in we did eventually add on another small room at the end with a fireplace and in the

40

years to come we would gather there on cold nights around the warmth of that fireplace and Mom would read to us. It sort of made me wish I could read, at times like that. That no-account little brother of mine, Farrel, who always got the light end of the work because of his injury, was reading everything by the time
he was seven or eight years old and the best I could do was look at the pictures.

If I remember right we finished the old cabin in early summer because the weather was hot when we moved in. Pop and Zodie and I built that place in just over two months. The most exciting part of it was making shingles for the roof. Pop borrowed a tool known as a "fro" and we cut eighteen-inch sections out of some bigger black oak trees and used that fro to split off oak shingles six to eight inches wide and less than an inch thick. We had put up rafters about fourteen or fifteen inches apart and we had to nail those shake shingles on, starting at the bottom and going up, while they were green. If they weren't green they would split when you nailed them.

Lordy that was fun! But building the chimney for the old cookstove was even more exciting because we had to really do it right or you could lose everything to a fire. In addition to the cookstove we were going to put a stove on the other side of the wall made from a 55-gallon metal barrel. I remember seeing that thing get red hot at times during the winter. And on really cold nights when the temperature would get down to twenty degrees or less, I or Pop would stay up and sleep in a chair close to that stove so we could rebuild the fire when it burned low. You might have to go out and get an armload of firewood, just outside the door, three or four times a night, to keep some warmth in that old cabin, which was without a shred of insulation.

The barrel would burn out by spring and Pop would get a new one. Lots of families in rural areas died during those depression days because of house-fires in the night. Dad thought about that in placing the two doors and four win-

Coming Back to the Ozarks

dows at strategic spots and we made that chimney strong and straight, and packed it with clay mud mixed with water to make a mortar which would seal the rocks and hold them together. Those rocks we used had first formed a fireplace in the old G. W. Harris cabin back in the 1800's where Mom had lived as a girl, and now we were using them all over again.

You might wonder where we got the nails to nail those shingles on with, and where the windows came from. I'm glad you asked that! As the depression came on, lots of families just moved out of the rural areas and into small towns to survive. There was an old homeplace on a ridge about a half-mile or so above us to the east, known as the old Barker place. It was falling apart and the roof had collapsed. Pop and I took the unbroken glass out of the windows and pulled every nail we could get out of the roof and doors and we gathered the best boards to make our doors with.

We made a lot of long hard trips to that old place bringing back all we could use but that was easy work compared to carrying those ten, twelve and fourteen-foot-long logs down the hill after Pop had them ready. Zodie and I carried the longer ones down, with her on one end and me on the other. But sometimes I'd carry the shorter ones down by myself. I remember when I'd put one on my shoulder and carry it down to the cabin site, I'd see stars and flashes of light shooting every which direction in my eyes. I thought that was the neatest thing. When they went away I'd head back up the hill for another one.

The last thing we had to do was mix clay and water and make a mortar to fill in the cracks around the logs. Man, that was fun too. It was something I could do without any help and I took it serious. When I got through there wasn't a crack or hole big enough for a gnat to get through between those logs. Because of that mud work I did, Pop named our new home "the mud-daubers nest". It sounds a little less impressive than it was.

To me it was a mansion. I was awfully proud of that old cabin. And for most of the depression we would live there and survive quite handily. We weren't living on caviar and crackers like the rich folks but heck we weren't boiling shoe leather either like they were doing in some of the cities. Maybe we would have if we'd had any shoes!

But you can live off the land if you work at it, even in the rocky hills of the Ozarks. And that Big Piney river close by was our strong foundation. It gave us fish and ducks, and turtles and frogs and inspiration. When Dad went to the river he came back a happier man, a little of the worry gone from his face. At times, Pop was a religious man, and at times he wasn't. I don't know if he ever went down to the river and talked to God, but I think, from time to time, God talked to him.

Little brothers, Vaughn and Bryce, look like indians...
and acted a lot like Indians as well.

Pop was a great trapper and the price of furs each
year determined how well we fared the next.

Chapter 5

Running the Deadfall Line

The Great Depression wasn't hard on coyotes and chicken hawks, and there wasn't a crawdad in the whole creek who fared any worse because of it.   It was kind of like that for our family, because we weren't all that well off before it started, or after it was over.   In the best of times, times were hard for us.   But at the mud-daubers nest, our new home, we were back close to the river again where Pop was happiest.   And I was just learning what a great place the Big Piney was for a boy like me. We were moved in and well settled by summer and Dad said I had proven I was a man with the work I had done on the cabin.   I was only a couple of months from my tenth birthday. He said it was time he began to teach me about the outdoors and it would begin with an ambitious project.

Pop was a heck of a trapper and fisherman and he had done well in the late 20's, before we went to Louisiana. He didn't have a job before the depression, nor during it, nor after. He had learned to live off the land, and raise a family there on the river by what he caught and cultivated and made with his own two hands. He had been raised on the river, he loved that life and the freedom it afforded him. He never knew a day when he had to do what someone else told him to do.

As I said earlier, in the late twenties, Pop was the F.C. Taylor Fur Company's leading individual fur trapper.   But those years of running the river traplines during the dead of winter, staying out for days and weeks in all kinds of weather and sleeping in caves and bluff shelters, had affected his health.   Doctors said exposure had taken a toll on him, and in 1932, he was having a rough time just getting in a day's work.   That was partly because of the damage done by being kicked in the stomach by a horse while he was in the army during World War I.

In the fall of 1932, the depression was on and Pop

45

couldn't do what he once could. We were faced with the difficult task of surviving! And so we did it just like the coyotes and chicken hawks did, we took advantage of opportunities, and lived off the land.

I had a lot of responsibility by the time I was seven or eight years old, but I loved my life. I got up every morning looking forward to whatever was to come, and all the time I got to spend with Pop was great adventure. That's why, in the late summer of 1933, when he told me I would have to help keep the family fed because of his failing health, I could scarcely contain my enthusiasm. In October, we set out to establish two long deadfall lines which I could run in the fall.

Pop had his steel traps of course, and he meant to trap the river, but I could add to that by running a deadfall line, and deadfalls didn't cost money like traps did. A deadfall was a trigger apparatus like a figure 4 (see photo and drawing) with a big heavy rock propped on top of it. If a furbearer got under it, attracted by bait, it tripped the trigger and the rock fell and killed it immediately. You ran part of the line every two or three days so you would disturb the area less and allow for the taking of more fur. But in some ways, a deadfall might be considered humane. Furbearers were killed instantly in deadfalls by a big flat rock and they were covered by that rock until you got there. The idea of deadfalls and traps are hard for some people to swallow. It involves killing things which you do not eat. You are taking furs to sell and maybe for some it just isn't an ethical thing to do. But we lived off the land and with the land. I never saw myself as any worse for killing a furbearer than another predator which would do the same thing and leave it's remains for the scavengers. Life was hard and you did what you could do to make some money to survive.

I know lots of those movie stars have condemned those of us who lived from the land and utilized the wildlife around us. But we weren't cruel, merciless people. I expect we had more reverence for life than most of those folks in Hollywood. None of us ever had much doubt about what was right or wrong, like they do in Los Angeles and New York. And I never understood why those people would criticize us country folks when we never once went to the city and criticized them for the way they live, and some of them live like heathens from what I hear. I think we should meet them half way. Let's outlaw trapping and hunting and fishing and guns inside the big cities and let country people keep living like they have for hundreds of years.

Instead of worrying about individual animals, lets concentrate on saving wildlife species by saving our forests and woodlands and keeping our rivers clean. Oh well, it's probably a little late for that! When I was a boy, the Ozark forests had already been hit hard by loggers, but the rivers were still clean. They aren't now.

For the trapper, the river was the place to concentrate his work because that's where the mink and muskrats were, and most of the money came from those furbearers. In my boyhood there were no beaver, nor otter. But fur, to someone running a deadfall line, wasn't mink and coon and foxes and bobcats. It was possums, skunks, an occasional weasel, and a wild house-cat every now and then. We got a few crows and bluejays on occasion and once we got one of Uncle Johnny's little pigs. I felt bad about that and just had to tell him about what I had done. I figured he'd get mad and call me a no-good-for-nothing *&%#$@*%A$ Dablemont , but he didn't. He said that little pig had no business rootin' around underneath my deadfall trying to get a fishhead when there was plenty of other food to be had.

A deadfall wouldn't kill a very large animal, like a dog or fox or raccoon. There were no raccoons to take back then anyway. Pop would get an occasional coon in his river traplines, but not many. In just a few years they had become very very hard to find.

I heard it said that coons declined back then because of a loss of den trees and I suspect that was true. For years every coon hunter who treed a coon in a hollow tree cut it down to get the coon. And the Ozarks had been heavily logged only 10 to 15 years before. Raccoons would come back and when they did they would began to hole up and have young ones in caves and under ledges, where they hadn't been known to den 20 years before.

Pop spent many nights in late summer cutting and fitting deadfall triggers, and when he had about 100 sets, he and I set forth to plan a line, starting near our old cabin, running up one creek hollow, over a ridge and down another creek. We lay out the lines in October, but I would begin running my deadfall lines in November, just about the time fur began to get prime. Pop explained to me that in the spring and summer and into the fall, fur wasn't at its best and not worth anything. The pelts came into prime as the winter came on and when they did I was ready. I had a small sack with replacement triggers and a big sack filled with fishheads that had been allowed to get a little bit prime themselves. Pop and I had gigged hundreds of suckers and we had saved that sack full of heads for bait.

The success of the deadfall line depended on one thing, finding big flat rocks large enough and heavy enough to kill possums, skunks and weasels. Pop carried the triggers in burlap bags, and used an old dulled axe to hack away and shape rocks which might need sculpting. All through October, we laid out that line, hauling, rolling or dragging rocks to just the right spots, busting away the excess, making them perfect for the job. He taught me how to set them, and how to use my knee to prop up the heavy rocks so I wouldn't get my arm broken. By late October, we had two lines laid out with thirty or forty rocks waiting on each.

I was happy because it meant the end of my school days. At the little Arthur's Creek country school, it had been me against the Abney brothers, and there were three of them. For a couple of years it had been a war, and I was tired of it. Besides that, I wasn't very good at learning, and I didn't like the teacher. I closed school down for a couple of days once by taking a skunk scent bag, setting it under a board on the front steps, and waiting 'til the teacher came to unlock the door, and step on the board.

You are probably thinking that a kid who traps skunks and skins skunks would smell like skunks but with deadfalls there was no scent released. It was a quick death and a skunk couldn't plant it's feet and lift its tail to expel the scent. When you skinned a skunk you just had to be careful not to cut into those scent glands. I remember thinking that should worse come to worse and someone got to insisting I had to go to school again, I would just skin a skunk and accidentally cut into those glands and become so smelly they would run me out. But now that I think of it, hauling that sack of fish-heads around on my back probably made me smelly enough.

Pop taught me, by the time I was nine, to skin skunks, possums and weasels, and scrape and stretch the pelts on a stretching board to dry like a sock turned inside out. I'd take a cart up to the Williams Brothers sawmill, a couple of miles away, and bring bag pine slabs to make stretching boards out of. We had dozens and dozens of them ready by November.

Running the Deadfall Line

In early November, as trapping season began and fur was finally prime, Pop and I took a big sack of fishheads and baited and set each deadfall. We got the fishheads from suckers we had gigged, and we had been gigging for a couple of weeks. Some of those fishheads were really ripe! But that's what was needed. Later, we would use some rabbit heads. There were lots of rabbits, and we made rabbit box-traps to catch them for eating, of course, using the heads for deadfall bait.

I don't ever remember being real hungry because there were so many rabbits and wild game, but I was small and didn't need much. Sis was twelve, and younger brothers Farrel and Vaughn were six and three. The government had given us Old Pie-Dough, but there were a lot of us for the milk she produced. Pop would actually grind up and mix rabbit meat and muskrat meat with an old meat grinder to make a kind of hamburger, and we ate lots of fish.

Pop was awfully stingy with .22 shells and shotgun shells, because they had to be bought. But sometimes we would have wild ducks to eat if he got a shot on the river or a small pond where one shotgun shell would kill several ducks. You never shot ducks flying, you found them sitting and pot shot them. Same thing with quail. There were lots of quail, and you could call them up in the summer and shoot their heads off with a .22 rifle. There were no turkey, no deer and very few raccoons and mink. Pop's river trapping was for muskrats, mink and raccoon, but beaver didn't exist back then.

Often during the summer I'd catch a bullfrog and eat it for breakfast, and on occasion, we'd have oatmeal when we could afford to buy it. Pop usually bought a little coffee from time to time because it was cheap, but we seldom bought sugar. If we didn't have honey, we sweetened most everything with a syrup made by boiling down river maple sap collected in buckets in the spring and fall, like they did in the North.

Our staple was wheat short bread, as I have already

pointed out in a previous chapter. Wheat shorts were sold in town as hog feed, 25 cents for a 50 pound bag. It was the husk that surrounds the wheat grain, and Mom made bread from it. We'd make whipped cream, when we had milk, and eat wheat short bread and whipped cream for breakfast when there was nothing else. I never remember having eggs for breakfast after we left the Hinkle place. We couldn't have kept a chicken around long at the mud-daubers nest because we had no pens or chicken house....something or someone would have eaten it.

We'd raise beans in the garden and can some, dry others, and have them all winter long. Mom would can some blackberries and dewberries found growing wild. But I learned to live off peanuts. We would grow bushels of them in the summer, and have them all winter. When I ran my deadfall lines, I took wheat short bread and peanuts and maybe a chunk of fish or a rabbit leg.

Thank God it was a mild November, that year when I became a deadfall trapper. I didn't have any shoes, and never wanted any. I lived bare-foot since I started walking, and for the first week I ran my deadfall lines bare-foot. The night before the first day, I couldn't sleep. I was mortally afraid of missing one or two of my deadfalls, of having one I couldn't remember and passing up a possum somewhere.

I set out at dawn that day, wearing a pair of Pop's old overalls with galluses shortened and the pants legs rolled way up. Pop wasn't a big man, but he towered over me. I had turned ten only a few days before, but I was terribly short, and so light the wind from a good storm could make a kite out of me.

I carried an old Barlowe knife which Pop had sharpened to a razor's edge, and when I found a possum or skunk, I skinned it on the spot. And that first day I had four or five possums, a couple of skunks and a weasel. I wasn't the fastest skinner, but I did a thorough job of it. A pelt wasn't worth anything if it had holes cut in it, and I wasn't about to risk Pop's scorn by nicking one. But it took all day, what with finding each deadfall, resetting and rebaiting them and skinning the critters found in them. When I got home that evening, Pop was really pleased.

A possum hide brought from fifteen to twenty-five cents, depending on size and quality of fur. I caught a couple of possums early in the fall which were females just rid of young ones which had almost no hair, just a bare rough hide. They weren't worth anything, of course. Weasels were good furbearers, but they were just too small, usually. If you got a big one it would bring fifty cents, but the average ones were less than that, sometimes a small one only brought a quarter or a dime.

Every now and then you caught a black house cat. Black cats were worth a quarter to fifty cents. And those occasional cats you caught weren't someone's pet, they were offspring of cats from those abandoned homeplaces like the Barker place, as wild as anything. Funny thing, a house cat of any other color wasn't worth a nickel. Pop and I often wondered if we could find us a couple of black house cats if we couldn't make some pretty good money raising them. Mom wouldn't hear of it though.

Star-black skunks were the real prize. That meant they had nothing but a little white star on the forehead and totally black on the back and tail. One of those brought up to a dollar and a half. On the other end of the scale was the broad-stripe, which meant it had a big wide white stripe from head to tail, sometimes with no black fur in between it at all. They were worth as little as fifteen cents, used for nothing more than making paint brush bristles. A star-black and a broad-stripe only showed up on occasion, each of them making up perhaps one in ten of the total of skunks you would catch.

Most skunks I caught were what they referred to as narrow-stripes, which had two narrow white stripes running back to the tail, or short-stripes, which had the white fur ending about the shoulders. Those two skunk pelts brought from fifty cents to a dollar, depending on size, but the star-black pelt brought from a dollar to a dollar and a half.

Pop had the brilliant idea of using soot and boot-black to mix up something to turn the white part of the pelt black, and it really looked good from the outside. He wasn't trying to cheat anyone, he just figured if he could make an all-black coat collar everyone would come out ahead. But when the skin side was stretched out, you could see where the white fur was. No furbuyer would be fooled by that.

And there were smaller skunks we called civet cats, which brought only fifteen cents to a quarter. I remember getting a great horned owl once and there was a bounty on them back then, so it brought fifty cents.

Well, for the first couple of weeks, things went pretty well, and my fur cache was fairly impressive. Then a cold snap came and there was some snow. That sends skunks and possums into short periods of hibernation. Neither is a true hibernator, like the groundhog or bear or chipmunk. But they can't live in extreme cold, and can't find food, and two days before a winter squall comes through, they know it is coming. They den up in holes and hollows when it hits and go to sleep. They may stay that way two or three weeks or even more if the cold hangs on. But when the weather warms and you have that week or so of forty degree days, they are back out again, hungry and hunting for food.

Pop fixed it so I could run the deadfall lines when the furbearers would be moving, and he knew all about such things. When a cold spell hit, we waited 'til it was over. And because we needed the money from fur so much, each day of sub-freezing temperatures was agony for me. But in late November, there was a stretch of good weather again. Wearing two or three of Pop's old shirts and an old coat, and a wool stocking cap, I set out each day to check the deadfall lines. Pop found a place in town which sold mismatched shoes for a quarter a pair, and got me two which worked pretty good. One was a boys shoe, and the other was a girls boot. The heel of the latter had to be cut down some, but they fit, and they worked.

Running the Deadfall Line

When there was a snow, Pop would use two quarter sections of an old Ford Model T inner tube as galoshes. First I put on a couple of pairs of old nylon stockings which had come from my aunts Bertha or Julia and then pulled on the section of inner tube over them. Pop wired the open end of the inner tube tightly closed at the toes and then wrapped burlap around my feet all the way up past my ankles. Then he securely wrapped the whole thing with binder twine and I had the best footwear you could get without money.

I remember that during the day I would have to stop and rewrap the burlap with twine on occasion but my feet stayed fairly dry and fairly warm. And if I got cold, I stopped and built a fire, did some skinning and got warm again. At dinner time I'd stop and eat some bread and peanuts and fish or rabbit or whatever had been cooked the night before for supper and then I'd reach into that bag of smelly old fish heads and start rebaiting deadfalls again. I couldn't help but think, as I went along, of those poor kids going to school up at the Arthur's Creek church-schoolhouse. It was a shame they couldn't have been as lucky as me.

Pop always cautioned me to beware of anyone in the woods. He told me about a man who lived alone across the river by the name of Art Van Stratten. He was rumored to be deranged, a real threat to women and kids. I remember seeing him once, on a ridge-top above a hollow where I was rebaiting a deadfall. I hid back against a small bluff until he was gone, but my nerves were always a little on edge after that. I was too fast for him to catch, but he always had a rifle with him. Once when my sister Zodie went with me to check deadfalls, Pop gave me his .22 rifle and told me that if it came to it, he expected me to use it. I knew he was talking about Van Stratten.

Pop also told me to always stay back from edge of the Mudhole Eddy bluff, which I had to cross to get to one of the hollows upriver. But one day I was in a hurry, traveling like a yearling buck and not paying enough attention to how close I was to that bluff-top. It was the same bluff where, a year before, Zodie threw the pine knot stump down to me and busted my head open.

But on that fall day running the deadfall lines, I tripped on some loose rocks and went over the edge of that bluff, faced with a fall of 25 or 30 feet onto the rocks below. What saved me was the bait sack I carried. Pop had rigged two burlap bags, one to carry the bait, and the other to carry the fur. He put a small rock in each corner of the bags, and tied a strap around the rocks from one corner to the other so that I could sling them over my back. Those straps were nothing more than braided binding twine, in itself too thin to hold anyone. But the braided straps Pop made were strong enough to hold me, and as I went over the bluff, a limb sticking straight up off a big oak tree hooked that bag, and ran up between the bag and my back. I came to an abrupt halt as the limb bounced, bent, and held me, the straps tight against my chest.

I hooked my legs around the limb, and got astraddle of it somehow, then whittled away the limb with my knife, got the bags from around it and slid down the tree safely to the ground, with nothing more than scratches and a slightly skinned back.

We built a small shed to store and dry furs in and sometime before Christmas I had about 120 furs dried and bundled, ready to go wherever Dad wanted to take them. There were big fur houses in Kansas City and St. Louis and before Christmas each year Pop would take all of his furs to St. Louis where there was the McCullough and Tumbach Fur Company, Maas and Stephan Fur Company and F. C. Taylor Fur Company. Pop was partial to the latter because they had bought so much of his fur back in the twenties just after I was born. They knew Pop well and I remember in years to come when I took furs up to St. Louis on the bus, they knew his furs the minute they saw them. They'd always tell me how they wished everyone knew as much about preparing furs as my Pop did.

There were also individual fur buyers who traveled

around the Ozarks buying furs from people who didn't have enough to take them to a fur buyer in the city. And there was some advantage in selling to them. Dad's mink and muskrat and coons and foxes were worth more money per piece but my possums and skunks and weasels, though they made an impressive pile of pelts, weren't worth much for the weight. A fur buyer wouldn't pay you what a St. Louis company would but he could accumulate a truck load of furs and make some money for his efforts. In turn an Ozark trapper who sold to that individual buyer could escape the expense of traveling so far and have a whole day or two to concentrate on work at home. Mr. Richardson was such a buyer and that year of my first deadfall line, the Williams brothers passed on word to him that I had some of my own furs which Pop might sell, even if he wouldn't sell his own.

He walked down to our place from the road up on the ridge and I remember thinking he might never make it back uphill. He was a big, hefty man, a one-time professional wrestler. He came on a day that Pop had walked into town for supplies and I remember he flirted with Mom something terrible. She ignored all that, my Mom was a one-man woman and I always figured she knew she had the best there was. But Mr. Richardson had in mind getting a good price on those furs and he offered Mom 25 dollars for the whole bunch. I near about swallowed the overalls gallus I was chewing on!

You can't imagine how much money that seemed like to me, back there in the depression days. Pop would have told him to get out his money and there would have been a deal made in a hurry. But Mom said she thought Fred was pretty set on taking all Norten's furs with his to St. Louis, since he was gonna make the trip anyway and they'd "sure bring 40 dollars up there, according to Fred".

I wanted to say something but I knew I'd best not get into this. I knew Mr. Richardson was going to leave without the furs and Pop would come home and rant and rave

Pop caught this gray fox in one of his few dry land sets. Foxes were plentiful back then in the Ozarks, coyotes were not.

at Mom for two days because she lost that 25 dollars. But Mr. Richardson pawed the ground with his foot, fumbled with his hat, talked about how cold it was and said maybe he could go 26 dollars. Mom said she could let them go for 30 dollars and at that she was worried that Fred would be awful mad.

Well it went on for thirty minutes, with the fur buyer looking and figuring and writing with his pencil on a tablet he had in his pocket. He said he wasn't about to go above 27 dollars and Mom said she just couldn't sell those furs for less than 30. Then he had some coffee and thanked us for the hospitality and told Mom again what a pretty lady she was and how he couldn't believe she had a kid my age. He said he'd have to be getting along but he would go way out on a limb and give her 28 dollars and that was his last best offer.

Mom thanked him for coming and said he should come back sometime and deal with Fred. I knew it was all over and I could have cried. When Pop found out what she had done, I knew good and well he'd take that broom he had made for her and whomp her with it. That man had 28 dollars and he was leaving with it. Of course Mom had the upper hand. If Mr. Richardson actually got very far, she knew I could catch up with him in a blink of an eyelash and say she had changed her mind.

But almost across the creek he turned around and come back and said that he had been willing to compromise and Mom wouldn't and that hurt his feelings something awful. Mom said she could understand that and it wasn't like her to be that way. She said she knew a man had to make a little profit in those times, and finally she said and she'd let him have those furs of mine for 29 dollars. Mr. Richardson reached for his pocketbook.

When Pop got back from F.C. Taylor Company before Christmas he wasn't happy with what his furs had brought. Prices were a far cry from what he remembered in the twenties. But he was sure tickled with what Mom had got for my

58

furs. He said he might let her do all the dealing in the future. Pop almost never splurged for anything, but at Christmas that year we felt rich. You can't begin to imagine what 29 dollars was in that day and time, unless you are one of the old timers who can remember the depression. But make no mistake about it, most of my fur money went in that can that was buried in Pop's secret place. Just because you had a little money didn't mean you spent it. Pop figured hard times might come someday!!!!

Still, it was a happy Christmas! Mom sung Christmas carols and read Christmas stories, and there were some toy pistols for Christmas that year, as always, and some socks and a pair of shoes for everyone. They weren't new shoes, and maybe not matched shoes but not worn out either. There was some hard candy and fruit and a coconut for Vaughn. It didn't take a lot to make Vaughn happy. I think that was the year he got a little tin cup and we had a half-grown pig running around the outside of the cabin that someone had traded to Pop for a boat paddle or something. Vaughn was outside playing in a pile of sand with that cup when the pig came along and stepped on it. Vaughn was about four or five and not much bigger than the pig but he wasn't going to take that sitting down. He chased down the pig, jumped on his back and bit the heck out of him. We heard the pig squealing and found Vaughn on top of him with his teeth sunk in it's back.

I got a Christmas present that year too, so significant it is the only one I ever remembered. Pop got me a small "Keen-Cutter" axe, just made for my size. And though I was small in stature, I developed some pretty good shoulders cutting wood and clearing sprouts over the next few years for the neighbors. I started growing a little, and getting stronger because of all the work. Looking back on it, that hard work helped prepare me for future scraps with the Abney brothers, and for the paratrooper training at Fort Benning, Georgia about ten years later, and coping with the cold helped me survive those awful days and nights at Bastogne and in

Pop began to have more faith in me in the years
after my first deadfall line

the Ardennes Forest, fighting the Germans in the cold and snow.

After Christmas that year, I got my first pair of honest-to-goodness boots, matching ones at that. A truck driver friend of Pop who came down into the woods to haul out stave bolts and railroad ties had a brother who was very small, and he had been killed working for the Civilian Conservation Corps, a work project developed by President Roosevelt for the thousands of unemployed down-and-out laborers. The boots fit me, and they were just about like new. You can't imagine what a new pair of boots is like for a ten year old who had always been barefoot. New boots and a new axe....how could times get any better for a ten year old?

If I had to point to a time I went from a boy to a man, it was that fall and winter, with the responsibility of running a deadfall line to help our family survive hard times. Was it tough?....shucks no! I never knew such an exhilarating time of freedom and joy and happiness. I guess God made me for such a life, because you know, skunk smell never did bother me that much, and I'd still just as soon have a bullfrog for breakfast as bacon and eggs!

The photo above shows the Harris family about 1910, my mom is second from right.

The old mud dauber's cabin below was built on the same site about 20 years later. That's Zodie and me to the right, and Farrel and Vaughn to the left

Chapter 6

Hard Times in the Hills

In the twenties, it seemed that country people were moving to towns because the living was easier. But during the later depression years poorer folks began moving back to the country from the towns because it was at least possible to live off the land if you worked at it. In town, if you didn't already have some money you weren't going to get any because there were no jobs.

When I talk about making 15 cents out of a watermelon or 50 cents out of a few fish, you have to realize how much money that seemed to be back then. Pop made a living because he grew watermelons, cantaloupes and big banana mushmelons which could be sold in nearby Houston to the folks who still had a little money-- doctors and lawyers and merchants who lived along the street we called "silk-stocking lane". It was four or five miles across country to town and Pop walked it often with a sack thrown over his shoulder with some fish in it, or several cantaloupes or a couple of watermelons, or maybe some of everything. At times, when someone was taking a team and wagon into town, we could catch a ride. But there were many times after I got to be ten or eleven years old that I carried a pair of mushmelons or watermelons into town in a sack tied in the middle and both ends, so that one melon would be in front and one in back. It would take most of the day and I'd come back with 50 cents if I was really lucky.

Our garden produced food to can and use in the winter. Mom scraped up all types of jars for the canning but quite often we had to buy some lids and rubber gaskets for the jars. And there were other necessities which had to be bought... flour, salt and some coffee and coal oil for the lanterns. Pop put money into the things he had to have to make a living. Trotline hooks for example and a minnow seine. But you didn't buy frivolous things like shoes or clothes. Kids went barefoot for most of the year and then wore old hand-me-

63

down shoes and clothes. Pop's sisters, Bertha, Nellie and Julia, came down from St. Louis about every summer and we'd have to work on the old road for a day filling the ruts with rocks and making it so they could get close to the old mud-dauber's nest. They'd bring old clothes and shoes and other things we could use. Pop would take off somewhere and stay away from them as much as possible because he didn't care for their husbands so much, but I think a lot of it was just his pride. All his family seemed to be doing better than he was and while we never refused all that help, he wasn't pleased to have to have it. Aunt Bertha had a camera and most of the old pictures you see in this book of us kids and Mom and Pop were taken by Aunt Bertha. During the depression they brought some awful stories about the hard times in the city and it made it sound like there were folks up there who were almost starving.

When Pops's sisters came to visit, we all got dressed up and took pictures

One thing about living like we did, the depression wasn't much worse than any other times. We were always a little bit hungry, always needing what we didn't have and always trying to figure out how to make a nickel or a dime.

It was a life dedicated to growing or catching something to eat or growing or catching something to sell.

Fishing was a big part of our life because that was the way to feed a family on the river during the spring and summer after you were tired of eating rabbits and quail and squirrel and ducks. Of course by fall, you were tired of fish. But the Big Piney had lots of goggle-eye, also known as rock bass, lots of smallmouth and largemouth bass, and an abundance of sunfish, long-ears, green sunfish, and even bluegill. Pop used sunfish, and small chubs and suckers, for bait for his trotlines, and then he sold the catfish. Some of those big flathead catfish would weigh up to forty pounds, and a twenty or thirty pounder was fairly common. Pop caught lots of them in the summer, and I'd help him seine bait, or catch bait on a pole.

I made my fishing poles from eight- or ten-foot hard maple saplings which grew tall and thin along the river. I'd take a knife and cut the limbs and twigs off and polish them until they looked like fishing poles. When we lived at the mud daubers nest, I remember paddling Mom around the big eddies nearby in an old johnboat, catching what we always called "perch",--- some of the various species of sunfish. Country people called long-ears "punkinseeds" and green sunfish were called "black perch" or "shade perch". Mom loved to get away and catch them, because she drew praise from Pop for catching so much good trotline bait, but she also got a big kick out of catching a nice smallmouth every now and then. And I remember once when she and I were fishing off a big rock down at the river and she hooked into a huge smallmouth, one of the biggest I had seen at that time. It must have been close to four pounds, and she fought that fish around that rock and landed it.

She took it home, so proud of that big bass, and when Pop saw it, he had a fit. It wasn't something he could sell, because even then, selling bass was illegal. And he sure as heck couldn't bait a trotline with it. He claimed brown bass weren't fit to eat....certainly not in the same class as a stringer of goggle-eye. None of us knew then that someday the smallmouth bass, prized by sport-fishermen in a future time, would help us make a living by creating a demand for Pop's johnboats and float-fishing service.

It was no easy job to land a good bass on a maple pole. The hooks in that day were good, but we had weak line, made out of number 50 sewing thread. We'd take about twenty feet of it, double it into a ten foot piece and then twist it and twist it, and then knot it every couple of feet. Pop bought hooks at the general store in Houston, two or three dozen for a nickel, but he didn't want them lost, and if you fished for big bass, and had your line broke, you lost hooks.

Off by myself, I fished for bass quite often, and hooked some dandies. I used worms to catch sunfish and chubs for Pop's trotlines, and I used a dough-bait concoction to catch carp and redhorse which could both be sold in town. But every now and then I'd catch some fence lizards or blue-tailed skinks or big grasshoppers and use them to fish for bass. From the time I was a little kid, big bass fascinated me, and I'd just drop those lizards around big logs and rocks, and watch those bass come up and inhale them. I lost a few hooks all right, but I landed some bass by the time I was ten years old that would cause today's bass fishermen to drool. You couldn't believe how many bass were in the river back then.

One Saturday afternoon I was down at the Bell Rock Eddy not far from the house catching goggle-eye and bass on a maple pole and line. Pop had a catfish tied up there by me which he had taken the night before on a trotline. I was just trying to catch a mess of fish for supper. It was May and we had picked some mushrooms and some fresh cow-pasley greens, also known as crows-foot, which grew along the river bottoms. In case you don't know what cow-pasley is, it's a small plant you can pick in the spring and boil or fry in grease to make something similar to spinach. There are quite a few plants like it in the Ozarks, like poke and dandelion and watercress and others.

I was looking forward to a pretty good supper that evening. But while I was fishing, Doc Wommack came floating along with another fellow and they hadn't caught much. Wommack was the town doctor from Houston and a fine man too. He stopped and talked to me a long time and admired the fish I had, maybe a half dozen goggle-eye and three or four bass a pound or so apiece. But he knew and I knew that it was against the law to sell them because they were game fish. It was legal however, to sell that catfish and I came up with one heck of an idea. I told Doc Wommack I'd sell him the catfish for 50 cents and throw in all the rest for free.

It took a little longer to catch supper after they had gone but Pop was so tickled to get those two quarters he would have gone without supper. And I had learned that I could use a bass or two, given away as a gift, to sell about anything... watermelons, tomatoes or rough fish. And that really made me a big-time fisherman.

Something else came out of that chance meeting on the river with Old Doc Wommack. I was always very small in stature, shorter for my age than most kids when I was 10 or

11 but stronger and faster than some that were two or three years older than me. Doc Wommack took note of my shortness and he contacted someone with the government and got us a milk cow. Pop went to town and led it back, an old Holstein cow which would provide us milk. We named her Pie-Dough, and started planting turnips and cutting grass to get her through the winter. I filled the little storage shed we had with hay which I had cut, just native grasses growing along the river, cut and dried and stored. We ate the turnip greens, or the leafy tops, but the turnips were saved for the old cow. (Thank goodness... there ain't nothing I hate worse than turnips.)

I had to cut them in pieces for her so she wouldn't choke on them. But she liked those turnips and produced lots of milk. I learned to milk her and take care of her and that became my job. But I got lots of milk and it was just what I needed. We'd cool it in the spring-fed creek near the house and make butter and whipped cream to go with the wheat-short bread.

That's when I began to grow a little. But not enough. The tallest I ever got was about five foot, five inches tall, but that was fine with me. My brother Farrel made it to six foot, three inches, and he's always hitting his head on something. I don't think I ever hit my head on anything. Farrel and me were so much different it was hard to believe we were brothers. He was a scholar from the time he first started to school and loved to read. I wasn't able to read anything and wouldn't go to school unless I was forced to.

The first year or so at the mud-daubers nest we cut out a door and built on another room at the end. We just didn't have enough room for everyone to sleep and Pop wanted a fireplace there to provide more heat. I will remember as long as I live sitting in that room in front of that fireplace listening to Mom read to us kids. Even Pop enjoyed that and for a time, those books she read took us to different places and times, with adventures you could only dream about there in the Ozarks hills.

I know that fireplace meant something special to my mother because it had been made from the same rocks in the fireplace of old G.W. Harris' homestead where she had first learned to read as a little girl. My mother was well educated for that time. She had finished the eighth grade and had passed some type of teacher training and testing which gave her the right to teach. Before she was married, about 1918, she had taught for a year or so as a mere teenager at Paddy's Chapel near Paddy's Creek on the lower Big Piney. The school was about ten miles away and she stayed with a family there during the week, then road a horse back home on weekends. Mom talked about that time in her life as if it were pretty rough at times, since there were teenage boys there who were only in the second or third grade and very difficult to handle in that old one-room school where she was trying to teach all ages and all grades.

Old homeplaces were found all along the river when I was a boy, some of them from way back in the 1800's, back as far as civil war days. Lots of them were just small cabins and frame houses and many were in shambles. But about anything you could live in was being lived in. The old Johnson place was a mile or so to the north just above the bend of the river and the eddy which still bears their name. Ben and Andy Johnson were brothers and Andy Johnson was sheriff of Texas county for awhile. His brother Ben was a deputy. They were about Pop's age. I remember that Ben Johnson was one of the meanest and toughest men in the whole county, always into some type of fight or brawl at every dance or community picnic.

A half mile away was an old broken down place where Millie Clark lived with her three kids. Their old house sat up on a hillside above the Cow Ford eddy. Millie was either widowed or divorced and her and Ben Johnson had a thing going. She would take off with him for two or three days at a time and just leave her kids home. They'd show up at our place about to starve and Mom would feed them like they were her own. So there were times during the thirties when

Mom and Pop were feeding seven kids instead of four. As poor as we were those kids gave new meaning to the word. But they were good kids and the youngest girl, Connie, was my first girl friend. It was fun sometimes to have some other youngsters our age to play with, though there wasn't much time for play with all the work we had to do.

One thing happened back then that folks around the Big Piney got quite a kick out of. Ben Johnson was perceived as pretty much of a bully and he got up in the air when a local teacher at Houston thrashed one of his boys who had been trying to follow in his father's footsteps. Ben headed for school the next day to teach the professor a lesson and folks figured there'd be one less teacher at school when Ben got done with him.

The teacher was smaller than Ben Johnson and had been sort of a meek fellow until that day. He had also been a professional boxer! Out on the school lawn, he gave Ben Johnson a whipping while lots of the kids looked on, and though I never saw it, the word was that Ben went around town for awhile with swollen eyes and lips and his nose bent crooked, a little meeker than he had ever been. There was always talk that Ben and his brother Andy were plotting revenge but nothing ever came of it.

I think we lived at the mud-daubers nest for almost three years and they were the leanest and most difficult times of our lives. The government gave us an old steer, as they did to many of the rural families with several kids. Sheriff Johnson brought it down to us and said that the rules stipulated it had to be killed and butchered on the spot. Pop and me spent all day working on that steer and Mom canned most of the meat. I'm here to tell you that was the awfullest job I ever had and that beef tasted bad enough to kill maggots. We ate it through the winter...at least some of us did. Sixty years later I still can't hardly eat beef.

Pop would go around the community butchering steers and hogs for other people who needed help. He'd get the head and the feet of the hogs and we'd eat the jowls and pigs feet and the brains. I know...you'd just as soon not hear this, but that's the way it was. Sometimes when Pop would butcher a steer he'd get the head and hide and the lungs. We'd use the lungs as bait for the deadfalls in November. Most of the butchering took place in late October or early November when it got cool.

In that day there were lots of free-ranging cattle and hogs, most of which were rounded up in the fall and sold. Folks marked the cattle with brands and the hogs with ear-markings of some sort or another. One farmer might have three notches in the left ear and that was his mark, while another would have two notches in the right ear and one in the left and that would be his mark. When the hogs were rounded up, usually with the help of dogs specially trained for that job, the hogs were separated and sold or butchered and the young ones ear-marked for round-up the next fall. Folks who owned hogs usually had smokehouses where the meat was hung and cured and smoked and thereby preserved for the whole winter and into spring.

When we got any pork, Pop packed it in salt to preserve it and stored it in a box in the loft of the house. When it was prepared it was washed and boiled and then cooked. Still, it was awful. I couldn't figure out why we'd fool with beef and hogs. There were rabbits and quail and squirrels and bullfrogs and fish to eat and that's what I preferred. In the winter time I remember eating young muskrats which Pop had trapped and they weren't bad. In fact Pop used to say that mom was such a good cook that she could bake a muskrat so you couldn't tell it from baked possum. I sure would rather eat a young muskrat today than deer-meat or beef or some of that salt-pork I remember.

And though I shouldn't tell it, Pop and I developed a way to have fresh ham and pork chops every now and then even though we never owned any hogs. I got to be an awfully good shot with that old .22 rifle and I'd kill a young shoate along the river about once a year when we knew where there were some of them. Those shoate's were not ear-marked, so they didn't actually belong to anyone yet.

Pop got worried that some farmer was going to bring the law down on us so he said he'd watch from some nearby hilltop and if I got caught cleaning and butchering one of those young hogs, he'd come along and give me a good whippin' and just raise heck with me for being such a no-account Harris so-and-so and make the farmer feel sorry enough for me to let me go. Thank God I never got caught. I caught heck enough from Pop without having to get a dose of it for doing what he told me to do.

Of course, we probably had a right to some young hog which hadn't been marked yet because so many of them got in our garden during the summer. We didn't have wire so we made pole fences and brush fences and kept ever vigilant against free-ranging stock. But there were always times when something was in the garden and had to be run off. Pop was particularly mad at one young steer that belonged to a neighbor to the south. He was always in that garden and I remember Pop saying that one of these days he'd get his rifle and clip that steers ear off and that would get rid of him for good.

Well one day in the spring of 1934, Pop and Mom were up the river setting trotlines and I believe Zodie and Farrel and Vaughn were with them. Pop left me behind for some kind of chores and that included keeping that steer out of the garden. He wasn't as large as today's steers of course, living on the kind of food there was for calves to find back then. Our garden was the horn of plenty. I ran him out of it once that morning and then there he was again. I remembered what Pop had said about clipping his ear off and I figured if he could do it, I could. Even Pop said I was a better shot than he was.

So I steadied myself against the corner of the cabin and took good aim and squeezed off a shot just as that young steer lifted his head. I hit him right between the eyes and he dropped in his tracks, stone dead. I got so scared I ran around the cabin three or four times just trying to figure out the best way to kill myself before Pop got back and did it for me. I could butcher that steer and try to save some of the meat before it spoiled but I've already pointed out that I hated beef and there was the chance that the neighbor would find out and Pop would have to pay for that steer. Then he'd rant and rave and say he expected about that kind of thing of me. "You #%&*$*@%$ no-account Harris, what the #&#@$*&...." he'd say, and then if you left out the cuss-words there wouldn't be much else left.

I couldn't stand the thought of several hours of that so I made a decision to bury the steer in the garden right there between the corn and the pole beans. He was a good 400 pound animal and I couldn't move him. So I got the pick and shovel and started digging a hole right behind him and in four or five hours of hard digging, you wouldn't believe what a grave I had dug. I was sure it was big enough and deep enough so I found a pry-pole and heaved and grunted and worked until finally that steer slid into it, with all four feet sticking up and each one several inches above ground level.

If only I would have dug a few more inches it would have worked great but I was already into rock and hard clay and I don't know how much deeper I could have gone. Anyway, I filled the hole back up as best as I could and started scattering the excess dirt and by four or five in the afternoon you couldn't tell there was anything different about the garden at all, except maybe it was a little higher in that one spot, where I had to build the ground up to cover the feet. I sat back and rested until everyone came home just about dark and they couldn't figure out what I had been doing to make me so exhausted.

It came a big rain a night or so later and Dad was already beginning to notice something smelling terrible around the garden. The rain and the settling soil left four hooves sticking up out of the ground and you've never seen such a puzzled look on a man's face as there was on Pop's when he came across that.

My mom and sister Zodie with a pair of
muskrats sometime about the beginning
of the depression.

He said pretty much what I thought he was going to say, for hours and hours and days and days. He really moaned about wasting that much meat. If I had only butchered it, he said. How could I let that much meat go to waste, he said. Must be because I was a no-account -#*&$@$%A#@* Harris so and so after all, he said. But he did what I should have done, he dug down and cut that steers legs off at the knees so any visitors would have no idea what happened. The neighbor looked for that steer for weeks and never did find it. But he wondered why Pop brought him some catfish and garden produce every now and then.

My sister Zodie really grew up during those years at the mud-daubers nest. She went to school regular at the Arthur's Creek school house, which was about a two-mile walk. You had to really want to go to school to walk two miles. It was a one room school which served as a local church on Sunday. Mom and Zodie would even walk to church. I went on occasion but not often. And if Pop had work to be done I stayed home to do it.

Surviving was more important than schooling. In the summer, when Zodie turned 14, she got a job working on the Towell farm a few miles away and she lived with Mr. and Mrs. Towell during the week and came home on weekends. She was getting a dollar a week if I remember right, working in the fields all day for awhile helping to bring in hay and storing it in the barn. And at noon, when all the other farm hands got to come in and rest for awhile at dinnertime, Zodie had to go help with serving the meal.

It was harder on girls in that time because they were thinking about being pretty and there just wasn't enough money to buy anything. Zodie wore Dad's old shoes and dresses made from flour sacks, which most women used in that time. Flour and chicken feed and wheat shorts came in sacks which had prints of different kinds and if you had a flair for sewing you could make some nice looking dresses and shirts out of them. Trouble was, we never had a sewing machine. Mom had to hand-stitch everything and that didn't produce many pretty dresses.

As isolated as we were, we did find ways to enjoy ourselves. There was always time to swim in the river in the summer and fish. Pop made a checker board back then and taught me how to play checkers but I got pretty good at it and within a week or so I won all the games so that put an end to checkers. Pop didn't mind losing every now and then but he got downright perturbed when he'd lose four or five games in a row and I still don't lose many checker games even today.

I remember how fascinated I was at all the fun things Pop knew how to do. Some of those fun things he showed me came back to haunt him. Like the time when we had a big sack of potatoes out of the garden and he set a dozen or so bad ones out for potato slinging. He cut a big willow sapling and showed me how he could whip that switch forward and just hurl that potato out of sight. That really amazed me. I threw a couple of potatoes three times farther with that willow stick catapult than I could with my arm.

A day or so later Pop was down in the garden below the house doing some hoeing. I found that switch and got me a handful of potatoes and climbed up on the hill at the edge of the woods and let one fly. It sailed way over him and he ignored it. The next one hit in the brush fence at the edge of the garden and Pop stopped and looked and took off his hat and scratched his head, wondering what that was he had heard. A third one landed short and he turned around to see what in the world was happening in his garden. By then I had the range and the next shot hit the hoe handle and went to pieces, splattering Pop with rotten potato.

One thing about Pop, it didn't take him long to figure things out and blame me. But I was way up in the woods by the time he got to the cabin and I stayed there. He'd kick my butt later but he wouldn't kick it as hard after he'd had time to cool down.

Pop invented some less dangerous recreation. One time

he leveled off a place out behind the old cabin, cleaned it off bare and dug four holes the ground in a diamond just like bases in a baseball field. Then he made four or five big round balls about the size of croquet balls, cutting them out of pine, whittling them down and filing them down with an old wood rasp and painting them until they were almost perfect. Then the whole family got out there and the object was to roll your ball into the hole at first base, then second, then third, and then finally back to home. First one to get home was the winner.

It made a good game because you could knock each other out of the way and spend all afternoon just trying to get around to home. And it was hard to cheat at that game, which made it a real challenge. Often everyone in the family would be mad after the game but the winner. It taught me that a family which plays together will have something to argue about way into the night.

The old Arthur's Creek school and church house, site of the Battle of 1934 between me and the Abney brothers.

Chapter 7

Copperheads and Confrontations

A month or so after I buried the steer in the garden I had some more adventure. Uncle Johnny Harris was my mother's older brother, and he was a little bit slow, but with a great disposition and a wonderful temperament. During World War I, he had joined the army and gone overseas on a ship filled with soldiers who came down with that awful flu which killed so many in that time. He survived it, but most of the men on that ship had died. Though he wasn't the smartest man I ever met, he was tough and a hard worker. He was also one of the kindest and gentlest men I ever knew.

Uncle Johnny worked hard to keep his family up as everyone did in the depression, but they had more than we had, a few cattle, hogs and horses and 75 to 80 acres of corn on the old farm. He called me 'Snort' and he really liked me because I stuttered a lot, and he had a little bit of a speech problem himself. He also noticed that I was always up to trying anything.

His wife, Aunt Nellie, lived to be 101, and he had two daughters older than me who are still alive, Velma and Beulah Fay. They only lived a mile away, and sometime just after Thanksgiving in 1933 he asked me if I wanted to go to town with him on Saturday morning.

Pop said it was a good idea, he gave me a list of things to give to Mr. Smalley at the general store in Houston. The river was up about four feet but Uncle Johnny had an old rubber tired wagon and two fine horses. Old Prince was a bay and Ginger was black and white. Both were high spirited, but Uncle Johnny was a wonder with a team of horses, and he made them do his bidding with a minimum of words. He talked to those horses, and they responded, I'm sure he never hit one in his life.

Copperheads and Confrontations

I walked over to his house early in the morning and helped him hitch the team. Then he set me up on the spring seat beside him and wrapped a horse blanket around me, and we took a shortcut to town at a crossing, which saved a mile or so. The river was high with heavy fall rains.... it had floating logs and a lot of current. Uncle Johnny judged where he had to put the wagon in above the crossing to come out on the open road downstream and he did it masterfully. Those big horses jumped in and the wagon floated. It all worked perfect.

Uncle Johnny put his life in their hands that day, because he couldn't swim. I wasn't scared much, I could swim like a duck. I held my feet up and across the river we went. Those horses hit the road downstream just right, and got out of cold water frisky as could be. We went up that Mineral Springs hill in a hurry and we were in town in less than an hour.

There were lots of wagons and horse teams there in front of Smalley's store and no cars at all, so Uncle Johnny went in and got groceries and supplies on Pop's list and his, while I wandered around looking at this and that. Then he had to drive the team up beside the loading dock where they began to load boxes of stuff behind the seat. I was holding the reins when a Model T Ford came around the corner blowing its horn... Ah-oo- gah! Ah-oo-gah!

Those horses went off the ground and took off at a dead run. The wagon was going full bore down the road, and I turned them up onto main street sawing on those reins to turn them, scared half to death. We careened along up Main Street in Houston, folks diving this way and that to get our of their way, and me yelling whoa, and pulling back on those reins for all I was worth. I couldn't stop them, but I turned them again in a large two or three block area, back to the store and passed it, back up to Main Street again, always around the corners on two rubber wheels.

The roads in Houston were just gravel back then, and I came within a fraction of turning over two or three times, cutting corners across a wooden sidewalk once, pedestrians scattering everywhere, with me screaming at the top of my voice for help. No one would brave those horses, but the second time around Uncle Johnny stepped out before them and grabbed the harnesses and held on. If he had fallen, he would have been hurt bad. It took him aways to stop them, with me using all my weight trying to stand on that brake, and then finally some men jumped in to help him get them calmed down.

It was a dangerous situation, because if those horses had straddled a pole it could have hurt them bad, maybe one or both would have had to have been destroyed. Uncle Johnny went on and on about what I had done, and bragged on me like no one ever had before...but I was just lucky. If that wagon had turned over at the speed we were going, I could have been killed. It was just another adventure for me. And I was about to have more narrow escapes.

Early the next summer Mom and Pop were upriver setting trotlines. Mom was pregnant, only a month or so away from giving birth to my youngest brother Bryce. She couldn't do much, so Pop took Farrel and Vaughn along to help get bait. Zodie and I had been left behind to do something but I can't remember what it was. Anyway my older sister had a little trinket box of some sort and I got ahold of it and was aggravating her with it.

Zodie was older and bigger but I was faster. That's one way of pointing out that if she could have caught me she would have killed me. But I ran out of the house and was jumping up and down on a board in the front yard teasing Zodie and reminding her that she could only wish she could get her hands on me. Beneath that board was a big copperhead and he took Zodie's side of the argument. He came out from beneath the board, half mashed and all mad. And while I stood there sticking my tongue out at my sister and daring her to chase me, the copperhead nailed me just above the middle toe of my left foot.

I remember it was a hot, burning pain, and when I looked

down, the snake was stuck on my foot, writhing around trying to get his fangs out so he could take aim again. I kicked him away and killed him with garden tool of some kind which was nearby and as I remember it that copperhead was a monster of a snake. It seemed at the time that he was as big around as my leg and six feet long. Actually, he was about 30 inches long and as big around as a golf ball, and that's a pretty good size for a copperhead. They didn't get much bigger than that in the Big Piney hills.

Zodie saw it happen and she told me to sit still while she went to get Pop. I didn't know much about what to do so I tightened an old rag around my leg just above the ankle and made a tourniquet. It took Pop about forty minutes to get back and you could tell he was scared, especially after seeing the size of that snake. There were three dangerous snakes in the Ozarks back then, timber rattlesnakes, which were very rare that far north, and cottonmouths, fairly common along the river and in the creeks which fed it, and copperheads which were very common.

I never knew anyone to get bitten by a rattlesnake, never even saw one when I was a kid. We knew a few people who were bitten by cottonmouths, which were extremely dangerous because they were big snakes, not so much in length but in weight. They carried more venom. Copperheads usually didn't have so much venom and I have heard it said that if they had eaten recently and used the poison in their venom sacks, it would take awhile for the venom to rebuild. I guess that copperhead that bit me hadn't had a good meal in awhile because I surely got a good dose of venom.

I was getting sick by the time Pop got home and my foot was swelling and throbbing. Pop took his razor and told me to look away and yell real loud. I did, but it still hurt when he incised the fang marks and began to suck out the poison just like the old-timers had always said you should do. When he finished that he poured coal oil in a pan and soaked my foot in the coal oil.

I asked Pop if I was going to die. He said copperheads

bites never killed anyone that he knew of and he had known lots of people who had been bitten two or three times. Then he added that sometimes it seemed like a snakebite made people about half crazy and I might never be quite right in the head again but there wasn't much danger of dying. That made me feel quite a bit better. I knew several people who weren't quite right in the head and they all seemed to enjoy themselves and not have any problems.

By nightfall my ankle was the same size as my lower leg and my foot was beginning to turn bluish-black. I began to run a fever and become delirious. Mom held me all night and I had awful, fitful dreams. I had never seen concrete that I know of but I dreamed that night that I was laying on a big slab of concrete in a sweltering sun, just suffocating in the heat. That went on for days and when I did come around enough to drink some water I was in great pain. By the second day my whole lower leg and foot were bluish-black and the skin on my foot and ankle was beginning to split. Mom was keeping it coated with grease.

For about three days I was delirious with fever, half unconscious and very sick. For those of you who are biting your fingernails in suspense, I didn't die! It must have been hell for Mom, with a new baby on the way and me laying there in that condition. Eventually the swelling began to subside and the leg began to heal. A large area of my foot around the bite actually seemed to rot with infection and it smelled terrible. I couldn't walk at all and Farrel had to pull me around in a little cart we had for hauling wood. He really suffered for a couple of weeks because every time I had to go to the outdoor john he had to take me. And all my jobs became his, like working in the garden and bringing in the cook wood. And I got all the attention he had been used to getting because he had gone through a long spell of recuperating from his burns.

I overdid it a little and had Farrel haul me around in that cart quite awhile after I became able to walk. If Pop hadn't have eventually put an end to it Farrel would have been pulling that cart 'til Christmas. But toward the end of that, my brother got smart and every time he had to haul me somewhere he ran that cart over the roughest ground he could find. It got to where it was easier to walk.

The snakebite had no lasting effect and I was fortunate. Many people who have had a leg swell and turn black and break open like that have lost it to amputation. I was bitten by a copperhead ten or twelve years later and it didn't even effect me, I suppose because I had built an immunity from the first bite. And since then bee stings and wasp stings have no effect at all and I pay little attention to the occasional stinging remarks of my wife, or the venomous insults of my adversaries. Some of them have said Pop was right...that anyone bitten by a copperhead will never be quite normal again!

I was walking pretty well by August, limping a little but ready for the Old Settler's reunion in nearby Houston. That was one of the big events of the year and it occurred in mid-August, I suppose because that's when it was least likely to rain. A carnival would come in and you could ride the rides for a few pennies or a nickel. Folks would camp on the campground there at the reunion grounds just outside of Houston and there would be dozens and dozens of families camping out of wagons for two or three days at a time. Pop always borrowed Uncle Johnny's wagon and horse when we lived at the mud-daubers nest and we loaded up bedding and food and went camping at the Old Settlers Reunion about every year.

They had a big tent set up where Farrel and I saw our first movie. We paid a nickel each to get in and they showed several movies all afternoon. Seems like they were all westerns, with big stars like Tom Mix or Hopalong Cassidy or Lash Larue or the Red Raider. And they all were about the same story... one or several bad guys, a few good guys, and one that was better than all the rest and tougher as well. There was usually a pretty lady in danger or being swindled or something like that. Then there was a gun fight and the bad guys ended up dead or in jail. Too bad they don't have any good movies like that today.

Somehow Pop always managed to have a quarter for Farrel and I back then. That put the Old Settlers Reunion up there on a par with Christmas. Of course Pop made money when he got there by bringing some mushmelons and watermelons and selling them. So you had some money to use if you used it wisely. I never spent any of it on the dancing ladies or the creature from the jungle or throwing at the bottles to try to win a stuffed bear. My money went for the movies, riding the ferris wheel or buying gum or an ice cream cone.

They'd have square dances at night and singing and all sorts of activities. There would always be a big fight during the reunion when somebody was dancing with somebody else's girlfriend and there was some moonshine along. But I don't ever remember anything serious.

Most of the fights back then were over a woman. Like everyone else, I had my first big fight over a girlfriend at the age of eleven, out in front of the Arthur's Creek church and schoolhouse. Zodie came up with her first boyfriend back then and of course I wound up being the chaperone for them. I remember her first date, when the three of us went to the Arthur's Creek School one Sunday evening in the fall for a singing. They had those kind of things back then and it gave people something to do on the day of rest without costing any money. The last thing I wanted to do was to go to church on Sunday evening and listen to a bunch of folks sing. But Pop told me I was to go along with Zodie and her boyfriend so it would look proper and so I went.

That's where I met Wanda Reinert. Her daddy had an almost-new Model A Ford and we snuck out of church and sat in the back seat of the car talking and holding hands. And I will say that the singing sounded just as good out there. In fact, I suspect the farther you got from it the better it sounded. Anyway it was just about getting dark and Wanda and I were getting better and better acquainted when along came the Abney brothers, Junior, Willie and Archie. I didn't know that Junior had his eye on Wanda himself and considered her his girlfriend. She in turn, was leaning more and more toward becoming my girlfriend there in the romantic setting of the back seat of her fathers automobile. Without any warning, Junior, a year or so older than me, punched me in the nose and blood started squirting everywhere. I came out of the car with a tire pump which had been in the floorboard and clobbered the closest brother with it. Luckily, it was the older one, Archie. The youngest one, Willie, headed for the church and Junior and I were out there rolling around in dirt while the sweet refrains of "Will There Be Any Stars in My Crown" wafted from inside.

In short order the fight was over and you could hear Junior Abney above the singing, screaming his lungs out. I got behind him and had my teeth sunk in the narrow part of the very top of his shoulder just below his neck. I think it looked worse than it was because of my nose bleeding the way it was but I fully intended to hang on 'til it thundered, just like Pop told me a snapping turtle would do if it ever got ahold of you. The church began to empty out, urged on by the younger Abney who was yelling that I had killed one brother already and was about to kill the other one. Some of the men were trying to separate us and not making much headway until Zodie came out and started prying my mouth open with a screwdriver. That's the only thing that freed Junior.

I guess they revived Archie and bandaged up Junior and went on with the singing but it was over between Wanda and me. I suppose she saw the violent side of me at the age of eleven and decided against a lasting relation-ship. But it was over between her and Junior too. There were rumors around the Arthur's Creek School that he might have rabies.

I had another run-in or two with the Abney brothers in later years and we remained arch enemies until we grew up. You know how you hear these stories about how kids get into a squabble and then get to know each other and become friends. Well that never happened with me and the Abney's. I hated them and they hated me and we fought about every time we ever run into each other. Still and all, I'll be willing to shake hands and forgive and forget at the pearly gates if St. Peter insists. But that's quite a concession on my part and I don't see any reason to do it until then.

Some good came out of that fight. Pop said I didn't have to go back to school anymore because the Abney brothers had me so badly outnumbered and Vaughn and Farrel were too young to help. I guess I would have fought Joe Louis if it would have kept me out of school.

In January of 2000, I returned to visit the
Old Arthur's Creek School and sat in the desk
where I once was so miserable.

Copperheads and Confrontations

But my luck wouldn't last. I suppose if we had lived another five or six years at the mud-daubers nest I would have been an entirely different person than I am today. But God works in strange and mysterious ways and without Pop knowing it, I think He put an idea in Pop's head which was to make our lives better and perhaps keep me from becoming a complete social outcast. We were about to move back to the old Lone Star Mill where I was born.

In the late summer of 1934 my younger brother Bryce was born there in the mud-daubers nest and it was rough on Mom. It took awhile to get a doctor down there and maybe that kind of worried Pop. But I think he also began to remember that things were better when we lived at the old Lone Star Mill. Now it sat empty and still, the old mill wheel removed and the weeds growing up around it. It was big enough for a family of five kids and the mud-daubers nest never had been big enough for a family of four.

And there was something else the old mill had. Old Highway 17 crossed the river nearby, just a gravel road going across the river with a rickety old steel bridge. A new Highway 17 had just been built crossing the river a couple of miles upstream, so there wouldn't be a whole lot of traffic but there was a campground there near the mill, where the old bridge crossed. Pop got the big idea of selling his produce to campers and renting johnboats he would build to those who wanted to fish or just have a Sunday afternoon excursion.

So at the beginning of the spring of 1935 Pop got ahold of Uncle Johnny Harris and he brought his team down to the mud-daubers nest. We loaded everything we had and headed up the grade on the rough old road leading toward town. I remember sitting on the back of the wagon and watching the old cabin disappear behind me. I would never see it again while it was standing. I said goodbye to my boyhood that day. At twelve years of age I would begin to become a man. I didn't know it but even before my twelfth birthday I would become a fishing guide and it was something I would be for the rest of my life.

The old dam which backed water up for the Lone Star Mill
can still be seen today on the upper Big Piney.

The window in the concrete wall behind me is one that Zodie and I cut out in the early 1930's to be used as an escape window in case the old mill ever caught on fire.

Lone Star Mill
1920's

Chapter 8
Return to the Old Mill

Pop didn't have permission from anyone to move into the old mill. It was there and it was empty and we moved in. There was a lot of that going on during the depression with old empty places out in the country. Folks had left the homes in the country before and early on during the depression, moving to towns to find work, but when life got so overbearingly hard in town and jobs just disappeared, people who were about to starve just found any old empty house where they could get out of the cold and rain. Sometimes a family of six or eight or ten would live in a little one- or two-room shack that had been abandoned for years. Some folks lived in old barns and some even lived in caves. Because in the country you could at least scrape up a little food--fish and wildlife and wild plants-- and you could cultivate a garden. In the city you had to find a soup line or starve.

Mr. Lindholme was in charge of the Lone Star Mill and he was a meek, mild fellow who liked Pop and would have liked to see us live there. So we put in a good garden and Pop built a couple of johnboats and whittled out some sassafras paddles in order to have boats to rent or sell.

My first job when we got there was knocking out a window in the basement. Pop was very much afraid of house fires because back in those days, with people trying to stay warm in the winter in rickety old houses that were half falling down, lots of country people had died in house fires in the night. He wanted the basement, where Farrel and Vaughn and I would sleep, to have a window to get out of just in case. It wasn't really a basement because it wasn't below ground. It was a cement-walled room which sat under part of the mill and had probably been used to store grain back in the days at the turn of the century when it was a grist mill. When I was a kid it seemed like a big room but it still stands today and it's only about ten feet by ten feet now. It must have shrunk some over the years!

Zodie and I went to work chipping away the concrete with a hammer and chisel and in a few days we had a window knocked out. And up the highway past Bucyrus, some fellow had a cow for sale for almost nothing. Pop and I hitched a ride with someone and bought that old cow, a Jersey which I named old Mary. She was so cheap because she had one caked udder which didn't produce milk. We were several miles from home so I set out walking and leading our new cow while Pop caught another ride back to the mill. It was slow traveling for me and the cow, it took me until well after dark and poor old Mary was worn out by the time we got there. But that summer I filled the concrete room where we slept with grasses to dry for winter food and Vaughn and Farrel and I slept on that soft grass. And old Mary gave better milk and more milk than old Pie-Dough so she was worth all the work.

We planted turnips for her as we had for Pie-Dough. Turnips will grow well into the winter and last in the ground

Old Mary and Me

92

until you pull them up. Even if the ground is frozen they are still good, you just have to thaw them out. They make great winter food to go along with the dried grasses but I had to always cut the turnips up into small pieces so old Mary wouldn't choke on them.

We had some great fishing down the Piney at the old mud-daubers nest but it was just as good at the Lone Star Mill and we were right next to the river. For miles below us there were deep eddies separated by shoals and hordes of bass and goggle-eye and black perch. There were some largemouth bass but many more smallmouth and they were the real prize of local fishermen. As I said before, Pop thought anybody who fished for bass and goggle-eye was crazy. He loved to trotline and his main goal was flat-head catfish.

No bass could approach the smallest of the flathead catfish Pop caught. Of course he loved to gig redhorse and yellow suckers in the winter but Pop never used a fly rod or casting reel that I can remember. Sometimes he'd lower himself to relaxing with a can of worms and a willow pole catching black perch or long-eared sunfish from the bank somewhere close to the house and he'd use most of them for trotline bait.

There were ready-made customers crossing the old bridge going to town and camping at the campgrounds and having picnics there. Pop advertised his boats for rent and campers would rent them just to spend an hour or so paddling around in the old Mill Pond Eddy. We also seined minnows and dug nightcrawlers which we sold for bait to those folks who wanted to fish. And Pop would occasionally take fishermen out in his boat and paddle for them while they fished.

In the early summer of that year, Albert Howell, one of the more successful big landowners in our area, rented a boat and asked me if I'd paddle it for him while he fished with his fly rod. Still several months shy of twelve years of age, I spent the afternoon paddling that boat for him and watch-

Mr. Albert Howell was my first fishing client

ing him catch smallmouth bass. He'd get ahold of some two or three pounders right there in the Mill Pond Eddy and you've never seen such a fight. I watched in awe as he worked that fly rod and I couldn't wait to learn how to do it. Mr. Howell took note of my interest and gave me an old fly-rod and reel, and finally I graduated to something well above a maple pole. I caught on quickly and used that fly-rod for a couple of years, and eventually saved up enough from what Mr. Howell paid me to buy my own, a brand new one from Watson's Hardware up in town. I think it cost about five dollars, and brother, that was some money.

Zodie was older than me of course and could paddle a johnboat as good as me or anyone else so she got to take the first long trips down river. The Paw-Paw Bottoms lay just above the Mill Pond Eddy and upstream a quarter mile the new highway crossed the river at a place called Dogs Bluff. You could load a johnboat in the back of an old truck and take it up to the Dogs Bluff bridge and float it back down to the Mill Pond and get in several hours of good fishing. The idea of float-fishing trips in our region was spawned right there, I believe. There were already similar types of trips being organized on the White and the James rivers but Pop's float trips were well ahead of the Jim Owen floats which he and his crew made known nationwide.

On the White River they transported johnboats back on empty railroad cars because the railroad ran alongside the river or near it much of the way. On the Piney we didn't have access to a truck to bring the boats back so we'd arrange for a car to pick up the fishermen and bring them back. Then Zodie or I would paddle the boat back upstream for several miles, wading and pulling over the swifter and shallower shoals. Our work really began when the fishing trip ended.

Just below the old mill and Mill Pond Eddy was the Peaked Rock Eddy, then the Sweet 'Tater Eddy, the Ginseng Hole, the McKinney Eddy and a long stretch of shoals and potholes above the mouth of Brushy Creek. Below that was one heck of a stretch of fishing water known as the Horse-shoe Bend Eddy and the Towhead Eddy and then after another half mile of potholes and shoals there was the crossing at Mineral Springs where you could pick up fishermen. That made a great half-day of fishing but if you wanted to fish all day you went on down to the Sand Shoals crossing below the old mud-daubers nest and you floated through big deep holes like the Cathcart Eddy, the Mudhole Eddy, the Casteel Eddy, the Dutchman's Eddy, the Farley Hole, the Bell Rock Eddy, the Cow Ford Hole and the Johnson Eddy, with lots of potholes and shoals in between.

I guess I'm going to have to throw in a map here just to give you a complete picture. If you look at it you'll see the Peaked Rock Eddy just below the old mill where we lived. Pop and I put a cornfield in right at the upper end of the Peaked Rock and shortly after I started taking people fishing as a professional twelve-year-old guide, one of my big adventures took place right there. It involved a boat paddle, a steep rock, and two lady fishermen in long dresses.

The women were in their late thirties or early forties and they said they had done quite a bit of fishing. I don't believe they had. They heard from someone that they could camp at the Lone Star Mill, rent a boat and hire a fishing guide. Pop was down in the corn patch the day they came so I told them I'd paddle them down to about the McKinney Eddy, then bring them back and only charge a dollar for an afternoon of fishing. It sounded simple enough until we got to the Peaked Rock Eddy, so named because of a huge rock in the middle of the hole which had a point at the top like the peak of a mountain. There were smallmouth and goggle-eye beneath it and back under it where the water was deep and dark and one of the ladies decided she'd like to get up on top and fish down beside it. I did that all the time but I was twelve years old and light and barefoot most of the time.

The sides of the rock were just too steep for her and the toe-holds weren't made for the shoes she had on. She

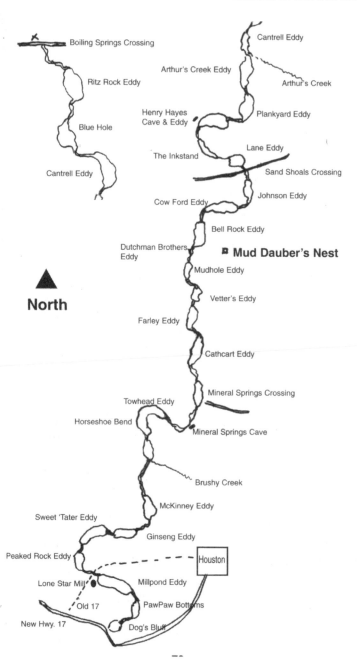

pointed out that she could do anything a man could do and certainly anything that a twelve-year-old boy could do and more. I've learned over the years that when women say that they can do anything a man can do, a man is better off just to let her make a fool of herself trying and not argue with her. At twelve years old, I didn't know that. I said "yes ma'am but when you step from the boat to that rock, the boat will move away and"...

The lady wouldn't hear it, she said to paddle her over to the big rock so she could climb up on top and I could hand her fishing pole to her when she got there. So I did as I was told and she stepped gingerly out to the steep side of the rock and planted her weight and started to step out. When she did, her weight pushing against the boat shoved it away and the best boat paddler in the world can't hold a boat long against the pressure of someone stepping out and pushing away.

I'll give her credit, she clung there to the side of the big rock for a second and then began to slide slowly down the steep face and into the water. Both ladies began to shriek and holler, and Pop, who was working in the cornfield nearby, ran to the bank to see what was wrong.

I couldn't figure any way to help her but I tried. I pushed the blade of the paddle against the rock right between her thighs and pried up as hard as I could. It worked for a second, giving her a much needed boost and lifting her enough to allow her to gain a little on the rock. But the pressure pushed the boat away and with the paddle gone, she begin to slip down slowly into the water again. I frantically paddled back, placed the paddle between her legs once again and pried up as hard as I could. Same result.

After several minutes of the futile attempt to help her gain the peak, I was exhausted and she was too. She finally just fell back into the water and grabbed the side of the boat. I paddled her to the closest gravel bar and she sat there dripping wet and fuming mad as she wrung out her clothes the best she could without taking anything off.

Trying to catch my breath after the ordeal was over, I apologized all over myself and told her I hoped she wasn't mad at me. After all, I had tried to tell her what was going to happen and the laws of slick rocks and water and gravity made it impossible for me to do anything about it.

She said she wasn't so much mad at me. She was peeved about the old codger over there on the opposite bank who was rolling around on the ground holding his sides and laughing. I told her I didn't know him.

The ground we cleared along the river was the best farm ground we had ever worked and we had the use of a horse and plow borrowed from Mrs. Meyers, an elderly lady who lived at the top of the hill above the mill. We grew watermelons and cantaloupes and banana mushmelons and roastin' ears (corn) which we sold there at the campground and in town. And that winter Albert Howell gave me a job after the trapping season ended, working on his farm clearing rocks and working with his giant Persian stud horse, Augustus, and his big Jack, named Roscoe.

The old Jack had to be kept in a stall because he went through a fence like it wasn't there. His hooves had grown so long they had to be cut down and filed down and I helped with that. We tied his head to a barn rafter and still it was the hardest job I ever did. But you expected that when you were making the kind of money I was making... ten cents an hour, ten hours per day and six days per week from January through March. For a twelve year old kid that was unheard of.

Old Augustus taught me a great deal about horses. I'd take him to the pond twice a day, or rather he took me. I'd hang on to the rope and get dragged to the pond at whatever speed he decided to travel. I fooled the big horse though when I drove a line of stobs in the ground from the barn to the pond and used them to stop him in his tracks by throwing a loop over one of the stobs when he got to going too fast. One thing I remember about that job. Every morning, the wheels of the wagon, which we used to haul rocks and firewood, were frozen to the ground. And it was a job to break them loose.

When spring came there was bad news. Mr. Lindholme, the caretaker of the old Lone Star Mill came to say we couldn't live there anymore and had to be out in 30 days. The owners of the mill were afraid it was dangerous and that if someone would get hurt, they would be sued. In thirty days the sheriff came down and evicted us and Pop and Mom and us kids helped move our meager belongings out in the yard. When the sheriff and Mr. Lindholme left, we just moved it all back in again and received another 30 day notice.

But by then, the owners had figured out a new strategy. Mr. Lindholme came to Pop and told him that if he would tear the old mill down he could have the lumber and be paid for the job as well. So we asked Mrs. Meyer if we could rent the old house she owned just across the road from the mill, a house in such poor condition no one had lived in it for years. She agreed to rent it to us for three dollars a month. That was a real blow to Pop but he figured we could make enough tearing down the old mill to come out ahead.

We moved during the summer and Pop and I began to tear down the old mill, board by board. It would take the summer and most of the winter to get it done because of the other things we had to do as well. That winter when the weather was mild and fur would move, I ran a deadfall line for miles down river and another nearly as far upriver. By then I knew enough about it that Pop didn't have to help me at all. On winter nights when the river was cold and clear, we would gig fish up and down the river and sell them in town.

And that's about the time we tried our hand at school again. Zodie and Farrel and I were enrolled in Houston schools and even though I was three years older than my brother, they put me in the same grade as he because I was so far behind. Of course, Zodie and Farrel loved it and did well, but I was miserable the whole time. I wasn't having too much trouble with the grades though, they were pretty good. I just copied all of Farrel's homework and when I had to give a book report, he would read the book for me and tell me what to say. I was doing just about as good as Farrel was doing, except he was enjoying it and I was bored stiff.

I think my teachers knew that so they made me the Captain of the Schoolboy Patrol. Now that spiced things up considerably. I got a cap and a white belt to go across the shoulder and a stop sign and a whistle. There were five or six of us and we all had assigned crossings to watch. I got the best one, up town. Just before school was out I'd head to the crosswalk up between the bank and the drug store and I'd stop traffic when school kids needed to cross.

A little power in the hands of the wrong person is a terrible thing and I proved it. I really gave those drivers what-for if they didn't stop where I wanted them to. And when I told a kid to get across that street he'd better do it quick and walk within the lines. I was amazed that some-one in a big car with a suit and a tie would stop and wait when I blew my whistle. I blew it often and loud and if you came by my crossing at the wrong time of the day, you'd best be prepared to wait. If you didn't pay attention you might get your fender kicked.

And then there was Donald White. He was my age but a couple of grades ahead and he made fun of me because I was so far behind. So I turned him in to the principal for shooting paper clips at the girls legs with rubber bands. He thought it was great fun but it made big red marks on the girls legs and hurt bad so I decided I'd put an end to that. I did too. Donald had a little pain of his own to contend with when the principal got through with him so he waited outside and conked me in the head with snowball which had a rock in the middle of it. I chased him around the playground throwing rocks at him without the snowballs, until I nailed him pretty good and knocked him about half silly.

That afternoon we both went to see the principal! It would come down to a show-down between me and Donald, I knew.... and finally, just before Christmas it all came to a head. I was sitting on the school bus beside Rosemary Cross, who was older than me and someone I really liked. Rosemary could drive and she'd come and pick me up on Sundays in her dad's new pick-up and take me to the church at Bucyrus. In fact, her folks owned the Bucyrus country store and they were good people. But Rosemary was very big, and sensitive about it. Kids back then were like they are today I suppose. They liked to make fun of the kids who are poor or dumb or heavy. I was poor and dumb and Rosemary was heavy so we both caught our share of the teasing.

Anyway, that morning Donald White got on the bus and started in on us. "Look who's sitting beside old fat Rosemary," he hollered. Well he could have made fun of me all he wanted but when he called Rosemary fat, he got himself in a pickle. I got up and started flailing away at him and Donald started swinging back. The bus driver stopped the bus about a mile from town and put both of us out to walk. When he drove away, I think we were both a little stunned. Fighting on the bus was one thing because you figured who ever came out on the losing side would be saved by the driver before he took too many lumps. But there we were out there on our own with no one to break us up and fighting seemed like less of a good idea than it had been.

But then I remembered this was the guy who was shooting paper clips at my sister and had hit me in the head with a rock and called Rosemary fat. And the next thing I knew we were rolling around in the snow in the ditch and Donald White was learning that sometimes the littlest guy in a fight has a greater incentive. Finally a car stopped and broke up the tussle and I walked home while Donald walked to school with some knots on his head. We didn't have any more trouble, outside of glaring and snarling at each other every now and then. But old Donald was learning manners, he never did call Rosemary any more names.

I started thinking about quitting again, what with trapping season going on. One of my teachers sat me down and told me that if I would just stick with school and get an education I could do great things. She said she had seen good things in me and that I was a natural leader. I could be anything I wanted to be, she told me. Trouble was, I didn't want to be anything but what I was. I liked the Big Piney and the fishing and hunting and trapping and guiding fishermen. I could do that but I just couldn't get the hang of readin' and 'ritin and 'rithmetic.

I just couldn't learn what everyone else seemed to already know. But I was sure of one thing. I could teach those teachers and principals and everyone else something about trapping a coon or paddling a johnboat or setting a trotline for a big catfish. And there wasn't anyone from the fifth grade to the twelfth who could handle an axe like I could. But no one seemed to care about that.

By Christmas time I was finished with school and never would go back. My education was over. My brother Farrel lasted quite awhile longer and learning came easy to him. In fact, he was the only one of the family who actually finally did get a high school diploma and he went back to school in his forties to finish it. Farrel and Zodie and I were constantly at odds because they spent so much time reading and learning and I couldn't. But I remember once when Farrel and I had a good time together at school.

That was the time they had a big school carnival in the fall and we decided we would make some money so we could go and win a cake in the cake-walk. One October night Farrel paddled the old johnboat up and down the mill pond eddy and I gigged about fifteen nice big buffalo fish. We sold them in town and split the money, about three dollars or so. But we would have had more fun if Pop had stayed home. He found out what we were doing and went along, because of course parents were invited too.

They had a big room where there was a walkway mapped out on the floor with numbers and you walked along it until the music stopped and they called out a number. If you were standing on the number they called you won a cake. Farrel and I spent all our money at that carnival and we won a cake two between us. But Pop won two of them all by himself as I remember and made a big deal of it, talking to all the teachers and bragging on his kids. It was pretty embarrassing, walking along behind Pop while the music played, trying to pretend I didn't know who he was while trying to get the attention of some of the girls whom I was beginning to notice. It became clear to me that a thirteen-year-old boy would never have much of a social life if he had a Pop who went to cakewalks. And I also learned that girls weren't impressed with boys who smelled like bait.

In addition to winning all those cakes we had some more good fortune that fall as we chipped away at the old mill, demolishing it a little at a time. Up in the top floor, or attic, I found a baking soda can in the corner, hidden away behind the rafters. It was full of silver dollars, about twenty-five of them if I remember right. You can't imagine what a great day that was in our lives. I took them to Pop and he couldn't believe his eyes. For the first time in a long while, he had some money he didn't have to squirrel away for hard times or sickness. He took it to Houston and bought an old 1927 Model T Ford and we made plans to haul our fish and produce to town and back, expand the float fishing business and join the lower middle class or the upper lower class, either one being a step up.

There were other treasures in the old mill in the form of lumber which Pop could use to make johnboats and that summer he really began to produce and sell them along with the sassafras paddles, to people who wanted to float the river... trappers, fishermen, giggers and joy-riders. The Big Piney was finally beginning to get attention for the recreation it could provide and in that day it was some river for recreation. Sadly, only a glimpse of that river remains and no one who sees it today could envision it as it was then. It was becoming my playground, with more and more people coming to take float trips and Zodie and I making good money guiding them.

The new car made it easier because we could float all day down to Sand Shoals, not far from the old mud-daubers nest, and Pop could pick up the clients in the old car and bring them back. We didn't have a trailer then so I still had to bring the boat back upriver and that was a much harder job than going down. But I was good with a paddle and could usually get back up to the old mill in two or three hours, pulling around the shoals too swift to float and paddling through the eddies. Usually, it was dark before I got back but that was O.K. I'd take along a can of carbide and one of Pop's old miner's caps with a carbide lamp mounted on it and I'd catch some frogs and put them in a wet burlap sack and have them for breakfast the next morning.

I'll always remember that summer night in 1937 when my little brother Vaughn begged to come back upriver with me. He was only about six years old and he tagged around after me constantly, walking right in my footsteps when he could. He couldn't pronounce "Norten" very well so he called me "Nutt". When dad came to the Sand Shoals Crossing to pick up the fishermen that day he brought me a sandwich to eat and I prepared to head back upriver with the boat. Vaughn came along that evening and he threw a fit to go back upstream with me. He had never made the trip and he figured that at six years old he was as big as me and ought to be able to go. Pop finally agreed, though he probably knew Mom would also have a fit when she found out about it. He told me to hurry a little so I didn't get home too much after dark.

So we headed upriver, Vaughn helping me paddle and having the time of his life, riding in the boat when I pulled over the shoals and finally laying down on that wet boat floor to take a nap. He was sound asleep about sunset and that's when I first saw it coming. We were about halfway back, heading in a southerly direction up the Big Piney, and there they were, boiling thunderheads and black sky and stabs of lightning coming down on us fast, probably already closer to home than we were.

I wasn't about to head into that storm so I bore down on the paddle and made the old johnboat jump. The Mineral Springs cave was just ahead and I meant to hole up there where it was dry and the lightning couldn't reach us and the wind couldn't blow any trees down on top of us. We got there with a little time to spare. I pulled the boat up high on the bank and tied it so rising water wouldn't take it away. Vaughn helped me get things up the bank and we piled up dry leaves in the cave to sleep on, and dry wood for a fire.

When that storm hit we were ready, with a fire going and Vaughn safely curled up on a burlap bag like a groundhog in a den. Outside, all hell broke loose. You could hear the wind roaring and limbs snapping and lightning crashing as loud thunder rolled across the valley. The rain pounded the earth and then hail behind it, for what seemed like nearly an hour. And then the storm abated and a gentle rain came in behind it, with occasional thunder and lightning across the sky as if the heavens had overcome it's rage and had decided merely to grumble for awhile.

I built up the fire and lay down beside Vaughn on the dry leaves to drift off to sleep. I knew how scared Mom must be right then but I knew she'd not want me heading into that rising river in the dark. We'd head home at first light and she'd soon know we were safe. And I was tired. The gentle rumble of thunder and the patter of rain on the forest floor outside the cave sent me off to a sound sleep.

I awakened to a calm, peaceful morning, with a little fog laying across the valley and birds singing as water dripped from green foliage. The first rays of sun burnt through the mist as Vaughn and I headed up the swollen Big Piney. It was a few feet high and muddy, carrying some drifts along with the current. I paddled hard and skirted the main channel, to pick my way along the edges through flooded willows and across submerged gravel bars. Vaughn was crying a little, he was hungry and he was homesick. I reminded him that he wanted to be like me and I wasn't whining so he shouldn't either. I was hungry and tired but still happy and I told him he needed to be happy when he saw Mom or she'd never let him go along again.

Mom was standing on the old mill dam when we came around the bend just above the peaked rock and she ran down the river wringing her hands and crying her eyes out. She was about half mad at me for taking so long to get home and hugged both of us so hard it just about turned into punishment. Every muscle in my arms and back was hurting from working against that flooded river. And for once, I was ready to take time to eat.

Pop told me later how mom had spent most of the night pacing the floor and bawling, keeping him from getting any sleep. Finally he sat her down and explained to her that he had raised me and taught me how to run the river and meet all it's obstacles. I was a grown man, he had said, and knew where every cave was between the mouth of the Little Piney and Arthur's Creek and that's where I'd be, safe and sound, waiting for the dawn. Pop said he told Mom she needed to realize that when he got mad he said some awful things he didn't really mean, like how I was a no-good Harris and never going to be worth a damn.

"But he ain't no Harris," Pop told her that night, "not by a long shot he ain't. He's a growed man and a true Dablemont and they ain't nothin' on this river he can't handle."

If I'd have had any buttons on my shirt, my chest would have popped every one of 'em off that day.

Catching bullfrogs at night is still a pastime of Ozark Rivermen because the meat is such a delicacy. For our family, in 1937, bullfrogs meant big money

Chapter 9
Bullfrogs and Boat Paddles

It was no great job to catch bullfrogs on the Big Piney. Back in the 30's they were everywhere, in the river, the creeks, the ponds. At night, a bullfrog will sit stone still when blinded by a light and you can sneak in quietly and grab him by hand. I used Pop's miner's cap, which had a little carbide lamp attached above the bill, like the miner's used back in that day. You filled the bottom half of the lamp with carbide and screwed it back on to the upper half as tight as you could. A rubber seal kept gas from leaking out. In the upper part of the lamp, you added water, and a little lever at the top controlled the drip of water into the carbide chamber. The gas spewed out the nozzle with a polished reflector around it and when you lighted the gas, you had a pretty good, bright glow, directed wherever your hat was pointed.

Today's battery operated headlamps are much brighter of course but in that day, the carbide lamps did pretty well if you kept the reflectors polished and the nozzle unclogged. You used them to run and rebait trot-lines at night, to hunt coons in the winter, to run the river after dark, and to blind bullfrogs.

One evening I was looking through one of Pop's magazines wishing I could read, when I spied a picture of a bullfrog. I showed it to him and commented on how real it looked and he started laughing about how some dern fool city folks were trying to pull another fast one on country people. Pop had learned the hard way not to pay attention to magazine ads. He sent a quarter to one of those companies which had promised to send a pamphlet telling the art of whittling and how to do it without ever cutting your fingers. They sent him back a sheet of paper with the statement, "To keep from cutting your fingers when carving, always whittle away from your hands."

Pop vowed no shyster would ever get any of his money

again and somebody offering to buy bullfrogs for a quarter apiece couldn't fool him. My ears really perked up when I heard that. I kept the page out of the magazine and went up town to see Christy Raddish, who owned the Houston Trucking Company. I showed him the ad and he said the company was known as Melito Seafood Company out of St. Louis. He drove deliveries there every Friday and he said if I'd get enough bullfrogs together to fill a lard can, he'd get ice from the ice house in town, pack them so they'd stay cold and deliver them for 50 cents. I told him I didn't have any money at the time, but I'd pay him when the company paid me. And that's the day I went into business with the Houston Trucking company, selling bullfrogs.

I didn't tell Pop of course, just in case the whole thing fell through and the people were shysters like he said. I kept the frogs alive until Friday morning and then cleaned and skinned them, walked to town and helped Christy Raddish pack them in ice. And then I went back home and forgot about it. About two weeks later a letter came from Melito Seafoods Company in St. Louis and inside it was a check for better than three dollars. The letter thanked me and told me they were looking forward to getting more bull-frogs from me. There was a price list enclosed and directions for preparing the bullfrogs for shipment.

They didn't want them skinned, just beheaded and with entrails removed. Pop read the letter by lantern light and then danced around the house waving that check and declaring that we were going to be rich. He officially took over the Norten Dablemont-Christy Raddish bullfrog venture and we became big time bullfroggers.

The first thing Pop did was dig a big pool out behind the house along a little drainage ditch and enclose it with chicken wire. It was about two feet deep and ten feet across and we filled it water and then filled it full of crawdads. It was to be our bullfrog holding pond and they'd have to be stored there until each Friday morning so they had to have something to eat. I figured frogs all ate flies but Pop

110

said it was crawdads they'd prefer over anything else. He was right and I marveled at how he seemed to know everything.

We worked the Big Piney hard during the summer of 1937, catching bullfrogs and sending them to Melito Seafood Company in St. Louis. Pop was right about them being a little bit crooked too. Their price list said they paid 10 cents for a small frog, 25 cents for a large and 35 cents for a jumbo. Well we never sent them anything that wasn't large, so they never paid us for any small ones, but no matter how many frogs you sent, they only paid for a half-dozen jumbos. Sometimes, we'd send them a couple hundred bullfrogs and half would have legs like a Russian bear wrestler, but we'd still only get paid for a half-dozen jumbos.

But Pop didn't care, he'd never made that kind of money before with so little work. Things were looking up for the Dablemont family. We started driving that old Model T up to Houston and buying things like regular people did... shoes and overalls and sliced bread and even a jar of mayonnaise. Lord in heaven, I still remember how good that first piece of white store-bought bread tasted with mayonnaise on it. Mayonnaise sandwiches were good enough for me to live on.

Mom got a job about that time helping to deliver commodities from the government to poor families along the Piney River. We were eligible too and she brought home cheese every now and then to put with those mayonnaise sandwiches. I figured that was what those folks along silk-stocking lane up in Houston were living on, mayonnaise and cheese sandwiches. It was about then that Pop took the whole family to see a movie and for awhile, when the bullfrog selling was good, we'd go once about every month.

That fall, Zodie and Farrel and I walked to Houston on occasion to see a movie with some of our Harris cousins, and one of those evenings Farrel got hit by a car by some drunk while we were crossing the street in front of the theater. He was skinned up some but nothing was broken. His overalls

Bullfrogs and Boat Paddles

and shirt got torn and bloodied and he was bawling pretty good like he was about half killed. And I guess the old man who hit him figured he might get sued or throwed in jail because he took Farrel over to the clothing store and they washed him up and fixed him up with brand new overalls and a shirt and the old guy paid for everything.

Nothing like that could ever happen to me. I'd step out in front of a car and they'd stop before they even got close. Farrel was just naturally lucky. He got hit twice by a car, once years later when he was riding a bicycle, and he got outfitted again that time if I remember right, with a new tire for his bicycle.

Our bullfrog adventures led us to Arkansas once during that summer. Ed Moore, one of Pop's best friends, had an old Ford pick-up and he said we could catch a million frogs out of the White River down in northwest Arkansas. It was a bigger river and it stood to reason that the bigger the river, the more frogs and bigger frogs you would find. We drove through the little town of Rogers, Arkansas just as a cattle drive was going through town, men on horseback pushing several hundred steers and cows down a dusty gravel street. I was disappointed because they didn't look like cowboys. They were just a bunch of hillbillies like us, dressed in overalls with ragged flannel shirts and brogan shoes and hats with the brims broken down to shade their eyes. I guess they hadn't seen those movies with the cow-boys, because they weren't anything like them. They looked just as poor as us.

Years later, I would live in Rogers, Arkansas, in the heyday of Beaver Lake, when it was fairly new and still had some good fishing. There is no resemblance now to the sleepy little country village I saw back then. And of course the White River is buried and mostly forgotten. It was some river too. Back then it was green and clean and flowing and bigger than the Piney. And there were a few frogs but not as many as we had figured until we got to going up some of the little creeks and tributaries. Quite aways up one of

112

those creeks I came upon a big pond with a fence around it and signs saying 'keep out' everywhere. But I couldn't read so I didn't know what they said, and when I looked up over that pond bank and saw those bullfrog eyes shining back at me from every angle I was glad I couldn't. In an hour I filled two burlap bags with huge bullfrogs.

There were so many and they were so heavy, I could only carry one sack back down the creek. When Ed Moore and Pop saw what I had they couldn't wait to get back up that creek. But the fence and the 'keep out' sign stopped them in their tracks. Something else caught Pop's eye. There was a sign which pointed out that the private property I had entered was a fish farm and trespassers would be prosecuted. I crawled in and found the sack of frogs I had left and we went down that creek with no lights about fast as I ever traveled in the dark.

It took most of the next day to get back to the Piney, especially after one of Ed Moore's wheels came off the truck and bounced halfway down a mountainside. We had to find it and get it back on. Some of the bullfrogs didn't survive the long trip in the heat of the summer. But most did. We ate the dead ones and shipped the others to Melito Seafoods company that week. We didn't get rich that summer, but we did awfully well, and Pop figured another year like that one would have us living high on the hog. Little did we know that hard times were coming again. The selling of frogs and fish became illegal in 1938 and we had a new enemy... .the Missouri Conservation Commission.

The agent in our county was a man named Leonard Rowe and he came out to tell us what the laws were, how we couldn't sell frogs any more, nor game fish. It would still be legal to sell rough fish but you had to buy a license to do it. The first time he showed up, Pop went off his rocker and the guy left. But he was persistent and he tried his best to win Pop over. And you know, he about halfway succeeded. Within a few months he could come out and talk to Pop without getting cussed at and they'd set there on the river and argue about things like how to tell a wolf track from a dog and how big coons got and what kind of tree made the best boat paddle.

I don't know if Mr. Rowe was so smart that he usually let Pop be right but I know he kept telling him that he was the best woodsman and riverman he had ever met and Pop liked that. Every now and then they even agreed on something more than that.

We went into the spring of 1938 figuring on being poor again but there were new things coming up which helped us make a living. For one thing, the lumber from the old mill, which we finally had dismantled, made some nice johnboats and people were beginning to see them and buy them. They were the best boats you could get back then. Pop kept improving them and he learned how to put rudders on the bottom, how to curve the sides around forming braces, how to put live wells in them for fish and bait.

Pop never used caulking or rags to seal the bottom of our boats, because he said that if you used it, and the boat ever dried out, as sure as the world a chunk or two would fall out and then it would never seal tight again. He nailed on the bottom boards horizontally, with good-sized cracks between them. When the new boat was put in the river, it quickly filled with several inches of water. The bottom boards swelled tightly together and within a day or so, you could dip out the water and the boat bottom was sealed tightly, without the slightest leak. But if you ever dried one out, you could reseal it time and time again just by putting it back in the water.

Our johnboats were becoming well-known, as was our float-fishing service. By 1938, Farrel was big enough to start guiding a little and there were three of us kids who could take people fishing and several boats on hand to rent. The Missouri Conservation Commission actually advertised Pop's fishing camp in one of their publications and Mr. Rowe sent us some occasional business.

Johnboats were sold for about six dollars each back

then, usually about fifteen or sixteen feet long. And before the last snow of the winter had completely melted, Pop had a half dozen of them under construction to be sold to a pair of fishing resorts up toward St. Louis, one of them on the Meramec river. Each boat came with a pair of hand-made sassafras paddles and they were the strongest, most beautiful paddles you've ever seen.

You could sell those paddles for $50.00 each today. In fact, I have made and sold several since the 1980's for just that kind of money. But when I made my paddles I had power tools to form them with. Pop used a draw knife, a plane, his pocket knife, and some old wood rasps and horse-hoof files.

I've always marveled at how quickly he made them and how straight and symmetrical each one was. There are photos here to show paddles he made which are on display in my nephew's office, one from as far back as 1927. In fact, the last paddle Pop made, in the summer of 1970, was given to one of his old friends, Joe Richardson of Houston,

Missouri. In 1997, Joe brought that paddle to my nephew, (Pop's grandson and Farrel's son Larry), and gave it to him. It was a treasured gift and amazingly as well made as the first ones he built when he was young. You know how it was made, in that era of power saws and sanders? Of course, as all of them were, with a plane and draw knife and those old wood rasps.

Pop's ability and ingenuity amazed me then, and as I think back on those depression era days I am still amazed at how efficient he was with so little to work with. Since I was a small boy I remember how he asked everyone he knew to save match-boxes for him. Some of them never knew why--- but on the side of those boxes there was a strip

Pop made his last paddle in 1970, the one on the left. The one on the right, he made in 1927.

of rough sandpaper used to strike the match against. Pop used those strips to sand and polish down the boat paddles he made and wooden handles for tools, minnow seines or trotline spools. He never bought sandpaper, it was one of those luxuries he couldn't afford. I don't know if anyone else ever came up with such a use for common match-boxes. But there were no rough spots or splinters on Pop's tool handles or paddles.

In May of 1938, the man who owned the resort on the Meramec river near Sullivan, came to our place to pick up three johnboats and he hired me to take him on a float trip down the Piney. His name was Alton Benson and he was quite a business man. He owned a restaurant, tavern, dance hall and gas station combination at Sullivan and developed a river floating business from that. When he saw me paddling that johnboat all day from one side, he really was impressed with the fact that a kid my age could do such a thing. That evening he asked Pop if it might be possible for me to come to Sullivan and work for him as a guide on the Meramec.

Of course I was all for it. I hadn't seen much of the world and I figured at fourteen years of age, I was a grown man, ready to seek my fortune. It was a hard thing for Pop to go along with but the money which Benson agreed to send back to him each week was enough to allow our family to do well, even without selling frogs and fish. The agreement was made and that night I got everything I owned ready to take with me. Mom cried her eyes out, and so did Vaughn. Farrel and Zodie were tickled pink!

Alton Benson had some heckuva place there at Sullivan, a gas station and a restaurant and club with a dance floor. It was called the "Swing Inn" There was a small room behind the kitchen which was mine and for me it was a penthouse suite. I had never had a room of my own, I had always slept crowded in with Farrel and Vaughn wherever there was room to throw a pallet on some straw. This place had a bed, a real one with a mattress and quilts and a feather pil-

My sister, Zodie, was guiding float fishermen on the Big Piney when she was only 15. When I left, she had it all to herself.

low. Finally I could see why some folks spent so much time sleeping!

I was to guide fishermen on day-long trips on the Meramec and the Bourbeuse Rivers and get paid two dollars per day which was to be sent back home to Pop. But I got to keep my tips and I could earn extra money at night pumping gas and cleaning the dance floor after it closed. That summer I had a float trip somewhere about everyday. The Bourbeuse and Meramec were much different than the Piney. The Meramec was a beautiful river with lots of fish. It had fast shoals and big deep eddies, some with the same names as those on the Big Piney. And there were walleye in

Bullfrogs and Boat Paddles

the Meramec, a fish I hadn't seen before.

The Bourbeuse was big and slow and more colored but it was a great bass river and we took a lot of one-day floaters on it just to catch bass. Benson had purchased three or four boats from Pop, all sixteen-footers but one and it was an eighteen-foot commissary boat. He had been using boats with the floor boards lengthwise and they were costing him sixty dollars apiece and leaked like sieves. Things got better for his float business when he started buying Pop's boats. They floated higher, handled easier, didn't leak and were only twenty dollars.

He often had me paddle that heavily-loaded commissary boat because he knew I could get it there without swamping it, while his older guides would bring the fishermen down river behind us, usually six fishermen in three boats, sometimes four in two boats. I loved to take the commissary boat down because I was by myself and I could get downstream ahead of the guests and do some fishing on my own. And in doing so I began to develop my fishing skills, learning how to cast and present a lure, and where the likely places were to catch bass.

Usually a commissary boat went on the three day, two night trips. I carried the canvas tents and cots and bedding and the cooking gear and food. For that I was paid fifty cents a day more and might get up to five dollars in tips for a two or three day trip. Benson's wife would drive in across a farmers field and meet us at the gravel bar campsite that second night with more ice, beer and food. And on many of those trips there was hard liquor. Guides and fishermen alike were often pretty much soused by the time the sun went down. I took care of everything, cooked fish and potatoes and beans for supper, set up the tents and cots and enjoyed listening to the stories and watching the show that went on at night. At sunrise I was up fixing a breakfast of bacon and eggs and biscuits and coffee.

Sometimes the clients we took fishing stayed completely sober but usually there was someone, or everyone, drunk

120

but me. I never touched alcohol, had no taste for it and didn't care to develop a taste for it, like some of the guides said you had to do. I remember one night in June when we were camped on a gravel bar at nightfall and one of the fishermen decided he'd take a swim before turning in.

One of the older guides told me to keep an eye on him because he was really looped. He made it to the river and decided he would dive off the end of the johnboat. Problem was, it was pulled way up on the gravel bar and in shallow water. He flopped off the back of that boat into about ten or twelve inches of water and just sort of stuck there. It's a wonder he didn't kill himself. Except for a scratched-up face and belly he was alright.

I never drank because I never wanted to lose control of myself and what I was doing and I was enjoying life so much I couldn't see how alcohol would make it better. I did drink cokes, so many that I got hooked on them. I just couldn't get through a day without three or four Coca-Colas and fishermen I guided always brought them for me. And there were plenty of them back at the inn and filling station for only a nickel a bottle. I couldn't figure why someone would prefer to drink beer or whiskey when they could have a coke for a fraction of the cost. I still can't figure that out!

At the age of 14, I was guiding float-fishermen for Alton
Benson on the Meramec and the Bourbeuse Rivers.

Chapter 10

Good Times on the Meramec

That summer on the Meramec I saw anglers using lures I hadn't seen before, Lazy Ikes and Flatfish and Heddon Midget-Didgets and River-Runts and Arbogast's Hawaiian Wigglers. Boy did those lures catch fish back then. It wasn't uncommon at all for fishermen to catch a four-pound small-mouth or walleye and every now and then a largemouth of six -pounds or better.

When I'd get in from guiding fishermen all day I'd tack-le my other job, delivering groceries around town for the Red and White grocery store. To do that I had to get a bi-cycle and for the first time in my life I bought something on credit. The bicycle was a beauty and I don't know if I ever wanted anything more. It was there in the picture window at the Western Auto store and if I remember right it cost 24 dollars. With Alton behind me, they agreed to let me make weekly payments and with it I could deliver groceries half-way across the county.

One night I had finished cleaning the dance hall floor before the crowd started coming in and so I headed down the highway to visit a friend I had made, a young man a couple of years or so younger than I by the name of Roder-ick, who worked at a tavern known as the Green Lantern. He and I were pretty close friends back then and had a lot of fun when we weren't working. A few months after the first printing of this book, he contacted me from his home in north Arkansas. We hadn't seen each other in more than 60 years, but he read the book and remembered me. Since then we have done some fishing together.

Anyway, back then, that highway I was bicycling along was the old route 66, now a famous thoroughfare but back then just another two lane concrete highway. It was after sunset but there was enough light to see well enough. I had a headlight on my bicycle but the batteries were dead. I was going down a hill meeting oncoming traffic when a state patrolman passed a car and in the dusk he didn't see me. He nearly hit me and I wound up in the ditch, indignant about the whole thing. The patrolman turned around and came back with lights flashing, mad as an old wet hen.

"What are you doing on that bike in the dark with no lights?" he said.

"What the heck are you doing passing a car on a hill?" I answered. Boy I shouldn't have said that! That patrolman chewed me out good! He said he had the authority to pass anywhere, drive any speed, and haul bicyclists off to jail and confiscate their bicycles. I crawfished pretty quickly and got over being mad at him in a hurry. Thankfully, he let me off with a warning and I got batteries the next day.

It was right at a hundred miles to Houston from Sullivan and late in the summer when I got a couple of days free, I rode my bike back home. It took most all day and I had some problems on the hills between Rolla and Licking but I figured out how to get up them. I'd wait for a truck to come along, one of the big commercial trucks which were loaded down so heavily they could barely get up those hills in low gear, and I'd grab ahold of the back and let them tow me to the top. I'd let go when we got to level ground and they began to pick up speed.

It was good to get home and see my family. And they were all anxious to see me and hear about my new life. Farrel was doing more guiding, as was Zodie, and that money coming in from Alton Benson every week was surely a big help. While I was there I got some of Dad's old traps and found out that I could get a ride back to Sullivan on the film truck with the guy who traveled back and forth to Sullivan where he picked up movies and delivered them to theaters. His name was Ed Doddard and he loaded my bicycle and gear in the back and we were there in only a few hours. I told Pop about the film truck coming up to Sullivan every night or so and he decided he had to see those rivers and the great fishing so he caught a ride up during toward the end of summer and floated the Bourbeuse.

He didn't like it near as much as he did the Meramec but he said it surely had some giant catfish in it and lots of fur for a trapper. Pop lamented that he was too old to join me, he said he wished he could set trotlines in that big river. He was envious of my good fortune.... but it was his good fortune too, he was getting good money from Alton Benson for the work I was doing.

Back on the Meramec that winter, after the float fishing was over, I kept working at the inn and gas station and I set up a deadfall line and a steel-trap line along the river. I caught lots of possums and skunks and muskrats, and a few coons and a pair of mink. The two of them brought about ten or twelve dollars each. I saved enough to buy a single-shot, bolt-action .22 caliber rifle for six dollars from the Western Auto. I put it to good use, hunting rabbits which I sold to the Red and White store for ten cents apiece. I don't know how they got away with selling rabbits to their customers but somehow they were doing it, making about a quarter for each one they sold.

I worked hard through that winter, cleaning that dance floor and working in the restaurant, pumping gasoline and running my trapline and taking care of my furs. I still didn't sleep much, only a few hours every night. And it was my good fortune one winter evening to run into a girl about my age when she stepped off the curb and into the path of my bicycle. I mean that literally. I ran into her with my bicycle.

She was skinned up a little but not hurt bad and after she pulled herself together and quit crying, I asked her if I could make it up to her by taking her to the movies. I couldn't believe my ears when she said yes. Just a few minutes earlier I was running her down with my bike and now I was taking her to the movies. It was a good one too, "The Streamline Cannonball" starring Roy Acuff. But I had to be careful about hugging her, 'cause she was pretty sore in places from getting hit by my bicycle.

She wasn't all that ugly and we hung around together for much of the winter. But I eventually lost out to an older fellow who worked for the Civilian Conservation Corps and had an old car, which he never had run into her with. I didn't care much though. Even with all the skinned places healed up, she still wasn't all that pretty and when you didn't have a girlfriend you saved a little more money. I paid off that bicycle before the winter was over.

I met Herb Kenley in the Spring of 1939. He was a big-time client of Alton Benson who loved to fish. Kenley owned a strip joint down on sixth street in St. Louis and he always hired one of the older guides named Hendricks, who was big and tall and strong. But that one day in the spring of '39, Hendricks was sick and Alton told Kenley I would be his guide. Kenley threw a fit. I was small and young and he just knew I couldn't do the job. Benson told him if he wasn't satisfied with the way I handled a boat the trip would be free. I heard Kenley tell him that if I couldn't do the job he "might just drown the little S.O.B."

Alton had a lot of confidence in me. He knew I had spent more hours in one of those johnboats than all his other guides combined and I could paddle a circle around Hendricks or any of the others. But Herb Kenley, who had something of an obnoxious temperament anyway, griped and complained from the get-go. It didn't make it any easier that I forgot to load a dip net and just below a stretch of shoals known as the fish-trap, he caught a monstrous walleye on a yellow Midget-Didget.

It weighed 14 pounds, the biggest I had ever seen or any of Alton's guides had ever seen. There we were with that big walleye and no dip net. I just knew this guy would kill me if he lost it and Alton wouldn't get paid so I got out in the river up to my knees, grabbed that big fish by the gill cover on his first pass and hoisted it out of the water. I didn't know much about walleye, we didn't have them on the Piney. I knew they had a mouthful of teeth but I didn't know about those razor-sharp gill covers and that one sliced my thumb like a sharp knife. It was a long, deep gash, and Kenley actually seemed more concerned with that than his fish.

Not me. I had been cut, bit, bashed and slashed since I could remember but I hadn't ever seen anyone catch a fish that big. I didn't even notice the blood dripping off my elbow. Kenley insisted we get back up river and get it taken care of and it was my turn to throw a fit. I told him I could paddle him down the river and handle that boat without any thumbs if I had to and I wasn't going to be bothered by a little cut that far from my neck. I wrapped it up with a piece of my shirt, bound it up with string, and we continued on.

Herb Kenley didn't do any more complaining... he caught more fish that day than he ever had, and back at the Swing Inn that walleye really got some attention. He gave me a five dollar tip and I heard him tell Alton Benson that from that day on he wanted me in his boat whatever the cost. "That kid," he said, "is my guide from now on."

The fishing was good in the summer of '39 and I developed several regular customers. I got even better with that boat paddle and learned to fish with the old casting reels and braided line so well that I could catch more fish from the back of the boat, while paddling, than most of my clients could from the front seat. On days when I didn't have float trips, Alton would take me over to Meramec Caverns and I'd guide tour groups through the cave. Back then the cavern was pretty much without development and there were no lights in it. We took groups through the cave with flashlights. That's when I really began to learn to talk to people and enjoy it.

Of course I had never been shy. On occasion people said they thought I was about the most talkative kid they had ever run into. But by dealing with people on a regular basis as a guide on the river or at Meramec Caverns, I really began to develop confidence in myself. I felt there wasn't anything I couldn't do.

About September of that year I had a day or two free and Alton Benson told me I could go home for awhile if I wanted to. There was a break in the float-fishing and he said the other guides could handle the work for awhile. I loaded up some gear in an old bag, tied it to the basket on the back of my bicycle and headed for the Big Piney bright and early one morning.

I made it home with enough light left to go down to the Mill Pond Eddy for a quick swim and there I met the love of my life, Verda Mae Jones.

Verda Mae (right) with my sister Zodie

I was nearly sixteen years old and Verda Mae was a few months younger. If only we had been a few years older. Verda Mae was the most beautiful girl I had ever seen, with long black hair and a dark complexion, half Cherokee Indian. Her mother and father had come to the Lone Star Mill campground for a vacation, all the way from Tulsa, Oklahoma where he was the head of the city water department. They had two younger kids, a boy and a girl, and Verda Mae. They had already met Pop and Mr. Jones wanted to take a float trip the next day, so I took him. But my mind had never been farther away. I simply pushed that boat along, anxious to return and see Verda Mae.

When the day was over I

got up the nerve to ask him if I could take his daughter for a boat ride that evening and maybe go for a swim. I knew that he liked me really well by then because I had done everything to get on his good side. I found out he was a Republican and I let him know I was too, even though I didn't know the difference between a Republican and a Revenuer. Since he was Indian I told him that Pop and I were both about half Cree Indian because I knew one of Pop's grandmothers was a Canadian Cree and his grandfather a French-Canadian trapper. I told Mr. Jones he was one of the best fishermen I had paddled for and how much I'd like to have a job like his. You'd have thought I would have had him right where I wanted him. But he thought about it awhile and then said it would be up to her mother. I had climbed the mountain only to be confronted by a cliff.

Verda Mae got permission to go out swimming and boating with me only if I took her younger brother and sister with us. Her brother wasn't much problem. He was Vaughn's age and the two of them were content to play around the house. But her little sister was a real pain in the neck. She was a little younger than my brother and Farrel was only about eleven and darn hard to get along with. When I asked him to come along and keep her company while I was sparking Verda Mae, he said he wasn't about to.

I don't know what I did to change his mind but I did something that worked because that evening there he was at the swimming hole being as obnoxious to that little girl as he could be to keep her out of our hair. I can't imagine me having enough money to pay him but I must have. Farrel didn't have much use for girls at that age so we're probably talking about a dime or maybe a quarter! I guess that tells you what I thought of Verda Mae.

Her family spent the whole week there at the campground and we went frogging and fishing and gigging and swimming and just had a great time. Verda Mae and I started getting off to ourselves and love blossomed. It was a romance made in heaven but all hell was about to break loose when we told our folks we were going to get married.

It wasn't so much her folks that objected. They said they'd go along with it if I'd move to Tulsa and work for the water department with Mr. Jones and Verda and I could live with them and she could finish her schooling. She was an accomplished pianist and had a promising music career ahead of her. I agreed almost before they finished the proposal. For Verda Mae, I'd go to Texas and live with the Comanches.

Mom didn't say much, she just bawled and squalled and carried on like I had been killed and was already buried. And Pop ranted and raved and called me a no-account @A%$*&#*%$#*@ Harris nit-wit. I don't know, maybe they had my best interest in mind. I was too young to be getting married, though lots of Ozark kids were married younger than I was. I think maybe they were worried about losing that money Alton Benson was sending them every week too. Pop said if I got married she'd have every penny I made and eventually I'd be back there on the Piney and he'd have to be supporting me and her and a passle of kids. I almost told him that he had never supported me.. .why would I bring a family back to where there had been so little support in the first place. It was a pretty dark time. All I wanted in life seemed so easily accessible and my mom and dad were standing in the way.

That night Verda Mae and I sat on the old mill dam throwing rocks into the river at sunset and I told her I loved her and she told me she loved me and we vowed to be together forever someday. Little did we know we'd never see each other again. The next morning the whole family was gone and I went looking for Ed Doddard's film truck.

Alton Benson was glad to have me back. He had wondered if I was dead or in jail or something. He knew I wouldn't quit a job I loved so much for any other reason. And then I told him about Verda Mae and he forgave me for being gone so long. For awhile I was the saddest-faced

130

guide the Meramec river had ever seen.

My heart just wasn't in my work. I thought about Verda Mae constantly but couldn't even send her a letter because I couldn't write. Mom was getting the letters she wrote to me and throwing them away, worried I might yet go to Tulsa and marry her. I might have if I had known where it was... just a few days bike ride down route 66. But for me, Oklahoma might as well have been overseas.

The rest of September dragged by and finally it was late October. I turned sixteen years old, was completely independent, and in my eyes, a grown man. On my sixteenth birthday the leaves were turning and the ducks were starting to arrive on the rivers and Herb Kenley wanted to take one last float trip on the Bourbeuse. He wanted to bring his wife along, or maybe it was his girlfriend, I don't know. She was younger than he and really a gorgeous woman. That's why I figured it was just his girlfriend. I was learning that girlfriends were most often younger and prettier than wives.

Anyway, Kenley told me in advance she hadn't been out in the wilds much and she was scared of everything, the water, snakes, sunburn, fishing guides....everything. She was just going along for the ride, she wouldn't fish and couldn't swim very well. I told him I'd make it the smoothest, safest, most unstressful boat ride she had ever had. Wrong!!!

I had bought myself a used .22 pistol from somebody the week before and I was enjoying shooting it. So when I saw the water snake on the limb we were about to float under I drew my pistol and blasted it.... four or five times I think... and it fell into the water just before we got to it. You'd have had to see it to believe it, it was just like one of those western movies. But Kenley's wife went all to pieces and we had to stop and calm her down. Kenley gave me heck but I told him if I hadn't killed that snake it might have been in her lap.

The fishing was pretty good but the day was unseasonably hot for the fall. I saw the thunderheads building in the west and I knew we'd probably not make it to the takeout point before the storm got us. It was before noon when we began to hear the distant rumble of thunder and the skies began to darken. I told Herb and his wife we were going to have to make a run for it. There was a nice bluff shelter cave about a half mile downstream and I wasn't sure we'd make it before that storm was in the boat with us. I gave it everything I had and streaks of lightning were playing across the sky right behind us when we got there. The thunder was crashing by then, not rumbling, and Kenley's wife was about to go to pieces some more. We got her and most of the gear up to the protection of the shallow cave and pulled the boat up high and tied it, just about the time the hail started. I'm here to tell you, that was a storm.

There was lightning and wind and hail and sheets of rain so heavy you couldn't see the river below us. And it got so dark for awhile it was almost like night inside that cave. Herb Kenley tried to calm his wife down with a few nips from a bottle he had brought along and in an hour or so they were calmed down quite a bit more than they needed to be. I was worried because even though the front had passed and the violent lightning and wind had abated somewhat, the rain was pouring down. I knew I was going to get wet anyway so I went down and emptied the boat, half surprised to find it was still there, and I pulled it up higher, out of the rising current.

Two hours later we were still sitting in that cave and the rain was still steady, the river rising as the rain came down. I told Herb Kenley that we just couldn't wait any longer. The wind and lightning weren't a threat anymore but we had to get down that river before it got so high it was unsafe. We just had to get wet, grin and bear it, bite the bullet and ride the high water.

Herb's wife wasn't dressed for the weather. It was cooling off as the front came through and she had on shorts and a thin, short-sleeved shirt. She began to shiver as we raced down that rising torrent in the rain so I gave her my shirt.

It didn't help much, she was cold and scared both. But it didn't take long to reach the creek where Alton Benson was suppose to meet us and we weren't really very late, as fast as we had been traveling. I paddled up the creek there at the take-out point to the old road which came down through a field and the creek was nearly out of it's banks already, flowing strong and muddy with the heavy rains. And Alton wasn't there!

I scraped some leaves and wood together under a little cliff there beside the creek and got a fire going somehow. We huddled together just below the overhang and warmed up a little with the fire. Kenley and his wife were drinking heavier now and were feeling better. I wasn't. Alton Benson was almost two hours late. He had tried to drive across that creek and his truck had washed off the low-water bridge. So he hired a farmer with a tractor and trailer to come down and get us. In the steady rain I heard the chop of that tractor motor and was so relieved I could have hugged that old farmer.

We tied the boat and left it and the farmer agreed to take us all back to Sullivan. There wasn't room for me in the truck, I sat in the back with no shirt and nearly froze to death while Kenley and Alton Benson sat on each side of Herb's wife and passed that bottle back and forth.

I don't know what happened that night but I heard later that Herb Kenley got so drunk he passed out and Alton Benson and Kenley's girlfriend or wife or whoever she was, took off somewhere alone and were caught by Benson's wife. All I know is, I never saw Alton Benson or Herb Kenley again and I didn't ever get paid for that last trip. It would be the last trip I took on the Meramec and Bourbeuse for many many years.

The gas station closed down and Benson's partner, a man named Bushman, kept the inn going for awhile. I was doing all the cooking and serving and cleaning and by November there was hardly anyone coming in the place. Finally Bushman told me he was going to Ft. Leonard Wood

133

to see about a job and he just lit out, leaving me there alone. I think he knew something I didn't because that evening several patrolmen came in and closed the place down. They said I had been violating the law by selling liquor at my age. I objected, I told them I had turned sixteen on October 26th and I could do anything any man could do. I wasn't drinking the stuff, I was just selling it. I could keep things going until Alton came back and if they closed down the Swing Inn, I didn't have any place to stay, or an occupation, or a future.

Then all of a sudden I was looking up into the face of that big patrolman who had threatened to haul me in with my bicycle that night out on Route 66. "You ever get lights

Me and my bicycle in 1939

on that bicycle, kid?" he asked me.

I was too mad to give a darn anymore, "You ever quit passing cars on a hill?" I fired back.

As soon as I said that, I wished I hadn't, but he just smiled and shook his head as if in disbelief. "Where's your home, kid?" he asked.

I told him where I had been sleeping in the back room and where I had come from, down on the Big Piney.

"You get a good night's sleep," he said, "and we'll come back tomorrow and see if we can get you home."

That night I bundled up everything I had.... my traps, (which I had been about ready to make a killing with down on the Meramec)... my rifle, my boat paddle and my clothes and all the money I had in a tobacco can under the mattress. I tied it all on the back of my bicycle at first light and started peddling. I'd be darned if I'd stay around and let those patrolmen change their mind and haul me off to jail and confiscate that bicycle and everything I owned.

In the early dawn I headed out onto Route 66 and paused one more time to look back at The Swing Inn. I was gonna miss it. In just a few short months I had lost it all, Verda Mae Jones, a good job and a good life. By the time the sun began to climb over the eastern hills above the Meramec River I was almost to Rolla and all the tears had dried. I still had the Big Piney.

Ted Kelly was a neighbor across the Piney a few years older than me. He became one of the Ozarks true war heroes.

Chapter 11

Goodbye to the Piney

Once again, Mom had all her kids home for Christmas, at the end of 1939. It would be the last time in many a year but we didn't know that. By then Zodie was practically a grown woman, almost 20 years old and about to get married. Farrel was happier to see me come home than anyone. He loved that bicycle. He was coming up on thirteen years old and taller than I was. Pop told me how Farrel had been running his first trapline and had been so excited about catching his first muskrats he wanted to check his trapline in the middle of the night. That was the year Farrel caught the big mink, bigger than any of us had ever seen.

Vaughn was nine years old and learning to shoot. In fact, it amazed me how good he was with that .22 rifle of mine. You could tell he was going to be a sharpshooter, he was just a natural. And Bryce was old enough to start school. By Christmas of 1939 he could already read better than I could.

Fred and Myrtle Kelly had bought the place across the old bridge along the river beside the Sweet Potato eddy. Fred Kelly and Pop had really hit it off good and would be lifelong friends. And Myrtle was a sweetheart of a lady who became a close friend of my mother. In years to come, Mom and Pop would go camping and fishing with Fred and Myrtle Kelly and play cards with them in the winter when there was little to do. I got to know their son Ted that winter and I don't remember meeting a finer person.

We didn't know then about the heartbreak ahead for Fred and Myrtle. Later that year Ted went off to join the Canadian Air-Corps and eventually became a flyer for the RAF in England. He was one of World War II's most decorated pilots and is a hero today not only in his home state of Missouri but in Canada as well. In 1942, on a bombing run over Germany, Ted Kelly was shot down and killed. A monument to him and other Canadian flyers stands today near Toronto.

Ted was about four years older than me. We fished together often in the spring of 1940 and played horseshoes at their farm. I had never played horseshoes before and he taught me. I love to pitch horseshoes even today and I think about Ted every time I pick up a pair. But he also talked to me a lot about going to school and learning to read and write. He kept telling me that with an education I could do great things, that I wasn't dumb at all and that learning to read and write would open all the doors for me. I hated to hear that. I wanted nothing to do with school and after all, I had been there before and just couldn't get the hang of it. I was convinced I was just too dumb to learn anything.

But still, Ted Kelly put that spark in my mind that maybe someday I should try to learn to read. I started practicing writing my name and looking at words and tried to memorize what they meant. That summer, Ted came by to tell me he was going to Canada and he'd be back some day to go fishing with me again. I stood out on the river bank and watched him cross the rickety old bridge in his dad's truck and he stopped just a minute to wave at me. I didn't know much about what was going on in the world and I didn't know what Ted was heading into.

It was several months before Pearl Harbor was bombed but England was already catching hell from German bombers. I like to think Ted Kelly helped turn the tide. A few years in the future I'd be following across the English channel to fight the same enemy that would take his life. But that day, as the old truck rattled away up the hill across the river, I didn't know. No one knew!

Just after Ted Kelly left we were busy setting trotlines and Pop was building boats and I was back to guiding float fishermen again. A fellow by the name of Tedford, who was a nephew of the local drugstore pharmacist, came to visit from St. Louis. He hired me for a day-long float all the way from the Lone Star Mill down to Boiling Springs. He told me that morning that he had never caught a big bass and he said that if I could get him a four pounder he would get me a job at Curtis-Wright Aircraft in St. Louis where he was the personnel manager. I wasn't all that interested at first and then he told me that Curtis -Wright paid 55 cents an hour. I nearly fell out of the boat. I had never dreamed of making that kind of money every day, day in and day out. I asked him if he was kidding and he said he wasn't. All I had to do was see to it he got that big bass.

Back in those days, every fisherman caught some nice bass on a float trip. Usually there were lots of smallmouths from a pound to two and a half pounds, and quite often someone landed a brownie from three to four pounds. Most of those bigger bass didn't make it to the boat because we used braided line on those old South Bend and Shakespeare and Pflueger casting reels, with a leader of monofilament which was often weakened and frazzled after an hour or so of casting. And the knots weren't usually tied well. Fly-fishermen using fly-rods lost most of the bass above two and one half pounds because they didn't have the hooks to hold them or a rod with the backbone to wear them down and land them.

But there were plenty of big fish to be caught and one of the best bass holes was only a mile or so below the Kelly place, at the McKinney Eddy. Back then it was a long, deep bluff hole where there were flathead catfish in the thirty to forty pound range, and largemouth which would have weighed seven or eight pounds. Many a four-pound smallmouth came from that big deep eddy in the thirties, forties and fifties. As much as any other place on the river, the McKinney Eddy typifies what has happened to the Big Piney. Back then, the swift water shoal was three or four feet deep and it swirled into pockets from eight to ten feet deep, where smallmouth fed. Big rocks and ledges beneath the bluff provided hiding places and the water was so clean you could drink it at any time of the year. In fact, we often did.

In the slower, wider part of the eddy there was fifteen

feet of water in places and a rock bank on one side, with a mud bank on the other where logs and rootwads lay, providing cover for largemouth and catfish. Today the McKinney eddy is filled with gravel and silt and algae and slime and there's a gravel bar only a few inches beneath the surface right in the middle of the hole. The ledges and rocks at the head of the eddy are buried under several feet of gravel and silt. The big catfish and big bass are gone and have been for some time.

Every now and then I hear the tourism department talk about Missouri's rivers and the Conservation Department boasts of how many stream teams there are. If they only knew what these rivers were compared to what they are now, I think they'd say nothing at all. The Big Piney that I knew died years ago and now it's just a shadow of what it was, left to carry lines of shiny banging canoes which scrape through the gravel and admire the scenery. They can't begin to know that under the gravel are the rocks where big smallmouth once lurked and that the slimy water they don't even want to wade through in the heat of the summer was once clean enough to drink.

The Big Piney became fair game for the gravel companies and the timber cutters and the cattlemen who have a thousand head of cattle for every cow which lived on the same watershed in my boyhood. How could it survive? The land has been drenched with chemicals and fertilizers for years, and the river carries the effluent from several sewage treatment plants on the headwaters. But I'm not placing the blame on one group or another. We are all to blame for what has happened to the Ozarks. And maybe you could argue that it was inevitable because of the ever increasing numbers of people and the demands they place on resources of any kind.

Life is so much better today than it was then, maybe we have to sacrifice the quality of the earth to have a quality life. I don't know, if there are answers, I certainly don't know what they are. Not many people alive today saw the

McKinney eddy in the summer of 1940. But I did, and I can see it now, the water deep and green along that opposite bank where submerged logs harbored big largemouth. God knows how I miss it!

Mr. Tedford fished down the bluff side of the McKinney Eddy first and caught some smaller bass. And I almost headed through the shoal at the lower end without going back up that opposite bank. But at the last minute I decided there wouldn't be many better spots for a four-pound bass and we headed back upstream to see if there was just one hungry one there.

It was fairly early in the morning, and Tedford was using a big Heddon topwater Lucky 13. About halfway up the eddy the lure ruffled the surface and sat still just a second too long. A hefty bass flashed from beneath the log and the water exploded around it. Tedford leaned back on him and the hooks set well. The bass came out into deep water beneath the boat as I waited with Pop's old homemade dip net and prayed. Sometimes it's best we don't get what we pray for. Maybe if the Good Lord had just given me what was best for me, that old bass would have worked those hooks loose and we'd have never seen him again. But I wanted that job and he answered my prayer, reluctantly perhaps.

There was one last surge to the surface and the big bass came out of water, tailwalking in an attempt to shake the lure. He would lose the battle and minutes later the beautiful largemouth lay on the floor of the wooden johnboat, flopping his tail and flaring his gills, a whole lot closer to five pounds than four.

Later that day Tedford hooked and landed a smallmouth which would have been close to four pounds too, from the Arthur's Creek Eddy well down below the old mud-daubers nest where we had lived years before. If I remember right, he caught that one on a Hawaiian Wiggler. He was really proud of those two bass and took them back to show to everyone in town. In that day no one ever turned back a big bass. There were more of them than there were fishermen and when you caught a prize fish, you kept it. You might turn back the little ones but you kept the big ones and most were eaten. Mr. Tedford took his bass back to St. Louis and said when I was ready for that job, it would be there. I guess he didn't really like living there so much as I thought. A year or so later he jumped out of a ten story building in St. Louis and killed himself.

Mr. Tedford and I after summer fishing trip in 1940.

Goodbye to the Piney

In the fall of 1940 I packed all my clothes in a couple of grocery bags and headed for St. Louis on the bus. Farrel said he'd take care of my bicycle until I needed it again and Mom said if she heard from Verda Mae she'd let me know. Little did I know she was getting a letter every week and burning them all. I moved in with Aunt Bertha again and when I walked into Curtis-Wright with a note from Mr. Tedford. I walked past about 200 men standing in line to apply for jobs, and I started to work that day.

Some of the older guys resented me. They called me a Flat River hillbilly for some reason, even though the Flat River was an East Missouri stream miles from where I grew up. They were right about the hillbilly part, I was one if there ever was one and proud of it.

That first day I was sent to the paint room and the guys in there gave me a five gallon bucket and told me to go to another part of the plant and get a bucket of "prop wash". Prop wash, of course, is the term for the wind coming off the propellers of an airplane on the ground or in flight and each department sent me somewhere else, laughing hilariously as I went. Finally one of the supervisors heard me and he took me back to the paint room and chewed everyone out. I was beginning to learn you couldn't trust just anyone.

They gave me the job of washing and preparing planes for priming and painting. The work wasn't really that hard but I had never seen so much waste. They were constantly redoing something just to keep everybody busy. It didn't matter to Curtis Wright, they were being allotted great sums of money from the government and wasting it was of no concern to anyone.

It took me better than an hour to get to work from Aunt Bert's place. I had to take to street cars and then a bus in the morning, then the same thing in reverse to get home at night. But it was a better life in the city back then, even though there was no air conditioning. People stayed outside in the evenings when the sun dropped low in the sky and neighbors knew one another. Kids played in the streets

143

Goodbye to the Piney

and there was baseball at Sportsman's Park. Uncle Jabe
took me to see my first Cardinal game and we went to see
the Browns on occasion too. Man did I get excited about
that. I loved baseball from the first time I saw it. Every
chance I got, I went to see a game.

And on week-ends we went to the local park and played
baseball and softball, sometimes all day on Saturday. Uncle
Jabe was a man I will always remember, so much different
than Pop. He didn't hunt or fish, he was just a common
working man, a boiler operator who made just average
wages. But he never ranted and raved about things like
Pop did. He was easy going and had lots of friends. He became a second father to me and taught me more in a year or
so than I had learned all my life... things like taking care of
myself, brushing my teeth and keeping clean and selecting
clothes and general appearance. He didn't smoke or drink
and he was a very religious man. Every Sunday we'd go to
the Tower Grove Baptist church.

And as good as he was he raised a son who was as bad
as they come. Al was several years younger than me and I
guess he was destined to be a criminal. We got into it over
some stupid thing he did to me and I took his pants off and
threw them in a tree. He was only eleven or twelve years
old but he looked at me and told me, with a cold calculating glare, that he'd kill me someday for that. I knew the
kid meant it. He hung around with some older kids from
another part of the neighborhood and all they did was talk
about how much they hated the cops and how to pull some
job that was against the law.

Uncle Jabe knew what was going on... he'd take a belt
and whip that boy every time the cops would bring him
home for some kind of trouble, but it never fazed him. He'd
never act like he felt it and he'd shrug any punishment off
with that cold glare. When he grew to manhood he took up
a life of crime and got in with some small-time organized
crime bunch in St. Louis.

I don't know how many people he killed but he became

144

a hit-man of sorts and early in life was trying to bomb a gas company for a rival gas company in southern Missouri when the bomb exploded in his car and critically injured him. He died a few months later from those injuries while serving time in prison. And if you want to talk about heredity, here's a real puzzler for you. Al had a son everyone called Little Al and Aunt Bert and Uncle Jabe raised him. You couldn't have asked for a finer boy and he became an outstanding, law abiding young man whom everyone liked. How do you figure something like that? All I know is, Uncle Jabe was a great man, and I'll remember him always. Much of what I was to become that was good; and some may say there wasn't much; was due to Uncle Jabe, my second Pop.

With the coming of the new year, I got a raise at Curtis-Wright because I was working hard and getting along well with everyone. They fixed that 'getting along well' part. My supervisor started a new thing about keeping the plant neat and orderly and he made me the "Good Housekeeping" supervisor. My pay went to sixty-five cents an hour and I was really starting to feel good about my job. I would be taking home another four dollars per week and if you think that wasn't a lot of money in 1941 you weren't around then.

The supervisor told me it was my job to see to it that the plant was neat, clean and orderly and I took it seriously. He said one of the things that bothered him was the lunch boxes and jackets and bags everyone left around. There were lockers for the employees to store such things in and it should be impressed upon them to do just that.

There hadn't been many seventeen year old, five-foot, three-inch supervisors at Curtis Wright and maybe that's why it was so hard to get through to anyone, but I did my best. For several days I lit into everyone who left a jacket or a lunch box out and everyone pretty much ignored me. So I decided to teach a few of them how the cow ate the cabbage and I told the janitor to go around and throw everything in the trash bins which should be in the locker and wasn't.

145

Goodbye to the Piney

Right away quick, I became the most hated man in the plant, and there was an uproar of immense proportions. In order to stem some sort of uprising, I was stripped of the title of Good Housekeeping supervisor and transferred back to the paint room...

In late October of 1941 I turned eighteen years old, working for Curtis-Wright Aeronautics next to the airport in St. Louis where Charles Lindbergh had flown not too many years before. But it was an awful long way from Uncle Jabe's place. He had an old 1928 Chevrolet and more and more he was taking me to work. It was a long drive and I decided it would be best to move out and get a room closer to work. I had a friend by the name of Beasley who had a car and he lived fairly close to Curtis-Wright. His folks had a room for rent pretty cheap, so I took it. I went back on weekends to see Uncle Jabe and Aunt Bert but I knew it was best not-to live with them until I got to be a burden.

November of 1941 was one of the worst months of my life. Painting airplanes wasn't exciting anymore and it was dark by the time I got off work. There weren't any baseball games any more and it was too cold to do much on weekends. I thought about the Big Piney and in my mind I could see the leaves falling and collecting on the surface of the clear cold water. I knew there would be flocks of woodducks and mallards in by then and I figured Pop was doing some gigging. He'd have a trapline and if I was just home, l could have a deadfall line five miles long.

But I wasn't home. I knew things were a lot better for my family if I stayed in St. Louis because I was sending back quite a bit of money every week, enough to provide a lot of things for my younger brothers they wouldn't have had. And too, there wasn't much work to do at times. I spent quite a bit of time on the job, for which I was being paid sixty-five cents an hour, stretched out napping on an overhead duct pipe, out of sight of anyone. It wasn't because I was lazy, there just wasn't anything to do.

One Sunday afternoon in early December, Beasley and I

were out riding around in his old car, just seeing some of the city I hadn't seen before and admiring the girls. I told him I was thinking about quitting because there wasn't enough to do and the job was awfully boring and I was missing the Big Piney and home. About that time there was an interruption to the music we were listening too on the car radio and a newsman announced that the Japanese had bombed Pearl Harbor.

It was grim news and the city was abuzz with rumor and speculation. Some said the entire U.S. Navy had been destroyed and the U.S. mainland was about to be attacked. I remember hearing the first reports about the number of servicemen that had been killed and it just seemed impossible to imagine. On the way back home I remember Beasley saying I didn't have to worry about not having anything to do at the plant. "From now on, he said, "we are going to be awfully busy."

I decided I wanted no more of it and I had Beasley drive me to the Bus Station on Sunday. I had seventy dollars saved up and most of my clothes in a sack. My rent was paid through the month and so I left most of my belongings in my room, and said I'd be back to get everything as soon as I could. That night I didn't care if I ever came back, I just wanted to get home. But there was one obstacle! She was sitting there on a bench inside the bus station crying her eyes out, a young girl about my age, pretty as a picture and as sad a sight as a lost puppy. She had long brown hair and brown eyes and was sitting there sobbing as if the world was coming to an end. I just couldn't walk by and do nothing. So I sat down beside her and asked if I could help.

I have often wondered, if I had climbed on a bus that afternoon and made it back to the Big Piney, what my life might have been like from that time on. Where would I have gone from there, what would I have been? Sometimes I wish I had just made it to the door of that bus. But I didn't. Mary Jane Belshe sat squarely in the way.

Chapter 12

The Quest for Wings

Mary Jane Belshe had grown up in the Ozarks too. She was from Pierce City, but had spent much of the past year in a sanitarium in Mt. Vernon being treated for tuberculosis. Her mom had moved to St. Louis, where she had a boyfriend, and Mary Jane had taken a bus to the big city only to discover that her mom wasn't home. She was barely eighteen years old and scared to death. And it was my chance to be a knight in shining armor.

I introduced myself and dried her tears and told her there wasn't anything to worry about. I got a taxi and asked him to take us to the address where the young girl's mother was suppose to be. She wasn't there. So there was nothing left to do but take her back to my room at Beasley's place. We talked way up into the night and she wasn't crying any more.

I was a perfect gentleman and I slept on the floor while Mary Jane slept in my bed. My valor backfired because the next morning Beasley's mother found out about my visitor and didn't even care to hear the circumstances. She told me to get my stuff together and get out.

Now we both were homeless. So we got another cab and filled it with my belongings and asked the driver to take us to that address of Mary Jane's mother on Delmar street. She was home that morning, though a little bleary eyed. She had been out honky-tonkin' with her old boyfriend, who was now her new husband.

I found a new place to stay on Delmar, not far from Mary Jane, who asked me to call her Janie. And though it was plain and small, it was priced right, at six dollars per month. Once again, life was exciting. Three weeks after I met her, on Christmas eve of 1941, Janie and I were married. It was a dumb thing for us to do but we were only eighteen years old and it seemed like the thing to do then. We rented a place on Oakland Avenue for fifteen dollars a month and I got transferred to the second shift, working nights, doing riveting on the bulkheads of airplane fuel tanks and pressure testing them. I did that for several months and had little opportunity to get back to the Big Piney. It didn't take me long to realize that Janie and I had made a big mistake. We got to know each other after we were married, rather than before and we weren't as compatible as we should have been. She wanted to have a baby and I said no. I knew that wasn't a smart thing to do with the money I was making. She tricked me, telling me a doctor had told her she couldn't have any babies. I believed her and she got pregnant. Our daughter Carolyn was born in the spring of 1943 and it was a responsibility I wasn't ready for.

During 1942 and 1943, life for me was very unrewarding. I didn't get back to the Big Piney very often, probably only three or four times for a couple or three days each time. My folks were crazy about Janie and the baby and of course they never knew the problems we were having. And when I was there on the Piney I forgot I had any. That old river was so beautiful and peaceful I never wanted to leave it. I'd get to fishing or trotlining or gigging and forget everything. Going back to the Big Piney was like going from purgatory to heaven.

The city life wasn't very exciting. We went to see the Cardinals and the Browns during the spring and summer and played baseball at Forest Park every week-end with guys from work. A friend and I noticed that the lake at Forest Park had bullfrogs in it and so we went there one evening about midnight and caught a bunch of them, using a flashlight to shine their eyes. I don't know how we got away with it but we did.

Well after midnight, we caught a bus toward home and I sneaked that bag full of frogs in and stuffed it under the seat. We were wet to the waist and I'm surprised we got on the bus, but it was late and there weren't many passengers. Things were going well until some woman behind started screaming her lungs out and the driver stopped to see what was wrong. She was still screaming when he got back there and standing in the seat, pointing to a big bullfrog trying to climb the side of the bus so he could jump out the window.

I heroically defused the situation by catching the frog and told the driver I had seen that kind of thing before during wet weather, frogs just moving everywhere, looking for new habitats. He didn't buy it and he saw that bag under my seat and wanted to know why it was wet and moving. Then he kicked us out and we had to walk home with about forty pounds of bullfrogs. I said right then that the bus line would get no more of my money. From then on we would get a taxi to transport our bullfrogs.

There were lots of problems at that time and not many happy days to remember. Folks were worried about the war and the country was gearing up to perhaps invade both Japan and Germany. Young men my age were going into the service everywhere. I had a deferment because of the baby and Jane's sickness but I felt the pressure to do my duty for my country and I wanted to be involved in it somehow.

The turning point came just after the beginning of 1944, one of the most formidable, darkest periods for our country. I was at work one night when a woman came up to me with tears in her eyes and anger in her voice. She looked at me with contempt and told me her son was my age, and he had been killed in battle. "Why," she asked, "are you not over there fighting the enemy like my son was?"

I couldn't rest at night after that, I kept seeing her face and hearing her voice and imagining that everyone I met was thinking the same thing. I had mentioned to Jane that I was thinking of enlisting and she outright laughed at me. She had mentioned that because of my stature the armed services probably wouldn't want me. I wasn't as much of a man in her eyes because I wasn't very tall. It didn't matter, I knew better. I was only five feet and four inches tall but I had confidence in myself. I was quicker and stronger and tougher than anyone I knew because of the kind of life I had lived.

I didn't feel that I was contributing anything important at work and couldn't even afford an old car. I hadn't seen much of the Ozarks I loved so much and was beginning to think I could never go back there. Life wasn't very enjoyable and my marriage wasn't working so I decided it was time to join the men who were fighting for their country. It was my country too.

In early March, 1944, I took a bus to Jefferson Barracks in downtown St. Louis and went in to enlist. I told the man at the desk I wanted to join the air corps because I wanted to fly planes like the ones I worked on. I had heard all the talk at Curtis-Wright about what it would be like to wear wings on the uniform. That's what I wanted.. wings on my uniform. And so they sat me down and gave me a form to fill out and I had to tell them I had no education. I was learning to read and write a little but I couldn't handle that form.

The guy behind the desk was pretty blunt about it. If you couldn't read or write, you sure as heck couldn't get in the air corps and train to be a pilot. My temper got away from me then. I told him that I could fight Germans or Japs without being able to read. I could outshoot darn near anyone I knew and I wanted to fight for my country with wings on my uniform. That fellow had the most puzzled look on his face I've ever seen. I'm sure it dawned on him that the young man standing there before him didn't know a thing about the armed services.

But there was a man at a desk in the back who heard me ranting and raving and he got up and walked over to where I was. I thought maybe he was about to throw me out and there was the thought that all the fighting I might do would be on the steps of the Jefferson Barracks. Apparently Janie was right...the army wouldn't have me.

But he didn't act too upset with my temper tantrum. He shook my hand and introduced himself as some kind of Colonel and asked me if I had ever heard of the paratroopers. They wore wings, he said, and were some of the best trained, toughest fighting men in the service.

I had no idea what the paratroopers were. Heck, I didn't even know what a parachute was. I knew you could train to fly a plane but if someone had told me soldiers jumped out of them I would have thought they were crazy. But whatever a paratrooper was, I wanted to be one and I signed up that day. They gave me a date to report and told me to get things in order before I left.

Back at Curtis Wright, I found the lady who lost her son and told her I'd be going to war soon and I would avenge her son's death when I got there. The contempt in her eyes was gone but the sadness remained. I know she looked at me thinking the same fate awaited me. Janie seemed a little prouder of me though. She got a job that week and began making good money working overtime, with her mom taking care of the baby.

She wrote a letter to Mom and Dad and told them I was going into the army and I'm glad I wasn't there when they got it. I could almost hear Pop raising the roof all the way from St. Louis. What a danged fool %$#&A**$# no-account Harris I had turned into. I would have never had to go to war because of Janie's illness and the baby and yet I had gone down there and enlisted. Mom and Pop figured they were about to lose a son but for some reason, I never once thought about going and not coming back. Maybe I just felt invincible because of my age and what I had already gone through or maybe I just had no idea what was going on, what war was about. But nevertheless, I was sure of one thing...l wasn't going to die fighting the enemy... the enemy was!

I felt good about things those last few weeks. Janie seemed happy and I got a new job at the plant driving a fork-lift. In less than a month I kissed Janie and the baby good-bye and with nothing more than the clothes I was wearing, caught the bus once again to Jefferson Barracks. After I reported, I joined a group of six or seven other young men and we all just sat around for about two hours waiting. I couldn't stand that. I started complaining and before long we were all mopping floors in the barracks. I made six or seven enemies in a hurry.

When the mopping was all done we were put on a train

late in the afternoon and headed west into the sunset toward Camp Roberts, California. I think it took about two days to get there. I played penny-ante poker with several guys, slept in the chair and ate in the dining car. And the scenery was really something after we got about halfway there. I arrived well-fed, well-rested and with three or four dollars worth of pennies. I got to thinking that army life might be just great for me. We got off the train and were assigned to a company, platoon and squad. Then we got shots, and uniforms. Mine wouldn't fit, I had to take it back twice to find something small enough. Eventually I got something close to my size but I never did find fatigues which fit really well. Decked out in my new uniform with the new garrison cap they made us buy, we posed for pictures to be sent home to wives and mothers.

The first day I was there a Lieutenant came in and gave us a good grilling, and he said something that stayed with me all through the war. I never forgot it. He said "You can live through this war if you'll get under the army's coat-tails and stay there. Listen to everything you are told, remember it and live by it. You have to have discipline to do your job and stay alive and that's what you learn first."

That really sunk in. I couldn't read so I'd have to make up for it by listening. I made a good friend right off the bat. His name was Conley and I don't remember his first name because all I ever called him was Conley. He was from Wyoming and like me, he was a country boy. He could read though, and he helped me with learning all the rules and regulations and general orders. Looking back, I don't know what I would have done without his help. But no one ever listened harder or concentrated more on memorizing everything than me. I knew I had to work harder than everyone else because I couldn't read and I had to make up for it.

The first week in training camp wasn't all that hard on me. Heck, I had been getting up all my life earlier in the morning than they did and I never had better clothes or food in all my life either. But we had to learn to march and I wasn't real good at it. The Sergeant pointed out that when I walked, I bounced. He gave me a sack of sand to put on my helmet to keep me from bouncing. I don't know if it worked or not but I wore that sack of sand on top of my helmet all week while we worked at marching. There were a few snickers because of it and it was a little embarrassing but if they wanted me to wear that sack all the way to Germany, it was fine with me.

Right away quick, I was made the company runner, to take messages back and forth from my unit to another. I could run longer and faster than anyone there and the army took note of it. Conley tagged me with a nick-name, "Ridge-Runner" because of it. Back home in the Ozarks a ridge-runner was an old long-legged coon that stripped the cornfields and outran the hounds. Since I was the company runner, the nick-name stuck. I didn't mind. I kind of liked it and it was better than having your name mispronounced all the time. No one could get the idea that Dablemont was pronounced with a long 'a', like table or cable. People always pronounced it with a short 'a', like rabble or babble. I hated that so it was nice to be called something people could pronounce. And Conley said I reminded him of an old boar coon outrunning the hounds when I headed off with a message.

The first five weeks passed pretty fast and I liked the army. We learned to salute, how to care for our rifles, and the basics of hand to hand combat. Since I was the shortest of the group I had to learn to be quicker and react better to make up for my size. I figured it out early.

We finally got to the rifle range after the first five weeks and I couldn't wait. Conley and I had grown up shooting small bore rifles and we were really going to show the army some things on that rifle range. But I had always used regular iron sights and the M-1 rifles we were issued had peep sights. We started out in a prone position and I couldn't even hit the rifle range sign. Conley was used to peep sights and he was really drilling that bullseye. Every time I shot they waved the red flag they referred to as "Maggie's drawers" which signified a miss. That's all I saw all day and I was nearly in tears. I had been sure I would be the best shot of the bunch and instead I was the worst.

But I had been born to improvise. If something didn't work, you had to figure out how to make it work and I knew my problem was those darned peep sights. How anyone could shoot with those kind of sights I couldn't figure out. So I went to the supply room and found myself a file and went to work on those sights. I filed a gap in the top of the rear sight and got it to a point where it would function as the regular open sights I had been used to. The next day on the rifle range it was a different story, and I began to nail those bulls eyes. By the end of the week I was rated as an expert, and indeed, it was me and Conley leading the whole company. Unfortunately, we had inspection at the end of the week and a Lieutenant saw the filed sight. He just stared at it a long time and then looked hard at me and then back at the sight.

I was proud of how well I had adjusted those sights and I figured the army would really see some value in a soldier who knew how to improvise so well and could make something work that hadn't been working. Wrong again!

He sent me to a supply Sergeant and the Sergeant said I might be court-martialed for those little improvements I had made to government property. And he told me that if I had wanted to change the sights, all I had to do was replace the peep sights with regular sights which they had in the supply room. I was really in hot water and after chewing me out and telling me how long I might have to be in the brig, the Sergeant decided there was one other option. I could pay for the rifle. Ninety-nine dollars!

There wasn't much of a choice there, but brother, do you know how much money that was to me. To come up with that money I went to work at night in the officers bowling alley, sitting pins. And then I got the opportunity to buy an old washing machine for one dollar and fifty cents. With the washing machine, I made some more money on the side washing clothes for other soldiers in the barracks washroom.

I finally paid for the rifle and they issued me another one with peep sights just like the first one. But I never fired it again. I was demoted from expert rifleman to sharpshooter but I didn't care. I always thought a sharpshooter was an expert anyhow. I was beginning to think the army had a screwed-up way of looking at things. If they had asked me in the beginning which one I would rather have been, an expert or a sharpshooter, I would have chosen the latter. And I would have told them if they wanted country boys to shoot the legs off a fly at a hundred yards they'd need to put regular sights on their rifles. But as far as I can remember, all the time I was there they never once asked me for my opinion. And them willing to admit I was a sharp shooter at that!

At Camp Roberts I was an expert and then a sharpshooter and they made me pay for the rifle, but I didn't get to keep it.

157

After the M-1 training we received, they trained several us us to shoot a Browning Automatic Rifle and I was better with it. It was a big heavy automatic weapon with a bipod to support the barrel and it had sights I could use. But when you started to fire it, at distances of up to 500 yards, you watched tracer rounds and adjusted to that. Some soldiers never got the hang of it but I did and I liked it. The Army took note of that.

About eight or nine weeks into training we went on bivouac, camping in the desert for a week. It would get up to about 100 degrees during the day and down to nearly freezing at night. That never happened in the Ozarks and I'll tell you it was hard to get use to. Every time I hear someone bragging about California, I think of those days sweltering during the day, freezing at night. I did plenty of sweltering back home on the Big Piney and I did plenty of freezing as well, but not on the same day!

Actually, I was enjoying myself despite the work and the weather. I was raised to be a soldier. We listened to lectures out there in the desert, had war games with one company trying to plot strategy for taking the other and learned to fire a sixty millimeter mortar. When it was all over, we marched back to Camp Roberts with a full field pack weighing fifty pounds. The march covered about twenty miles in the heat of the day and some of the guys passed out and had to be picked up and returned by ambulance. Part of the problem was their age. We had some guys in that outfit that were nearly thirty years old.

Anyway, we were several miles into one hike when one of the officers found out we were missing the base plate and tube for one of the mortars. Somebody hadn't done their job and it had been left behind. The Sergeant sent Conley and me back to get it and we did. About an hour or so after everyone else was back in camp, Conley and I came in with that extra load and I was about to drop. But the army had to have taken notice. Not that they asked me for any advice yet, they still didn't. But everyone else was confined to barracks for the weekend but us.

The Lieutenant made exceptions for Conley and me because of what we had done and gave us a weekend pass. Everyone was mad at heck at us but I didn't care. None of them had volunteered to go back and get that forgotten equipment and we hadn't either. The Lieutenant knew that my wife was coming in that weekend on a train. I rented a room for the weekend from an elderly couple next to the barracks and I couldn't wait to see Jane. I had decided I was going to try harder to make our marriage work and I wanted her to have a great time while she was there, and maybe I'd even look a little taller in her eyes. After all, she never thought I'd make it that far.

But instead of a new beginning, it was actually the beginning of the end. She was excited about meeting an Indian from Oklahoma on the trip over, and she wanted to leave a few hours early on Sunday so she could take the same train back home that he would be taking. I was crushed.... and mad. I told her that as far as I was concerned it was over between us. But again, she was young and looking for excitement. It wasn't such a great life being married to a soldier, working her young life away in a city for very little money with a baby to take care of. Looking back, we should have gotten a divorce then and started over again, for her sake and mine. We were just kids and our lives were going in different directions. Getting married was a bad mistake and bringing a baby into the world so early in our lives was even a worse mistake.

But it wasn't the first mistake I had made and it wouldn't be the last. I was about to make another one. When our seventeen weeks of training was over, two men out of 250 volunteered to be paratroopers.... me and Conley. Neither one of us new exactly what they were but I knew they wore wings and they were the toughest fighting men in the whole army. Poor old Conley just went along 'cause he was my buddy and I asked him to.

160

Chapter 13

Ft. Benning:
Pushups and Parachutes

In the summer of 1944 we climbed aboard a train with all our gear and headed across this great nation to a camp named Fort Benning, Georgia, where they made paratroopers--- whatever that was. It was a faster trip than I had made from St. Louis to Camp Roberts, even though we went twice as far. I don't remember much about it but I didn't make as much playing penny-ante poker. Either there wasn't much time or the paratrooper recruits were a little better grade of poker-players.

When we got off the train in Georgia there was a truck waiting for us and we joined other soldiers to be trucked to Camp Benning. As we entered the army property there was a big banner hanging over the road and Conley read it to me. It said, "Soldier, your walking days are over!"

We all cheered and yelled and decided that being a paratrooper was going to be a great job. Then about a quarter mile down the road there was another banner which read, "Soldier, from now on, you run!" Nobody cheered.

We went a little ways farther and the driver stopped the truck and showed us four or five great high towers with four arms coming off each one. He said those towers were 300 feet high but they looked higher to me. There wasn't a bluff anywhere on the Big Piney close to that height. And then he said that in four weeks we'd be going off the top of those towers, and those who lived would become paratroopers.

At that moment my heart plunged to my belly and I was absolutely scared to death. I looked at Conley and he looked at me and I said, "Ol' Buddy, what have I got myself into?" Conley didn't say much but his face was a little whiter than normal and he looked at me as if calling him a buddy might be taking quite a bit for granted.

Ft. Benning: Pushups and Parachutes

At the barracks there were soldiers everywhere, coming and going in all directions. It was the largest class ever to go through Ft. Benning to that point. An awful lot of them would never make it. Some of them would wash out and go back to the regular army infantry or artillery. The ones that did get through it would make up an elite group of fighting men who thought they could whip the whole German army by themselves, the 101st and 82nd Airborne Divisions.

I didn't know it of course but men who had already trained there had jumped at the D-Day invasion at Normandy behind the lines and a large number of them had been killed when the planes missed the drop zone by miles and dropped them in the midst of German strongholds. And there were some who were yet to fight in Holland, and others of us who were destined to gather at a place called Bastogne and be trapped there in what was to become known as the Battle of the Bulge, where the nation would suffer it's greatest casualties ever in a single battle. I didn't know where I'd end up or what I'd do but I knew I was going to get those wings on my uniform no matter what. Whatever these darned paratroopers were, I intended to be one.

Over the loudspeaker we were told that everyone would get two sheets and two blankets and we'd better give them back when we left. Then the voice said we'd get one uniform and boots which were to be kept so black and shiny we could see our reflection in them.

We were assigned bunks and stripped naked to head for the showers. A corporal met us when we came out and I remember he had 'GOD' printed on his uniform in big letters. He started screaming at us to run and anyone caught walking had to do fifteen or twenty pushups. Conley and I ran to get our uniforms, but again, they didn't have one that would fit me. So I ran to the orderly room and was told to run in place while they got one to fit me. For the first time since I had joined up I ended up with a uniform which fit me perfect.

We lined up and an officer screamed at us to remember

we were troopers, not G.I.'s and we had better not look like G.I.'s or think like G.I.'s. He said he had better never see us unshaven and we had better never have hair beyond crew cut length. The next morning no one passed inspection and the training officers made us do push-ups while they yelled at us and put their feet on our backs to make it harder. When it was over we headed for the chow line and I couldn't believe how much better the food was than anything we had seen at Camp Roberts. There were eggs any way you liked them, sausage and bacon and ham and biscuits. From there we had to run back to the barracks and we spent the day learning how to make our beds the way the officers wanted them made and how to pass inspections. Then they gave us all medical inspections. One of the inspectors really gave me heck.

"What are you doing here?" he asked me. "Are you a midget?"

I told him, "I want to be a paratrooper.. .sir," loud and clear and with the emphasis on 'sir' the way the army likes it.

I'll never forget how he laughed at me and called attention to me with everyone around. "This little guy wants to be a paratrooper, " he roared with laughter. "Anybody think he'll make it through the second day? Bet we'll have to carry him home!"

I knew what was going to happen. The old army Colonel back at Jefferson Barracks said they wanted six-footers, men that looked like John Wayne, except better. "They'll give you hell," he told me, "'but when they kick you out of something, go back to the end of the line and go through again. If you don't quit and if they can't break you, they've got to take you."

On the second morning we were out in fatigues lined up and ready to run to breakfast, but at first light they ran us five miles. It was 80 degrees before the sun came up. When the run was over we went back to the barracks and changed into dry fatigues then went to breakfast and ate like hogs.

Ft. Benning: Pushups and Parachutes

Back in the yard they lined us up and the sergeant who had been laughing at me saw me standing there and made me go to the back line in the squad.

We started doing small arm circles, which sounds simple and looks simple. You stand with your arms straight out from your body in opposite directions, and wave your fists in a circle about twelve inches in diameter. When I first started doing that I thought 'boy what an easy workout this is'. After fifteen minutes of that we couldn't put our arms down when they told us to. I tried but they wouldn't go down. They gave us hell for that too.

It would be a week before we could do that and then put our arms down. That same day we got a lecture on the parade ground from a Lieutenant. He started out telling us how proud we should be to call ourselves paratroopers and he said the one thing we had to do to stay there and stay alive later was to be alert.

He walked over to me as if he couldn't believe what he was seeing. Then he asked me if I thought I could stay alert. I said "Yes sir!" loud and strong. Then he said that every time we heard him say the word "jab" he wanted us to hit ourselves in the chest with our fist and keep it there until he continued. And then he started lecturing us and every now and then he'd say that word and no one acted like they even heard him. Again, he raised hell with us until we listened so closely that we began to hear it and react. That was an exercise he did often and in a few days we began to hear and react as we were suppose to do.

I had stuttered almost all my life when I got nervous and there were times at Fort Benning when I was so nervous I stammered worse than I ever had before. One day a training officer asked my name and rank and I saluted and said, "P..P..P.. Private N..N..N. .Norten D.. D...Dablemont, sir."

I thought that officer was going to come apart at the seams. "What did you say to me trooper?" he asked. I repeated it and stuttered even worse.

"Would you listen to that...." he said, "this man is a reg-

164

ular burp-gun!" He called a Sergeant over and said, "Sergeant, take this burp gun around the camp and have him salute and address everything he comes to and give his name and rank until he can do it without stuttering."

I spent hours over the next couple of days saluting poles and trash cans and jeeps and everything I came to, trying to learn to say my rank and name without stuttering. And you know, it worked. I got to where I could do it perfectly. It was a week or so later when that same officer called me forward and asked for my rank and name and I gave it to him perfectly. But that wasn't enough. He asked me to recite the first general order. All general orders were something we were suppose to memorize, and I had. The first one was, "I will walk my post in a military manner, being always on the alert, repeating all orders to the guard-house more distant than my own."

But if you know how a bunch of trainees are. You know how they take something like that and make it into something funny. I had heard the butchered version a hundred times, "I will walk my post in a military manner, and take no crap from the company commander."

When the Lieutenant asked me to recite the order, I was so intent on not stuttering I gave him that idiotic reply before I could catch myself. He nearly came off the ground yelling and screaming at me and I did push-ups for an hour while he yelled at me. I was thinking to myself that if I had to do much more talking I'd probably get myself stood up before a firing squad before training camp was half over.

During the first two weeks it was damn tough. One day they had us lay down, side by side, four men together, and a railroad tie was placed on our chests. We were told to hold that railroad tie half way up and then on command, extend it up a full arm's length. But my arms were so short I couldn't keep my hands on the log. The other guys arms were so long they lifted it above my reach. Brother, that officer gave me hell that day. He stood there and screamed at me for being so small and said that I could never be a paratrooper because my buddies could not depend on me to do my part. He made me do pushups until I was nearly exhausted and then told me to get a pile of sand under my shoulders so I could lift my share of the weight. From then on, every time we worked on the log, I made a pile of sand to elevate my shoulders and the officer didn't say anymore about it. But he never let me relax, he tried his best to get me to quit.

One day while we were doing pushups in a sawdust covered field, he walked over and put his foot on my back and started giving me hell again, telling me I couldn't be a paratrooper because I couldn't do pushups. I could do pushups better than anyone else because of my short arms and upper body strength but the his foot made it impossible.

While he yelled at me and put more pressure on my back, I tried my best. He said again I couldn't be a paratrooper and wanted to know if I was ready to quit.

I looked up at him and said "Sir, if you'll take your foot off my back, I'll do pushups during the ten minute break while the others rest."

Something changed with that. He took his foot off my back and knelt down beside me and said, "You little sawed-off &*#%$#&*, you really do want to be a paratrooper don't you?"

That night, when we were running back in from the field, we passed about 100 men standing facing a building without shirts and there were Sergeants running around screaming at them and painting yellow stripes down their backs. Those guys were on their way to becoming regular infantrymen... G.I.'s. Of the 5,000 men who began that training only about 2,400 finished.

When the Sergeant ran past me, he asked me if I wanted to join them. I was exhausted and felt as if I couldn't go another hundred yards but somehow I did. And I yelled out as he went by that before I'd quit he'd see me dead. He acted as if he didn't hear me but he never bothered me

166

again and never again did anyone say I was too small to be a paratrooper.

The training got rougher. We went through the infiltration course, where you had to crawl under barbed wire with a pack on your back and a rifle before you. There was mud and obstacles of all kind and you had to crawl through it without ever getting up on your hands and knees because there were live rounds being fired over the course only 36 inches above the ground.

The hand-to-hand combat training was tough but we were trained to use bayonets and then pitted against other troopers. I took my licks but I learned to use my strength and quickness to make up for my small size.

One of the hardest parts of combat training was the bayonet training and the training involving using a knife. I thought that was all senseless because I would never be out of ammunition, and I'd never get that close to the enemy.

Before I had to use a knife or bayonet, I'd have to fire a great deal of ammunition and miss. But still, I learned what they trained us to do.... come up behind a man, put your arm around his face, your knee in his back and cut his throat with a knife. They had training dummies there, life-sized and filled with sawdust and we attacked them again and again. I was good at it. Thank God learned that! As horrible as it seemed to me and as horrible as it sounds to you, killing a man is killing a man no matter how it is done. It's easy to do it with artillery and bombs and not so hard at a distance with a machine gun or rifle because you can't see his face or feel his resistance.

It is a horrible thing when you are close enough to hear him and smell him, and you have to do it just to go on living. But when you want to go on living you do what you have to do and you learn that there's not much you can't do, nothing you won't do. I wouldn't have believed that when I was a kid growing up on the Big Piney. But at Camp Benning I became a man who could kill other men and do anything to stay alive. I didn't know it at the time, what was happening little by little. Maybe if I would have thought about it, it would have been a difficult thing to accept. But they taught us just to do the job and not think about it.

All the training was referred to in stages and when we had finished with A stage, B stage and C stage, I knew I wasn't going to be kicked out. But my Sergeant never let me get out in front. In everything we did, he made me go to the back of the line or the rear of the platoon. By then we were making fifteen-mile runs before breakfast and somebody was always carrying a 25- pound medicine ball. On those runs, you double-timed it ten minutes, (a little faster than jogging) and walked five. You couldn't ever look down or they'd nail you with that medicine ball and you had to carry it until you saw someone not looking and then you tossed it to him. If he caught it, you carried it. If he didn't he carried it.

Nobody had to carry it too long if they were running head up and paying attention but I made the mistake one day of throwing it to the Lieutenant and I carried it the rest of the day. What the heck, he had his head down and they told us when someone had their head down they were suppose to get the medicine ball. Someone should have told me Lieutenants didn't count. That Lieutenant held a grudge about that I think. That same week I spit in the sawdust on the parade ground and he made me pick it up that wad of sawdust where I spit with my teeth and carry it off the grounds.

The B and C stage training involved putting on a harness, attaching it to a steel cable and jumping off a thirty foot platform. You'd fall about ten or twelve feet, and then the cable would catch you and slide you down into a sawdust pile about fifty feet from the platform. Thank goodness for the heavy pile of sawdust below us because once I forgot to hook up to the cable and jumped off that platform and fell the whole distance. Even with the bed of thick sawdust, I'm lucky I wasn't seriously hurt, but I wasn't. It knocked the wind out of me pretty good but I got back up to the platform and the Sergeant wasn't amused by the fact that I had forgotten to hook up. I wouldn't forget again.

During that stage of training we learned to pack parachutes and how to jump off a small bench and roll on your side and shoulder. It seemed kind of silly but it had a purpose. You had to know how to hit the ground or you'd break your leg or ankle. It was said that at times you might hit the ground at nearly forty miles per hour. It all depended on whether you were under that chute or out beside it. You had to learn to catch only a portion of your weight on your feet and legs and then roll, letting your hips and shoulders catch the rest.

We spent an hour or so each day packing parachutes and learning about the different sized cords and the purpose of each one. Our parachutes were called T-5's and why they called them that is as much a puzzlement to me as it might be to you. They were 26 feet across and some were made out of silk and some out of nylon. The nylon was a much better chute because the silk would tear when it got wet and you could lose a couple of panels if you jumped during moist conditions. But even with a blown panel or two, you'd get to the ground. Maybe a little faster but not enough faster to worry about. Training chutes were white but the ones used overseas were camouflaged.

During the D stage, we were transported to the towers and I was scared half to death. Everyone said they were 300 feet high but I never saw a mountain in the Rockies any taller. Conley and me were trying to act like we weren't scared, but we were, and I think everybody else was too.

Parachutes hung from the arms of the towers already blossomed out and they were hooked to the harness you wore. Then they drew you up slowly to the top of the tower at about elevator speed. I had the dangdest case of butterflies I ever had. The only thing below me was my boots and troopers way down there who were about the size of bugs. They gave us all a newspaper sheet and when we got to within six feet of the arm which held us, it stopped.

Ft. Benning: Pushups and Parachutes

Then over the loudspeaker we heard our numbers called and each of us was to drop the newspaper if we were ready and hadn't passed out. They could see I was conscious because I was kicking around some but I couldn't drop that newspaper for anything in the world. Finally after calling my number several times, they gave up. Then the cable pulled me on up the last six feet, the parachute was released and my heart came all the way up past my ears. Then I was drifting down, still clutching that newspaper, and it was an unbelievable thrill.

We had been told at least forty times to grab the shroud lines when we hit the ground and dump all the air out of the chute. Out to the side there were a couple of planes running and a prop-blast producing about thirty mile-an-hour winds. I forgot the shroud lines and the parachute caught that wind and drug me across the field while I was trying to dump the air out. The Lieutenant was running along beside me screaming at me until I finally got stopped and he gave me hell all the way back. He told me that in combat that kind of stupidity might get me dragged into the ocean or over a bluff or into enemy fire. And all the way back he told me it had better not happen again.

They hooked me back up and it never bothered me again to be dropped from the tower. It was great fun, I would have liked to have done it all day long. In fact if you weren't careful you'd get to enjoying it so much you wouldn't be prepared to hit and roll. But I had little problem with that, I was good at it. And I never again forgot to grab the shroud line and dump the air.

No matter what the stage of training, all the other things continued, the calisthenics, the obstacle courses, the road runs and the lectures, and hand-to-hand combat training, always attacking those dummies. I did everything fine except the ten foot wall in the obstacle course. I like to never cleared that thing and the Sergeant screamed at me for an hour making me do it again and again. Finally I got over it and then went for the rope over the mud hole and missed it. I know that Sergeant would have liked to laughed when I went in that yellow mud hole but he didn't. He was really good at being mad all the time and screaming like hell. I guess it's something he worked hard at.

During the F stage, or sixth week of paratrooper training, we were herded onto C-47's, eighteen men at a time, and I went on my first airplane ride to make my first parachute jump. I was scared to death again....it seemed like the plane was having a hard time getting off the ground. It rumbled and vibrated and creaked and groaned and then lifted up and soared. There were little windows above us but I couldn't see out and didn't want to. Our chutes had been pre-packed and we had been trained. I knew exactly what to do but I kept going over everything in my mind. Pop said anyone who jumped out of an airplane was a darned fool and I was beginning to see the reasoning behind his thinking.

The plane climbed and vibrated and strained and my knees were so weak I didn't think I could get on them. The jump-master said to open our mouths to equalize the pressure and so I began to sing 'The Wabash Cannonball'. I saw the red light come on and the jump-master said, "Number 1 stick, stand up and hook up".

All nine men on my side stood up and I was the ninth in that line. We had been trained to hook up our own static line and then check the guy in front of us to be sure that he was hooked up properly. Then the jump-master checks the hookup of the last man in the line, which was me, and goes to the rear of the plane where the door is, and slides it open. He is hooked up to a cable in the plane so he can't go out, and he holds to a bar which he can swing from by his hands like a monkey. If you freeze up or won't jump or can't jump he'll plant his boots right in your back and kick you out. That kick he gives the trooper helps him to clear the tail section. The plane is going about 150 miles per hour and the prop-blast adds to that so you have to jump and turn your back away from the front, looking toward the tail section. If

171

you look into that prop blast it will almost tear the skin off your face.

When the red light over the door went off and the green light came on, the jump~master yelled 'go' and all nine men went out just seconds apart so that we would land together. You don't want your platoon scattered all over. To form an effective fighting unit we had to get together quickly. Still singing 'The Wabash Cannonball', I followed them all and didn't need to be kicked. I was so scared I was practically numb. I saw the tail section and for a fleeting moment I thought it was going to hit me. And then in another second it was gone and everything else was gone.

The jerk of the opening chute was a greater shock than I even imagined. They tried to prepare us for that but you couldn't be aware of what it was like until it happened. The back straps snap into your skin so hard it makes strawberries on the back of the shoulders and your helmet edge comes down to whop you across the nose. If your paratrooper boots aren't laced well and tight with parachute cords, your boots will come off when the chute opens. And you yell one thousand, two thousand, three thousand and if your chute hasn't opened you have to get the reserve chute opened fast. At 1500 feet you don't have much time.

I was alone, 1500 feet in the air, looking out at the chutes below me, remembering that I had to watch them and not get over them. If you fall faster than someone below you, you may come down on his chute and you have to run off of it to keep your own chute from collapsing. We had been trained about that too and I sure didn't want to get in that predicament.

I hit the ground hard and rolled as I was supposed to. Immediately after touching down you dump the air from your chute and look up to be sure nothing is coming down on top of you like boots or rifles or shovels or whatever might dump out of a pack. I remembered to do everything just as I was told and I felt ten feet tall, standing there watching the last stick of nine men sail down around me. It was an exhilaration words can't describe. I was ready to go back up again. I was a paratrooper, a 101st Airborne Screamin Eagle.

After jumping that first time you can jump several more times and it is great fun. It didn't ever bother me at all to go back up after the first jump but the next day after you sleep on it, the first jump has you weak-kneed and scared all over again. It's hard to explain it, but the second day I was as nervous as could be and it was even harder to get out of the plane. It wasn't just me, all paratroopers seemed to have the same problem.

We were told that we'd be jumping out of bed that night after the first jump and everyone laughed about it. Just after getting into deep sleep I was bailing out of bed hollering hup thousand...two thousand, waking up about the time I hit the floor. Nobody got much sleep that night because there were a lot of troopers jumping out of bed in the middle of the night, reliving their first jump in their dreams.

On the second day, there were thunderheads everywhere and convection currents to deal with. On my first jump I caught one of those updrafts just after my chute opened and because I was so light, the upshoot carried me up a hundred feet or so. We had been told what to do but I didn't know exactly what was happening. It was quite a thrill though. I saw the other parachutes going down but I was going up. So I grabbed the riser cord and began to dump air. I overdid it and began to fall too fast. I could hear the captain on the ground with a loudspeaker telling me what to do but I couldn't understand him.

Then I began to slow down and hit perfectly in that Alabama peanut field. I looked around and saw Conley laying on the ground out in the field. Medics were going to him and I could see he was in great pain... so I ran over to him. There were tears in his eyes because he knew he was through. I knelt down to console him and he looked up at me and said through the pain, "Looks like I'm washed-out, Ridge-Runner... but we'll still give 'em hell. You get 'em

173

I turned 21 in October of '44 with Fort Benning
and paratrooper training behind me.

from the air and I'll get "em from the ground."

I started to say something but about that time an officer came up and was on my back good. He screamed at me to get back to my position and leave the medics to do their work. I looked back over my shoulder as the medics took him to the ambulance and I never saw him again. In fact, I never even heard where he ended up. I never knew his first name I don't guess, or if I did I can't remember it. He was a great friend and it would have been tough going through training without a buddy like him. But he had flat feet and they had always bothered him. They hurt him even during the simplest jumps.

I'll bet he made one heck of an infantryman because he was nothing but muscle. Conley was from Cheyenne, Wyoming, with red hair, about 160 pounds and around five-feet, eight-inches tall. He could shoot an M-1 like no one I ever saw. I'll never forget him. I hope he got through the war and has had a great life.

Before shipping out in November of 1944, I got to spend a week at home with Janie & Carolyn and said goodbye to Mom and Pop.

Chapter 14

Preparing for the Enemy

It was rough that night after they took Conley away in the ambulance. I kept trying to find out if anyone knew anything but no one did. The Sergeant said it wasn't any of my business, I needed to think about my job and forget about Conley. He said I'd see a hell of a lot of troopers fall before it was over and I'd better get use to it. My job was to do what I was ordered and carry out my responsibility to the rest of my unit. But that empty bunk made it tough.

There were other problems ahead though. After the third day of jumping and training I was notified that my wife Janie was in the orderly room and I could go see her. I don't know why she came there or where she got the money or where she stayed, but she was there to watch me jump the next day and I was intent on showing her she had married a great deal more of a man than she knew.

When I jumped that morning I saw where the observers were and figured she'd be there, so I dumped the air out of one side of my chute and sailed toward them, way out of line with where we were suppose to land. I could hear the Captain again on the ground giving me instructions to stop dumping air and straighten the chute but I ignored him. I hit the ground on my feet as we were never suppose to do ran aways to get my legs steady, gathered my chute and walked toward the observers like John Wayne.

I didn't make it. The Lieutenant came up and threatened to have me court-martialed. He gave me hell for five minutes and it was awfully embarrassing to get berated like that in front of all those admiring onlookers. I figured the army would be proud of a trooper so concerned with public relations. Wrong again!

That night I got a two hour pass to spend some time with Janie, so they must not have been as mad at me as they seemed or maybe someone felt bad about the hard times they had given me that whole day. I didn't need the whole two hours. Jane still took note that I was the littlest para-trooper and how good some of those tall guys looked. We went to get a banana split and I flirted too much with the girl behind the ice-cream counter. We had one heck of a fight and I went back to the barracks early.

That fight nearly cost me my life. I packed my parachute that night thinking more about the argument Jane and I had than what I was doing and I tied the wrong cord around the mouth of my parachute. It is too complicated to explain but there's a breaker cord which is very small and must break in order for the chute to open. If you use the wrong cord it won't break and the chute won't open. Luckily, a trooper doesn't pack his reserve chute. But word had gotten around that we had lost a man that day because his chute hadn't opened and for some reason he never even employed the reserve chute. I didn't know him, don't know what happened. I guess when several thousand men are training like that you expect someone to get killed every now and then. I came awfully close to being the second but it wasn't entirely my fault.

We were suppose to jump only once the next day and it was to be our first night jump. We went through everything else during the day, the calisthenics and road runs, the lectures and combat training and then the big night jump. I was ready for it... it wasn't going to be any big thing, same routine, except we'd have to watch hard for the ground coming up in the darkness. No one figured on having some idiots piloting the plane getting off course but they did. And instead of dropping us over a peanut field at 1500 feet they dropped several groups of us from about 1000 feet over a swamp.

When my chute didn't open I was paralyzed with fear but I ripped that cord from the reserve chute and the spring shot it out into the black night. I really can't recall the impact of the reserve chute because it seemed like only seconds later that I felt limbs hitting my face and I blacked out. When I came around I was hanging from the limbs of

178

a tall tree, thirty or forty feet above the water. My back hurt something awful and my face was bleeding.

I could hear people talking in the distance and I started wondering if a limb might break and I would fall into that swamp and be eaten by an alligator before I ever even confronted the enemy on foreign soil. Later on, I think I might have preferred that kind of ending, but not that night. I started yelling at the top of my voice because we had been told to do that on this particular jump if something went wrong so that someone could find us. I could hear other troopers yelling and I wanted to be sure I was just as loud as they were.

In a little while there were medics wading around below me yelling up at me to shut up so they could listen for others. They had to tell me several times. They doctored me at the hospital that night and decided there was nothing seriously wrong. One trooper hadn't been so lucky. He had apparently hit hard in the water and drowned. The company Chaplain had broken his hip and there were a lot of other injuries.

The jumps continued during the day and we were jumping with rifles and full back packs by then. I weighed about 130 pounds and carrying that pack to the plane was a job. I never could straighten up. A full pack consisted of a bedroll and k-rations, a digging tool or hatchet, hand grenades and ammunition stored in the pockets of the jump pants, an extra pair of boots, and a field jacket. Then there was the weight of the helmet and rifle. Some of the 200-pound men had trouble with the pack. For me, it was a heck of a challenge. I hit the ground a lot harder and it jarred me good. But as we made more jumps I started to get the hang of it.

The last jump I made was a demonstration jump for a bunch of Generals the day before they graduated us. I was the only buck private in the group of eight, and was selected because I was standing in front of the orderly room trying to figure out what the newest bulletins said. The Sergeant walked up and said, "Ridge-Runner come with me." So I went, always one to help when I could, especially when I was told to and had no other choice.

All the other men on the plane were Sergeants, Lieutenants and Corporals. The chutes had been packed already and they were far different than the others. You didn't hook up, you jumped and pulled your own rip cord. And for the first time, I'd be jumping above the normal 1500 feet level... we were going up a mile high, 5,280 feet. They told me to follow and free fall until I started seeing other chutes open. The Sergeant said if I opened up too early I'd look like an idiot up there in the air all afternoon with all those Generals watching. The plan was to fall to about to about 1500 feet and then pull the cord.

That was the most enjoyable jump I ever made. It seemed like I was just laying out there suspended in the air with a tremendous wind hitting me. There was absolutely no sensation of falling. It took awhile to get straightened out because the horizon and the sky kept switching places but the free falling experience was really enjoyable. I pulled my cord at about 1500 feet like all the rest and floated down to land on my feet. I wished we could go back and do it again.

The next day they graduated us and hundreds of men stood at attention while General Taylor pinned the wings on us. He gave a speech but I don't remember much of it... just the part where he told us to shake hands with the four guys in front, behind and to both sides. He said that some of the men we shook hands with would not come back and I remember what a sobering thought that was. But I never even wondered if I would be one of them. I felt invincible.

I had to stand on a doggone little platform in one of the back rows because I was so short and they wanted the platoon to look uniform. But I stood there at attention for a couple of hours and watched as some of the bigger guys passed out in the heat. Eventually, that General made it around to me and pinned those wings on me and I was a paratrooper....the littlest one there maybe, but I was one anyway.

When he came to me he looked down at that six-inch bench I was standing on and he said, "Trooper, you know that as far as I'm concerned you are equal to three ordinary men now. Be proud of that, and act accordingly in combat." And he shook my hand and carried on but I saw him glance back at that bench I was standing on and wonder how in heck I got there.

I knew I wasn't really equal to three ordinary men.... I figured I was equal to two maybe but not three. But I can tell you, at that moment I was prouder of myself than I had ever been. My training had made me ready and capable and confident.

That night several busloads of paratroopers went to a big tavern in Phoenix City, Alabama. I went just because we were celebrating the end of training. We wouldn't have celebrated anything if we had known what lay ahead. But there we were with everyone getting drunk and I ordered a Coca-Cola, still addicted to them from my days of boyhood on the Meramec. I never liked alcohol and didn't intend to drink the stuff. All I wanted was a Coca-Cola and sure enough some danged guy had to make a wise crack about mixing milk with it.

He was a Mexican training officer by the name of Rodriguez and only a couple inches taller than me. That's when I remembered that General telling me I was the equal of three men and I figured if anyone ought to know, it would be a General. After all, you didn't get to be a General if you went around miscalculating things. And so I suggested to Mr. Rodriguez that if he didn't approve of me drinking a Coke he ought to go off and get drunk and mind his own business or I might put a couple of knots on his head with a Screamin' Eagle insignia on 'em.

One thing led to another and the two of us sparred around there for awhile and for some reason or another, I kept hitting where he wasn't and he kept hitting where I was. Come to find out Rodriguez had been some kind of professional lightweight boxer and he finally held out his hand and said he had had enough if I had. I had. We shook hands and talked awhile and he bought me another Coke and we got to be pretty good friends that night. In fact he shipped out with us, so I got to know him pretty good over the next few weeks. I think he was killed later in combat. But that little skirmish convinced me that sometimes Generals don't know everything.

We got a ten-day furlough to go home and say goodbye to our families. It took a couple of days to get back to St. Louis by train, where I picked up Jane and my daughter Carolyn and took a bus back to the Big Piney. Mom and Dad were beginning to show their age and Mom cried about half the time I was home. Pop cussed me out good for joining the service when I could have stayed out with my deferment. He said I had turned out to be a blankety-blank Harris #*@&%$@*&%%#* after all. Screamin' Eagles be damned, I had showed my stupidity and wouldn't never make it back. Folks around Houston that I had known since boyhood shook my hand and carried on like they never expected to see me again. A few wanted to know what a paratrooper was and why I hadn't got to be an officer.

I got away from it all and went down to the Piney to watch the clear, flowing waters carrying the red and gold leaves of the coming autumn. I wished somehow I had stayed on the river and never seen St. Louis. I wished the Germans and the Japanese had fought each other and let the rest of the world alone. I took a boat paddle and an old johnboat and paddled up the river aways and watched some woodducks burst from a slough alongside me. And I asked God to let them and me come back there someday if it was his will. Once again I was a little bit scared, wondering what it would be like to fight the enemy on a foreign battlefield. But I had been scared before, lots of times, and I always got over it.

Just before I left I asked Pop if I could borrow five dollars for the bus trip back. Still mad because I had joined up without talking to him about it, he said it would be stupid to loan me money because I wouldn't be able to pay it if I got over there and got killed. I went down to see uncle Thurman Harris and he loaned me the money. Jane and Carolyn and I climbed on the bus with Mom crying her eyes out and I waved good-bye to Houston, Missouri sometime in late October of 1944. In St. Louis, I spent a day with Uncle Jabe. We had a big ball game at the park and a good dinner and then I said good-bye. At the train station Jane didn't shed any tears. I hadn't grown an inch in her eyes.

It was cold at Ft. Mead, Maryland, and we went back to hard training of all kinds. That's where I trained on a .30 caliber machine gun and fired a perfect score with 100 rounds. They made a big deal of that, announcing it over the loudspeaker. It wasn't so much a matter of aiming and shooting but of calculating the numbers of cranks and clicks on the machine gun which placed the bullet in the targets as they rose and fell. One of my buddies said, "Ridge-Runner you're a damn fool... now they'll put you to shooting a machine gun in combat and you won't last two weeks."

Training with the .30 caliber machine gun.

Preparing for the Enemy

I got a three-day pass for that score and another three-day pass for throwing several live hand grenades in barrels at 35 yards without missing. The day I was suppose to take my six days we shipped out by trucks to Camp Shanks, New York. All those passes were just morale-builders apparently... I think they knew all the time we'd never get to use them.

It took a whole day to get to Camp Shanks and that place was heaven compared to the other places we had trained. It had really nice barracks and a recreation hall the size of a football field. We were just there a day or so, and the night before we were to head overseas they brought in bus loads of young women and had a big party in the recreation hall with food and pies and cakes and mixed drinks and dancing. There wasn't much country music so I didn't much care for it. And I didn't know a thing about dancing.

A little Jewish girl who was a bit on the heavy side but shorter than me, tried to show me how to dance. I wasn't very good at it. She said she was married and just came because she was bored back in New York and her husband was in the hospital. There were lots of girls there who had husbands overseas and I think maybe they were just there because the Army wanted to take our minds off what might be ahead and build morale.

But the paratroopers already had a spirit and a morale that was hard to beat. We were proud and confident and we looked at ourselves as being several notches above the norm. It carried us through some of the darkest days and the toughest times. Take that night at the recreation hall. I'm absolutely sure that I danced with a few of those married ladies who wished they were single that night even if their feet hurt afterward.

On the 30th of November, 1944, we packed up and boarded the Louie Pasteur, a big ship which had once been used to haul cattle and hogs and then had been rebuilt for troops. I stood at the back of the deck after my gear had been stowed below and watched the harbor disappear slow-

184

ly behind us, watching my country fade into the fog, proud that I was going overseas to fight for the United States of America.

The ship was packed, troopers slept in hammocks below deck. I stayed back on the tail end of the deck to see everything and I could see the propellers every now and then as the ship rose and fell. I thought they'd be a lot bigger than they were. For a few miles the boat shook as the motor began to build power. Five or six hours out into the ocean I saw some big fish in the water and decided I'd see if I could shoot one.

I got my rifle and ammunition and went back to shoot one of those fish but I only got off one round before one of the ships officers came running up and jumped all over me. He asked me if I knew why they were running a zig-zag course and I said I didn't. That's when he told me about submarines and the ships which had left port and never made it to England because they were torpedoed with everyone on board lost. I put the rifle away and promised I wouldn't even cough the rest of the trip. At first it worried me a little. They had trained us to do about everything except long-distance swimming. But being worried about shooting at a fish seemed silly to me. With all that ocean how would the Germans ever find us?

There were other things to worry about that after noon. As the ship began to rise and fall and pitch, the sea sickness came on. And the ocean spray mist had left me coated with a fine layer of salt to make me feel even worse. I was miserable. For two days everyone was throwing up and no one could eat. I just drank water and heaved. They gave us some pills which eventually began to help and I began to feel well enough to stay up on deck and play checkers and watch Rodriguez do some boxing.

Without the sea-sickness, you'd still get sick. The food was awful and the whole ship began to smell because there were so many sick troopers. I couldn't go near the commodes and I don't see how anyone else did. I don't think

I relieved myself all week in one of those restrooms but I didn't eat anything either. I bet I lost another ten pounds in five days.

We landed in Manchester, England late November or early December and though it wasn't the prettiest place I've ever seen, I have never been happier to see dry ground. I was really sick. I had a bad headache and a fever and was terribly constipated, but I was scared to death to go for treatment of any kind because I didn't want to get separated from my outfit.

And so I entered into a haze not unlike the fog that settled over England that first day I saw it. We were told we were heading to Holland to reinforce 101st airborne troops that had been fighting the Germans since mid-September. I was about to become a part of the war. I had no idea what to expect, but I wasn't scared. I was too darn sick to be scared. And I told myself that when it came time to go back home, I wasn't going by any boat unless I was paddling the damn thing.

Before we get much farther, I have to tell you that as easy as it is to remember my boyhood and those months of military training and even the years that followed the war, nothing is easy about remembering what happened after I got to England. Some of it is fairly clear in my memory. Some of it that I would just as soon have forgotten, I can't forget and never will. And though I don't know why, much of it is just a haze, even the days after we arrived before we ever even saw combat. I have tried hard to remember certain parts of it but I just can't.

I don't know for sure how long we were at any particular place, I have to go by what my papers say and by the historic accounts of the Battle of the Bulge. So I don't know that I can give any great insight as to what happened. I can only try to put together the parts of it I do remember and attempt to get the chronological order of events correct as best I can. From this point on, I have to say this is all to the best of my knowledge and the best I can remember. I am not going to try to give dates. You can find that in history books.

Part of the problem is, I never did know which direction we were going or anything about the places where we had been. My lack of education made Europe a whole new world to me. I can't remember anything about how we got to Holland but that's where we went and I think we went on a boat the day after we landed in England. I can remember going across the English channel a couple of times while overseas. It was the roughest water I had ever seen but it only took a few hours to get across it. I was always seasick when I crossed the English channel.

They sent us to guard a big arching rock bridge in Holland and we were housed in little Quonset hut barracks near it. Troopers who had arrived there back in September had been fighting the Germans for two and a half months and we were going in, I am sure, to replace them right at the end of it. But that battle was virtually over so they didn't really need us there. I was told to stop anyone who tried to cross that bridge and if they didn't stop, to shoot them. It was uneventful and boring and I never had to even lower my rifle. I was on guard duty with other troopers and we spent two hours on and four hours off.

It was there that I met Glen Cassidy. Our commanding officer began pairing us off and Cassidy was to be my fox-hole buddy. I was disappointed in him at first. He was from Maybrook, New York and a city boy through and through. He didn't know a thing about the outdoors and hadn't ever even camped out. Fox-hole partners were to watch after each other, one carried one shelter-half and the other carried the other. I carried a hatchet and he carried a trenching tool, a small shovel.

Cassidy was six-feet two-inches tall and weighed about 160 pounds. He was really particular about his uniform and always clean-shaven, as we were suppose to be. He was very well educated and could speak German better than I could speak English. And he was always talking about his red-headed girlfriend, a high-school sweetheart he intended

Foxhole partners, Glen Cassidy and me

to marry. In our squad there were men by the name of Dingler, DeMeer, J.R. Davis and Sergeant Balew was our squad leader. DeMeer was an athlete, a topnotch pitcher who was said to have had a shot at the major leagues. I think he was from Illinois.

Davis was short and stocky, not much taller than me and the only guy I ever met who stuttered as bad as me. Balew was from Oregon, of average build and several years older than me. In training, he had been a Corporal in our company and was promoted to Sergeant when we shipped out. He didn't talk to us much except to give orders. I never liked him much and he didn't care for me but that doesn't have anything to do with anything when you are in combat.

At 21, I was the youngest of the squad and the only one who couldn't read. But finally I was on a par with everyone because no one else could read that foreign language on signs in those countries. Cassidy could though and he kept me informed as much as possible. But hell, like I said, I never knew north from south or one country from the other. I had never heard of countries like Holland or Belgium. I knew about France, because our ancestors had come from France, my great grandfather and grandfather both had been born there.

We weren't in Holland very long. It seems as if we were just there a few days and then loaded onto trucks and buses and heading what they said was south. As best I can remember we traveled a couple of days and it was boring as hell. We spent time on what they called six-by-six troop trucks and buses I think. I can't say for sure. But I believe we went to Mourmelon, France, where most of the 101st Airborne paratroopers who had been fighting in Holland had been sent. It was a rest area at that time for the Screamin' Eagles who had been fighting since September.

There were a lot of troopers there, wherever we were. And every time you turned around someone was saying they heard we weren't going to fight at all, that the war was nearly over and the Germans were done. There were also rumors that we were going to be retrained and sent to invade Japan. I got to where I didn't pay any attention to anyone because there were so many versions of the rumors. I just knew that if this was a war I could survive it. The only thing to fight was boredom.

Wherever we were, they had tents there that would sleep twelve or fourteen troopers, and there were lots of them. The weather was fairly warm, not too bad for December. At that time there was no snow at all. They gave me an overcoat which was too long and I couldn't even walk in the damn thing without tripping over it. When they gave me a small one that didn't drag the ground, the shoulders were so tight I couldn't even get my rifle up. The overcoat was heavy too so I threw it away. It was cold at night but I used my field jacket to stay warm. It was enough then. Soon, I would wish I had kept the overcoat.

We were doing nothing so they put those of us who had good records on a truck to a train station I think and then on to Paris. Out of our squad, only Cassidy and I went. French people loved us, always hugging us and patting troopers on the back. I didn't know why, I didn't know much about the liberation which had taken place. But I didn't much like the people I met. They were always begging us for cigarettes and chocolate bars and most of the adults ran around with wine bottles in their hands, or so it seemed to me.

They took us to a nice hotel and changed money over for French francs. We bought some French food in a little cafe but I didn't like it either. I remember seeing some little kids go by pulling a long loaf of hard dark bread on a string down a dirty old brick street.

There were French prostitutes all around but we had been told about venereal disease to a point where I was afraid to run my hand along the hotel bannister. I sure wasn't going to talk to a woman. That stuff the army used to keep you from getting a sexually transmitted disease may not have worked on everyone but it did on me. I had seen some of the awfullest, scariest movies about that kind of thing you can ever imagine. I don't know if it was true or not, but it was effective.

Some servicemen, and there were a lot of them there who weren't paratroopers, were running around with French women who were anything but beautiful. And there was a lot of venereal disease over there and it was a problem for some of the military personnel. But I don't know why they would take the risk with women that downright ugly. It amazed me that so many European women were so plain and didn't shave their legs. But I didn't know about the abuse those people had taken under German occupation. It didn't pay for a woman to be pretty.

I went sightseeing in the afternoon that first day with Cassidy but I was worried about getting lost. Paris was a huge city with people everywhere and lots of American servicemen from all branches of the military. I even saw some sailors there. They had it planned so that about 150 of us went to a stage show in a theater that night not far from the hotel. It was the most vulgar thing I had ever seen.

I never dreamed that people would do such things for an audience and it was a little bit repulsive. But the troopers and soldiers there seemed to enjoy everything, you've never heard so much whooping and hollering and cheering. They offered soldiers something that sounded like a "sech au franc" to go up on stage and participate in something I don't even want you to imagine. Cassidy and my other squad members knew how tight I was. I held onto every penny I got. Cassidy started elbowing me in the ribs and hollering that he had the man for them. I just eased down in my seat and hoped nobody heard him.

"Ridge-Runner," he said, "are you going to pass up a chance at twenty bucks?"

I sure was!!!!

My friend, Yancey and I somewhere in France, December of '44. You can tell by our faces that we haven't yet seen combat. Within weeks, Yancey was killed in the Ardennes Forest

Chapter 15

The Siege at Bastogne

Very early the next morning a First Lieutenant began raising everyone with a sense of urgency. I thought we were all in trouble for something and some of the guys were complaining because they thought they were going to sleep late that morning and get to see Paris. Some were a little hung over.

They assembled outside the hotel and we were told that the Germans were on the offensive and we were going to stop them. We put on battle fatigues and turned in our barracks bags with all our personal gear, which would be sent back to Mourmelon. They issued us rifles and ammunitions, k-rations, full field packs and grenades, helmets wrapped with bandages and sulfur powder packets. I took my knife and both pistols with all the ammunition I had for each.

History says that before noon they loaded us into big trucks and we began to move out. I didn't mention this in the first edition of this book because I know no one will believe it, and looking back on it, I can't swear that I have it straight, but I have always felt that about fifty of us who had been in a special group due to good conduct passes, were taken on truck to three big planes waiting outside the city, and flown to Bastogne. I remember jumping into an area, and spending the night in the loft of an old building, and I think it was that day.

Everyone tells me the 101st went by truck to Bastogne and no one jumped. I think they are wrong. I think some of us jumped. But then again, I remember spending hours riding in those truck convoys too. All I know is, sometime while I was over there, we made a jump somewhere late in the evening and I am almost sure it was at Bastogne.

Anyway, no one gave us any details. I wasn't excited because I figured it would be like Holland. No one told us anything about what was going on. We arrived late in the day as best as I can remember. History books say there were more than 11,000 paratroopers trucked into the city of Bastogne but I don't remember seeing many of them. Where we wound up, no matter how we got there, was outside of the city, into the countryside. It was late and dusky, but I could see that the landscape was broken fields and trees much like it would look back home.

Some of the troopers got into the woods and assembled shelter halves to sleep in but Cassidy and I saw a building not far from us which was half barn and half living quarters. There was a dim lantern light in the house half and I assumed there were people there. We didn't bother them, we just quietly climbed up and slept in loft on some old musty straw. I even took my boots off and wrapped up in my blanket. It was the last time I'd have those boots off for awhile, and I'd not sleep so well again for many months.

At first light we climbed down and joined our group. There were hundreds of troopers around and all moving off in the same general direction. I heard later that we were southwest of Bastogne, some said later that it might have been as much as six miles from the town where General McAuliffe was holed up in a basement. I don't know anything for sure. But over the next few days I was in communication with only a small group of men, because the next morning Cassidy and I rejoined our unit and we were back with J.R. Davis and Dingler and Demeer and Captain Balew.

There were a few other troopers around I didn't know, and you didn't get a chance much to make acquaintances. We didn't travel far but we traveled fast. There wasn't much excitement at first, and then I remember a First Lieutenant I had never seen before came running by and said to find cover in nearby woods and get dug in, we were about to come under attack. The timber was good-sized but not heavy nor with a lot of undergrowth. It was much like a park with planted trees in rows.

Sergeant Balew was telling us this was it, saying to get

rifles ready and get dug in. "We are about to be under attack," he said, "and we are to stop any assault!"

I wasn't convinced. There wasn't a German soldier anywhere and I told Cassidy I figured we were on another damn dry run like in Holland. "We'll cut pine boughs to line our fox hole with," I said, as I reached for my knife. And that's when we first heard the distant guns and the whistle of incoming artillery. There must have been nearly one hundred artillery shells hit that forest in the next few minutes along a quarter mile front. The ground shook with the explosions and dirt and trees and limbs were in the air around us.

You could hear that shrapnel whizzing and buzzing through the air and the screams of troopers who were hit. I buried my face in the ground next to a tree trunk and tried to get as low as possible. Through it all I never looked up and I figured it was over for all of us. I didn't imagine anyone could live through such a thing. And then it ended and in the lull, everyone was trying to tend to the wounded.

The closest one to me was a trooper by the name of Fitzgerald who was also from St. Louis. His left knee was blown away and it looked as if he might bleed to death. Two or three men had been killed in our immediate area and all around you could hear the screams and moans of wounded men and officers yelling orders.

A medic began to give Fitzgerald morphine and they began to treat his wound. He finally stopped yelling and I talked to him for a moment, telling him he'd be back in St. Louis in a few days and be fine. He asked me for my an address and I gave it to him. Behind me, Cassidy was digging a fox-hole and when they took Fitzgerald away, I started to help him. Another outfit came in as we dug in. They brought in a bazooka and a Browning Automatic Rifle and our Lieutenant gave me the rifle. I had a good deal of experience with it during our training and I liked to fire it because it had open sights.

Before we really got very far, the order came along the line to move up, that we were too vulnerable where we were and we had to advance. That didn't make any sense to me. We had just been clobbered with artillery and we were being told to move closer to them. But you did as you were told and apparently the artillery had stopped because German troops were on the move, coming at us, and they wanted us in the best defensive position. We stopped at the edge of another forest where there was something like the old brush fence we had built around the garden back home to keep the hogs and wildlife out. But that barricade was made of bigger logs and limbs and it looked to be a good place to set up a defensive front.

Cassidy and I were sent to the end of the line to set up the Browning Automatic Rifle, which I'll refer to from now on as the BAR, and establish the flank of the line. It was a lonely spot. J.R. Davis and Demeer were digging in behind that brush barricade about thirty yards to our left and to our right was an opening which we were to guard and watch. I found out later it was an old road.

We were all numb with fear and the adrenalin was so strong I felt like I could dig a cellar. "Cassidy," I said, "back home we protect ourselves from tornadoes by getting in a cellar, and we can dig one right here. If we're going to stay alive, we've got to get it deep and cover it up with logs and brush."

I started digging down and cutting roots with the hatchet and Cassidy used that little shovel to dig it out. It probably took hours but I couldn't say for sure. I know that we worked on it until we had the thing six feet deep or better and then we began to expand it. It was really getting cold and a fog had moved in so thick you couldn't see ten feet away. I knew that Davis and Demeer were working on their fox-hole too, I could hear them but the fog was so thick I couldn't see them. Cassidy and I cut pine boughs and put them in the bottom of our cellar and carried every log we could find to cover it with, just leaving a small opening to come out of. You could hear the guns in the distance and not all that far away but they weren't shelling us. I guess they were shelling Bastogne back to the north. And in the distance, I could hear intermittent small arms fire. I think historians say it was December 16th.

Suddenly, the war was upon us, and it had happened damn quick. No man could sit in those fox-holes and stay normal during an artillery barrage.... I can't make you understand the misery and the fear that we all felt. I prayed, I cried and I swore, and sometimes I did all three together. Once, years later, a preacher told me that he didn't believe he could pray and swear at the same time. I told him not to worry, I did enough for both of us.

The Germans had rockets which the troopers referred to as screamin'-mimi's" which I never saw hit anywhere, so I don't know what they did. But occasionally they fired them over us and they screamed so horribly you were shaking after a few minutes of it. When that was combined with artillery you didn't think you could keep in control of yourself. Sometimes you just had the urge to throw everything down and take off running as hard as you could just to get away from it. Our nerves were destroyed by the days of it, but still we hung on and tried to get a little rest in shifts and stay on guard. I don't have the words to tell you what the terror was like. And I pray to God no one ever has to know anything like it. We could have hunkered down tight and took on those German troops and held our own just fine but the constant shelling eventually broke you down.

For the first couple of days I guess, we just stayed there, dug in and waiting. The snow began to fall and you couldn't see your hand in front of your face. We just kept working on covering that hole and expanding it, digging a shelf in underground where a man could perhaps sleep protected with soil above him and pine needles to warm him a little. We kept the end of it open and I would be on guard while Cassidy rested and vice versa. The artillery shelling would be intense for as much as an hour, then let up, and then in a couple of hours come again. Nobody slept, really, it was just a semblance of it. You stayed conscious but you didn't.

The Siege at Bastogne

Again, I can't tell you what it was like.

I saw some of the movie, "Band of Brothers" and didn't care to see much of it. Yes, it was a lot like it was all right, the timber and snow was about the same as it was in the movie, and the artillery hitting those trees was so real I couldn't watch it. But there is one thing in the movie I never saw, and that is the paratroopers sitting around at night with fires, talking about home. I never saw any of that. Anyone who moved was bringing orders or messages, or ammunition and grenades. We didn't get out and talk, and there were no fires anywhere that I saw.

They were shelling us even at night and during the snowfall; and it got so cold you just worked to keep from freezing to death. There were orders for no fires and we all knew that if there was smoke to be seen the German artillery would zero in on it. The snow was heavy. The flakes were round and soft and fell through a heavy fog. I'm sure there was a foot of it on the ground after the second or third day.

Fog would lift and blow and move slowly so you could see a little, then nothing. There were times when it opened up pretty good down low but the tops of the trees were enshrouded in it, like a thick blanket lay over the whole country. That really hurt us because without that fog, allied planes could have been hitting the Germans and dropping us supplies. But then again, it could be the Germans were having a hard time finding us too.

We were soon out of K-rations and Cassidy and I were eating hard, frozen chocolate bars, which was all we had left. My canteen froze and busted and the cold was nearly unbearable. None of us had the kind of coats and boots and clothing we needed for that weather. We had to go in too fast to be supplied with what we needed. It was a 'come-as-you-are' kind of thing!

I figured that we were going to freeze to death but when we were being shelled you didn't know it was cold. About ten in the morning the second or third day, the snow was light and the fog was opening up a little.

Cassidy was asleep and I began to hear a noise, squeaking and scraping and clanking a long ways off. It was moving slowly and I couldn't figure out what it was at first. Then I knew it must be a tank. There were the sounds of other tanks in the distance too but the one closest to us had a damaged track and wasn't getting along as it was suppose to. But it was getting closer and coming right at us.

When we finally saw it, it was close, and making so damned much noise you couldn't hear yourself think, with that track squeaking and grinding and clanking. I decided there wasn't much we could do, with only hand grenades and a BAR. If the bazooka was close, it would be a different story. When it was right out in front of us, some troopers led by Sergeant Balew sneaked in and doused it with gasoline cocktails made from glass wine bottles and gasoline and the whole thing went up in flames. It may be they hit it with a Bazooka, I don't know.

Of course, if you hit the right vents the gas goes inside the tank and the occupants have to come out. The occupants of the tank never saw the troopers who hit them and they started coming out of there with a couple of them on fire. There were three or four of them and I opened up on them with the BAR, firing it from the shoulder without using the bipod brace. I could follow the tracer bullets easily and I fired until they all were down.

They didn't get far from the tank, with several troopers firing the M-1 rifles in addition to my BAR. One of the Germans was alive and swearing at us in English. I never expected what I saw as we ran up to them. The dying German soldier was a woman. I have no idea why she was there, some said she must have been a girlfriend of the tank driver or something but she was in uniform just like the others. There was no way I could have known but I looked at her face, twisted in pain as she swore at us, and I was sick with what I had done. It was my first close up combat, and explaining how I felt isn't possible.

But there wasn't much time to think about it. More tanks could be heard in the distance and we began to see German ground troops coming at us. We all opened up and sometimes I was firing at forms 75 or 100 yards away, and sometimes I was just firing into the fog where I had seen them. For two or three days it was like that... ground troops coming and receding, machine gun fire, mortar and artillery. We would be ordered out in small groups to counter attack, and then returned to our foxholes.

We just stayed dug in and no one slept any more. One night after such a daytime battle, three or four German soldiers walked right up on Cassidy and me, coming along that little road. With the snow, it was easy to see them, and I opened up with the BAR. They never knew what hit them. They weren't more than twenty or thirty yards away when we fired. I don't know what they were doing but I expect they were on some kind of reconnaissance.

The thing about a BAR, even though it lays down a tremendous amount of fire in a short period of time, it tells the enemy right where you are because every seventh or ninth or twelfth round is a tracer. The tracer is to let you know where you are hitting, because a BAR fires progressively higher and to the right as you shoot it. The bipod rest sometimes digs down into the ground as you fire and the rifle is next to impossible to aim. You shoot it by watching those tracer rounds. And if you are out there blazing away all the time with it the enemy is going to figure out your position and in the night they are going to put some hand grenades in with you. Maybe that group of German soldiers in the night were looking to do just that. Thank God we were too cold to be asleep and we saw them first.

Later, when I was alone, I just didn't fire unless there were German soldiers close. There wasn't much use in firing unless you figured you were about to get overrun or you were certain to hit what you were shooting at. We were greatly outnumbered and my BAR would only call attention to our position, and it suddenly became important that you didn't waste ammunition.

As the fog broke up a little, more German patrols or reconnaissance groups began to come along and on occasion we would have fire-fights with them. Then we'd get shelled. Then they would all concentrate on another section of our perimeter and there would be a few hours of calm while they tried to break through somewhere else. Even so, you never relaxed, never let up your intensity.

I can't remember when it happened but I think it was only a few days after we got there... late one evening an officer came down the line of foxholes and called me by name. I didn't want to leave that place but he told me to come with him without my BAR. I just turned around and glanced at Cassidy and he was looking at me like we might never see each other again. I hadn't volunteered for anything so I had no idea what was happening but I went, and we covered a lot of ground by foot.

Two hours later in the darkness a considerable distance from where we had dug in, the officer explained what he wanted done. There were four of us there with him I think, or maybe three, but each of us was to take out a German sentinel. That was something we had trained to do at Fort Benning, again and again. There were dummies you sneaked up on, put your knee in the back and left hand over the mouth all in one motion and slashed the throat with the knife in the right hand. I had been good at it in training, because I was small and quick and it had all seemed like a game with that training dummy. It was a game I excelled at.

But this was no game! I was stricken with terror that night. I had never dreamed I would be asked to do such a horrible thing to a human being, and I told the officer that I couldn't do it. He said I would do as ordered and that I had been singled out by my commanding officer as a trooper capable of accomplishing what had to be done. I wondered for a time if the Captain of our company, who had seemed to hate me back at Fort Benning because I was so small, had singled me out to get killed. But I know now why he gave me the job. I was small and I was fast and I had very good night vision. They knew I could see very well at night, time and time I had demonstrated that at Fort Benning and it was something I had bragged about. I wished then I had not.

We had no firearms that night, nothing but a knife. If there were shots fired in desperation it would end the entire operation. The Germans were dug in there, too many and too close. They'd attack the following day, if we didn't get them first. We were going to get them first, after the sentinels were dispatched of. We were given white sheets with holes for our heads which slipped over and draped around us. They weren't coats or coveralls they were just white sheets which kind of hung around you like a superman cape, and there were white covers for our helmets.

The officer, and I don't know what rank he had because no one wore any bars or identifying medals out there on those front lines, took me through the timber of a small ravine, and we crawled to a point where I could see a German soldier on a high point next to a big tree perhaps sixty or seventy yards away. He whispered to me to go slowly and deliberately and do what I had been trained to do.

I was crying so hard and shaking so bad I didn't think he'd leave me there but he did. I was as scared as I have ever been, or ever will be, and it wasn't because I didn't want to take a German soldiers life, it was because I knew I couldn't do it without getting killed. He had a rifle and I knew I couldn't get close to him without him knowing it. The snow had a crunchiness to it because of the cold. It wasn't soft and fluffy, it was hardened a little underneath the top layer of new snow and as I crawled it made a noise. And I was crying so hard I was jerking, like a little kid does when he can't stop sobbing. I'm not ashamed of it, I was horrified.

And then the sobbing stopped and I just became sort of numb. It seemed like I was moving in slow motion, and yet I knew I had to get there and get it over with. The crying and the swearing was over, and I was just praying. It was sixty yards away and then it was forty. It was thirty yards and then it was twenty. He wasn't moving back and forth, just standing there with a long overcoat and a rifle in his hands that you could see from twenty yards away. He stomped his feet once and slapped his arms against his body. That German soldier was just as cold as we were.

A fog would move through every now and then and hide him and then it would pass and in the snow he was easy to see. I froze once as he turned a little. I had almost discarded that sheet but just then I was glad I hadn't. It hid me a little. I didn't move.....I didn't even breathe. He turned away and leaned against the tree and I prayed and prayed as I inched closer, my knife in my right hand, the snow scraping and crunching beneath my body. I felt that any second he would hear me and kill me before I could get to my feet.

I can't tell you much about what took place from that point. I can't remember it well. I just rose to a crouch and tried to do just as I had done so many times to those training dummies. I remember he had a scarf on and I didn't think I could even reach his mouth he was so big. Then my knee hit his back and it was over and there was no noise. I was crawling back down the ravine, so relieved to be alive I didn't even notice the cold. I waited where I was told to wait and the officer and the other men came in within a few minutes.

I tried to tell them I was sorry I had broke down like that but no one would look at me or acknowledge I was even talking. I think each of them was feeling like I was, with emotions that are difficult to explain. But the relief to be alive when an hour before you were sure you were going to die, is something which overrides anything else. I felt awfully ashamed of myself but the officer who led us told me to drop it. He said I did what I was told to do and the rest didn't matter.

The Siege at Bastogne

In the darkness a couple of hours before the dawn as we headed back, I heard hand grenades going off a distance away, where the Germans were entrenched. It was just a constant and heavy --poompf, poompf, poompf, which just lasted for a few minutes. I heard no cries or screams, and no small arms fire at all, just the sound of those grenades, and not very far apart.

Whoever had planned that, whoever had scouted that situation and figured out how it had to be done had done it well. I was back in my fox-hole by the time the artillery started just after dawn, so drained I felt as if I had run hard-out all night. I tried to get the blood off my hands and jacket the best I could in the snow but Cassidy knew I had been through something awful. I told him just a little and then just couldn't tell him anymore. We never discussed it again. I tried to put it out of my mind and not remember any of it until now and I think I have been successful at forgetting the worst of it.

Artillery barrages seemed to increase as the days went on and the fog thinned. But it seemed to just get colder and colder. I've heard it said that many times during that siege the temperature got down under zero. I don't know how cold it got, it was just tremendously cold, and paratroopers lost toes and even feet to frostbite.

It continued to snow off and on and for better than a week at least, the clouds enveloped the area completely. I don't think there was any sunshine during the whole time we were there. I don't know exactly when the events I de-scribe happened and I can't put any of those nights and days into a time frame. They say the fighting started about the sixteenth of December and the siege was broken by Patton's troops and tanks on the 26th. That means we were under fire there for about ten days but if I had been guessing I would have guessed we were there at Bastogne a month. I really thought it was.

We were foggy-headed from hypothermia and from a lack of rest and proper nutrition but we stayed and we fought. And when people say "I don't know how you did it," I tell them they could have done it to, because it was all you COULD do. You couldn't quit... you couldn't call for someone to come and get you or come and help. You sat there and you stayed alive if you could and anyone or everyone put in that situation would do what we did...sit there and try to survive.

Because we had no water, we had to eat snow for moisture and those chocolate bars. For days we were trapped there in that fox-hole just trying to survive the artillery. But there was so much of it---the shelling, you just knew sooner or later one would get you. It happened finally, to Cassidy and me, one night after midnight, maybe close to morning. Cassidy was laying down on the pine boughs trying to sleep a little and I was watching, determined not to let any German troops come up on us in the night. You always could see pretty good with the snow and maybe some moonlight above the clouds to help.

I heard an incoming German 88 mm artillery shell whistling in and saw it pass over us to hit about sixty feet behind us. The second one hit just seconds later out in front of us and I knew the third one would be between the first two somewhere, that's the way the Germans fired them. I dived under the logs, yelling to Cassidy that I thought we were about to be hit. Apparently that shell landed right on top of us. I can't remember anything else about it.

"The Battered Bastards of Bastogne," as we came
to be known, were saved by Patton's tanks and
Third Army infantry, which broke through south
Bastogne on December 26, 1944

Chapter 16
Battle in the Ardennes

I don't remember an explosion or a flash or anything. I just remember waking up lying on my back in the snow, completely out of the foxhole, sort of numb and my head hurting with a terrible ringing in my ears. I heard Cassidy moaning and screaming and I remember telling him I'd be right there to help. But I just couldn't move for a minute or two. I tried but I just couldn't get up, I couldn't make my body do what my mind was telling it.

My left arm was hurting and burning so I knew I had something wrong with it. I could taste lots of blood in my mouth and there was blood coming out of my ears and nose as well. I just kept telling Cassidy that I was coming but I couldn't make my body work. It took awhile to finally get my feet under me. Even then I couldn't walk, I just sunk down and crawled over to him. He was ten or fifteen feet from our foxhole and in the darkness I couldn't see much of what had happened to him. But there was a growing patch of blood beneath his right side and his overcoat was torn all to pieces.

I took my knife and cut away the overcoat and then his fatigues until I could see the long ugly gash across his right side, halfway to his breastbone. A piece of shrapnel had sliced through him apparently going through the ribs and his lung, it must have been the size of a dinner plate. He'd pass out for awhile and then come to and then pass out for awhile longer. I started putting sulfa powder on the wound and tried to figure out away to bandage him up. I took all the bandages from our helmets and tried to just wrap them around him as tight as I could. He came to and actually talked to me for awhile and that gave me some confidence.

He said, "Am I gonna cash in, Ridge-Runner, am I gonna cash?" Cassidy talked that way. He was a city boy through and through but he loved those old westerns and he never talked about dying, he always said he was gonna "cash" or

207

"cash in" or something that sounded western. To tell the truth, I figured with all that blood in the snow he was indeed gonna cash but I kept telling him he wasn't hurt bad and I'd get him some help. After I had wrapped him up the best I could, I packed some snow on the wound and the bloody bandages and I actually think that may have done some good. I wrapped him back up in his tattered overcoat and both blankets but I was afraid he still would freeze to death even if the wound was survivable.

The bleeding stopped and at daylight it looked as if the whole thing had frozen around him. But by then he was unconscious and wasn't coming around at all. J.R. Davis came over to stay with him while I went to find Sergeant Balew to get help.

I remember him saying, "Ridge-Runner, we'll get somebody in here as fast as we can but there are troopers hurt everywhere and there just ain't enough medics to take care of 'em all." We were at the height of the German siege and we were out at the very edge. I think we had Germans all around us and between us and no one was going to risk trying to move around much. So I told Sgt. Balew I would make an Indian travois stretcher I could drag and I'd take him in myself if they'd just give me directions. He said it would take awhile to get an O.K. but he would try. So I went back and cut poles with my hatchet and ripped up our shelter halves to bind it all with, and made something sort of like what you've seen the Indians pull behind their horses on those western movies.

I kept watching for Germans and checking on Cassidy and he kept breathing so I worked even harder. My hands were so cold they were numb but I would warm them the best I could against my body and go back to tying on cross braces and trying to be sure I had a stretcher that would stay together. If it didn't, Cassidy would never make it and probably I wouldn't either.

Sergeant Balew tried to talk me out of it but he said he had radioed for permission to leave my post to bring in a wounded man and after about two hours, he got that permission. He told me where to go and tried to tell me that the odds were good I wouldn't make it. If I could get to a certain area behind us there would be some help waiting.

We had some more shelling that morning but when there was a lull we pulled Cassidy up on the stretcher and wrapped a blanket around him and I secured everything the best I could. His boots were hanging off the end a little but I pretty much had him in a sling he couldn't fall out of. I headed back toward Bastogne with nothing but my pistol and at first it seemed everything was going to go fine. The snow allowed the poles to slide fairly efficiently. Then I headed across a clearing and I guess somehow the Germans spotted me because they began to shell the clearing and the timber around it.

I ran as hard as I could run and looking back on it, I think if I had remembered I was pulling him I might have dropped the whole thing. But I was so scared I didn't think... I just ran like hell. I got past the area where they were shelling and I think I pulled him nearly a half mile or more before I came across another line of troopers dug in and a couple of guys helped me pull him to a place where they had a stretcher. They put him on it, and onto the back of a jeep and we headed for a field hospital along a road which must have been the edge of Bastogne. The buildings were all in rubble but they had a tent like you'd see at a circus one with a big red and white cross above it. They took Cassidy in there and he was still alive, so I my hopes were revived a bit.

But there was a field there with rows and rows of soldiers under blankets in the snow, literally hundreds and they filled the field. In my mental state, I first I thought they were all sleeping, but then it hit me what I was looking at. I saw the blood on the blankets, the twisted arms and legs and the body parts separated from bodies and I staggered away, all of a sudden sick and demoralized as I had ever been. I hadn't seen that many soldiers in the whole time I had been there. And all those paratroopers under blankets were men who had been laughing and relaxing in Paris a few days before and now they were dead.

I started to go back to my post but someone stopped me and told me I could get another field jacket from the Salvation Army clerk. Mine was really shredded in the back and left arm. Blood was running down my arm but it worked O.K. except for a little stiffness. I didn't know there was a piece of shrapnel in it about the size of a nickel just above the elbow. They took me to another area and it was bustling with activity, even with the artillery sailing in from time to time. The Salvation Army people gave me a new jacket and blanket and a heavy turtle-neck sweater, and thinking back on it, I don't know if I would have lived much longer if I hadn't gotten that sweater because I came close to freezing to death over the next few nights. I also got some K-rations to take back and hot food on a tray, the first food beside the candy bars which I had eaten in days. I got some coffee and drank some water for the first time in days as well.

Lord in heaven knows I didn't want to go back to that hole but I knew if I didn't, I could be court-martialed and shot. And besides, where would it be any safer? The field hospitals were even being shelled and they were digging in to keep some of the less seriously wounded troopers underground. Cassidy would be cared for by people who could help him but it would all be for nothing if the Germans broke through.

I took off at a trot and figured I'd never make it but somehow I did, with some of the afternoon to spare. It must have been about that time that General McAuliffe, back in Bastogne, received those demands from the Germans to surrender. The story I always got was that McAuliffe was so beside himself for a moment he just said "Nuts" and then turned to an aide and said, "What should we reply?"

The aide said to him, "That's as good a thing as I can think of, General.

And so he just turned and gave them that message..

210

"Nuts!" Historians say that happened on December 22, about a week after the siege of Bastogne had begun. I think that must have been about the time Cassidy and I were hit with that shell. Apparently there was a fuel reserve there that the Germans wanted for their tanks and if they had gotten to it, maybe nothing would have stopped them.

General Patton's Fourth Armored Division had fewer tanks and though they were faster, they weren't the tanks those Panzers were. It would have been an awful battle if the Germans had obtained the fuel they needed to keep their tanks running. They didn't and I guess hundreds of them were abandoned outside of Bastogne and their crews were strafed by American planes as they walked back toward Germany.

Of course, I didn't know about any of that. I was alone and cold and scared so bad I was shaking much of the time. A fever had begun from the shrapnel wounds in my arm and back and the sky was beginning to open a little so it got even colder at night. And we kept fighting. Nothing slacked off. I know that for the next couple of days I was getting ammunition and wrestling that BAR, going out in small groups to meet German probes and try to keep them from breaking through.

We would make a counter charge against German troops that had tried to rout us and then retreated. Then we'd retreat back to our positions. I figured every time I left that foxhole I was dead. But about that time, our planes begin to get off the ground and they started dropping supplies to the beleaguered troopers. One parachute dropped right out in front of me and I threw caution to the wind and dashed out to retrieve the pack.

I know there are those who will think I am making this up, but I swear, there was nothing in there but several crates of cigars, beautifully wrapped with a name like La Frendlisch or La Frendrich or something. I couldn't read enough to know for sure. I stored a couple of the boxes in my foxhole and passed the others on. I got some K-rations that day that someone else had found up the line and brought by in the cover of darkness. No one had told me I couldn't smoke a cigar and as sick as I was, that first one was absolutely wonderful. It was like taking medicine, and that's the truth.

It calmed me enough to keep me from shaking so much and it smelled great. I ended up back in the hole that night alone and there was more shelling. That day or the next, allied planes began to turn the tide. They came through and strafed the hell out of everything in our area and they strafed the woods where we were. I lay down flat in the bottom of my foxhole and there was no way I was going to get hit because the bullets were coming in at an angle. But one of them came through the ground in front of the foxhole and landed on my back, and it was hot as a firecracker. I wondered how it could have gone through that icy air and through that frozen ground and be so hot after all of it.

I was back to eating snow again and my tongue was swelling badly, so badly I couldn't hardly keep my mouth closed on it. I was so cold I knew I wasn't going to make it much longer without some serious frostbite. My face was already frostbitten and the wool gloves I had been using to wipe my nose had frozen into my beard stubble. My feet were getting numb and I decided I had to do something.

This is something I know will bother many who read it and I thought about leaving it out of the account, as I have left other things out that I saw, which I just really don't think I can talk about even now. But it is what war and the horrors of war is made of and it will give you an idea of how desperate men get in such conditions.

The body of one of the Germans within thiry or forty yards of my foxhole was frozen and covered with snow. He was frozen to the ground and unmovable. I couldn't see his face. But he had on rubber galoshes-type boots which were no doubt warmer than mine. I crawled out to him in the dusk one evening and tried to remove them but there was no way I could do it. So I waited for darkness and crawled back out and took my axe and chopped off both legs just below the knee, broke the boots loose from the ground and took them back to my foxhole. I returned to do the same thing to the arms of the corpse because he was wearing a coat lined with rabbit fur.

I knew I couldn't get it off of him but I could get the sleeves off if I cut off the arms and that's what I did. In the cover of the foxhole that night, I worked and worked until I got the galoshes off, then cut the fur-lined sleeves off and threw the arms and legs out into the night as far as I could. I have had people ask me if it was a hard thing to do and I always tell them the truth. It wasn't at all. I was sick and had a high fever and I was freezing and all I wanted to do was find a way to ease my suffering.

By that time I hated the Germans as few people could understand. The shelling and the screamin'-mimi's and the attacks for days had turned me into something I would not have thought possible. It had hurt to see that first German that I had a part in killing at the beginning of the offensive. A week later I would have killed every German in the world. All I wanted was to survive and by then the Germans weren't humans to me, they were just objects to be destroyed. I don't feel like a barbarian or a butcher, I just kept wanting to live and had decided to do what it took to survive.. anything to survive.

I took off my own boots and wrapped my numbed feet in the rabbit fur sleeves. It worked well, because the galoshes were too big for me. I couldn't get the sleeves over my feet and put my own boots back on. That night I think I actually slept a little, so exhausted I just didn't care anymore. I think the shrapnel still in my body, in my arm and back, and the fever which it caused was close to killing me. If they found my hole in the dark and threw in a hand grenade, I wouldn't know it and there wasn't much I could do about it. I was beginning to feel that death was perhaps the answer to the misery. If it came, it wasn't because I hadn't done my best.

You might think that after what I had just done, I wouldn't be able to sleep. But I could, at least a little, and a little was enough. You never did really sleep out there in a fox hole, you did something that was akin to it but it wasn't sleeping.

I think that must have been Christmas eve, I don't know.. I can't clearly remember much about any of those days after the artillery shell hit us. And again, I'm not sure the things I have related are in the correct order. But it seems like it was the next day that I heard the distant roar of tanks behind us and I knew they were American tanks, I had heard enough of them to tell that. There was still a hell of a battle going on somewhere but it wasn't where we were. We weren't being shelled.

The pain in my arm and back was getting worse and worse and I was sweating a little every now and then even in that awful cold, and growing weaker. I knew I was just too weak to fight and so I left the foxhole to go find the rest of my squad and couldn't find them. Thinking back on it I think I just staggered out of there and went the wrong way. I was trying to carry that BAR and get back to where I had left Cassidy and I don't remember much about any of it, except that I came across a soldier who had dug in underneath a disabled American tank....

He wasn't a paratrooper, I don't think, but maybe one of the soldiers retreating from the German advance even before we had got there. He told me to get under there with him and I did. He had one heck of a shelter under that tank, I don't know how he did it. But I don't remember being there long, I either went to sleep or passed out.

The next thing I remember I woke up in a field hospital somewhere and it wasn't the one where I had left Cassidy. It was canvas topped, added on to brick or rock walls and a partially intact building with rooms where other troopers were being treated. They were giving me shots of penicillin and had already removed the shrapnel from my arm and some small pieces from my back. They didn't get it all out

214

of my back, I would find out later, but I didn't know it at the time.

My face was hurting worse than anything. They had shaved off the beard and pulled the scabs away, some with those wool glove fibers embedded in them. My face was raw and bleeding and they had put some kind of salve on it. I was badly constipated and they gave me the first enema I had ever heard of and that hurt like hell too. My company was brought back to Bastogne and reorganized, J.R. Davis was there without a scratch and so was Demeer. Sergeant Balew had been wounded and was gone, Dingler was either dead or injured too badly to go on. No one knew about where Cassidy had been taken or how bad he was. I figured he was dead.

Our new Sergeant was a man by the name of Graham and he was a great man in my eyes. I was feeling pretty good in a day or so but I don't know for sure how long I was laid up. My papers say that I was treated on January 2, 1945, but I think we were heading southward into the Ardennes Forest by then. I think it had to be within a day or so of the time Patton's tanks arrived, but I really don't have the slightest idea.

The Germans were retreating and we were chasing them. Much of the time it was an uneventful trek southward, but every now and then we had a firefight. The skies were clearing and I remember seeing wave after wave of bombers going from the right horizon to the left horizon.

I had to learn to walk in those oversized galoshes but my feet were starting to get the feeling back in them. I wasn't about to give them up. Our squad moved down a road with a good number of other paratroopers I had never seen before. Lots of them were green recruits. I don't know where the tanks were but apparently we weren't close to them because I never saw any American tanks after we headed into the Ardennes from Bastogne unless I just can't remember, and I guess that's possible. I do remember a lot of trucks and jeeps.

Battle in the Ardennes

And I did see plenty of those Third Army foot soldiers that came in with the tanks and they were a worn-out, scraggly looking bunch of men. They were suffering with the cold just as much as we were. They had come one hell of a long way in a hurry, and every one of them was a hero as far as I was concerned. When they got there, the Germans knew they were done for. Those of us who held on through the siege survived only because of Patton's tanks and those Third Army G.l.'s and we joined them in pushing the Nazi's back where they came from. If you think I don't love ol' General Patton, you're crazy!

The road into the Ardennes was snow-covered and packed and wound through open clearings and a few buildings and good-sized timber. Along it there were dead horses and cows and sheep, most of them snow-covered, and occasionally there were dead German soldiers, and even some dead civilians. We had been told never to investigate a body or pick up a discarded weapon because in their flight, the Germans had booby-trapped a lot of those things.

I was really afraid of mines because they designated me as right scout and when the order was given for "scouts out," I had to travel out in front of the company and well ahead on the right side. It was a bad place to be but fortunately I didn't come across any Germans nor any mines out where I was. The worse thing that happened to me was when I stepped in a snow-covered shell-hole and fell. I felt an awful pain in my lower back which nearly put me down for the count but I somehow regained my feet and went on. I didn't know it then but a very small piece of shrapnel they hadn't found was embedded in the muscles of my back just above the belt, not far from my spine. Some small shrapnel stayed in my back until the 1990's, when I finally had all of it removed.

I can't remember how many days we traveled, but it was weeks, I believe. As we marched on, the resistance became greater and toward the end we fought along every mile of it, it seems, chasing the Germans who would stop

216

every now and then and try to ambush us. We approached a small town and they shelled us for awhile but it wasn't very accurate. There was some machine gun fire and mortar from several hundred yards away and we started to dig in, but then the word came to move into the village and we did, carefully and slowly. I thought any minute they would open up on us but the Germans were gone when we got there.

They were stopping and firing to slow us up, and then retreating. The fighting was sporadic along that road until we got to a river called the Moder River. At least that's what I heard someone call it, but I can't say for sure. Anyway, on the other side of that river the Germans dug in and made a stand. The river was frozen and snow covered and they were entrenched on the other side. It appeared that they intended to try to keep us from crossing. We dug in there above the river on a forested bench within a half-mile of a bombed out village behind us where more troops were organizing.

Once you got through that frozen ground it was easy digging, the soil was loose and deep and sandy. I set up my BAR and actually fired it for the first time in days at enemy soldiers I saw easing down through the brush toward the river. They scattered and disappeared but I know they didn't all make it back with the fire I had put in there. You couldn't tell though. Most of the time you were firing at figures at a good distance or at the place where you thought they were. And they were firing at us as well. Snipers from across the river were the biggest danger. I climbed out of my foxhole once to relieve myself and they plastered the tree I was behind. You could hear the splat of bullets against the bark well before the report of a rifle. I crawled back to my bunker faster than a fence-swift lizard back home.

That night somehow, Germans scouts crossed the river and walked around among us apparently on some kind of reconnaissance. One sentry had been knifed in the night and there were tracks within thirty or forty yards of my position. I hadn't seen or heard a thing. Our C.O. said that no one would sleep that night, everyone was to be on full alert. We were going to catch those enemy soldiers if they came through again. Flares were ready and everyone was on guard. And in the middle of the night there was movement out on the ice and somebody opened fire. You've never heard such a battle as went on that night with mortars and small arms fire from both sides of the river continuing for ten or fifteen minutes. And then it was over and we were on pins and needles all night.

The next morning when it was light enough to see, there were no enemy dead out on the ice as we had expected. Out on the frozen river there was a collie-sized black and white dog, or what was left of him. Turned out it was a stray which our Captain had picked up on the road, half starved, and brought along. The poor dog never knew what hit him. We all felt bad about it but the dog was probably better off than he would have been trying to survive on K-rations. And the Captain said the dog had defied orders anyway.

After a couple of days we were relieved by incoming G.l.'s and moved back to the town for a day of recuperation. I was about half sick again with diarrhea and something they called trenchmouth, which causes your teeth to loosen and your gums to hurt something awful. A medic gave me something for the diarrhea and a mouth rinse that was a purplish-blue color, which really helped to take the pain away from my gums and mouth.

As more troops moved into the area some sort of attack against the German position was planned. A Lieutenant came and found me and said he understood I had experience firing a .30-caliber machine gun. I hadn't fired one since that time at Ft. Mead but I told him I could shoot it if he needed me to. I didn't want to, volunteering was something you didn't do if you wanted to stay alive. But I was a paratrooper and we didn't take lightly our assignments.

The Lieutenant took me and two guys I had never met,

neither of them paratroopers, to feed the ammunition and we set up a water-cooled .30 caliber machine gun on a point overlooking the opposite side of the river. He showed me an area they wanted raked with machine gun fire at an exact time during the attack planned on German forces. I told him that I couldn't really see the place I was to be firing at because of trees and bushes, but he said that when I began to fire, the machine gun would clear it out.

At the exact time I was to begin firing, right at dusk, I opened up with the machine gun and was amazed. In a matter of minutes there was nothing there in front of us and for several minutes we poured machine gun fire into the area across the river, three complete belts of ammunition. It was several hundred yards away and I can't remember much of it but naturally we couldn't see any enemy troops. The firing was to cease at a certain time and we were to get the heck out of there before they could zero in on us. We didn't quite make it.

Apparently we had been doing some good because the Germans had pin-pointed our position. And they hit us with several rounds of artillery fire. One shell hit only a few yards in front of us and apparently the shrapnel went up and over me. Looking back on it, it was a miracle that I wasn't hit.

The explosion knocked me back and rolled me several feet. I was so stunned I lay there for awhile but I was conscious of the fact that more shells were coming in so I got up and checked myself to be sure I wasn't hit. I don't know what happened to the other two guys, they were no where to be seen and I didn't hear anyone moaning or screaming. I figured they were both dead or gone so I picked up the machine gun and base plate and headed back to the village with it. The barrel was leaking, and the hot water poured down my back and burned me, but I ignored it. You can understand the adrenalin I had going if you realize what it takes to carry a .30-caliber machine gun and base plate but the Lieutenant had drilled into me that I had to take care of that gun and I did.

Chapter 17

The Last Skirmish

There was one hell of a battle that night. Flares and mortar and artillery from both sides just lit up the surrounding countryside. When it was over a large number of German soldiers had surrendered. But we didn't get them all. Somehow they mustered enough of a force to come across the river when we least expected it.

I'm not sure exactly when it happened. I remember that I had found a chicken, of all things, scraping around in the thawing snow around one of the old buildings, and I killed it. It didn't have many feathers and was too scrawny to make much of a meal but I skinned and cleaned it and inside one of the little houses which was still pretty much intact, I found a wood cook stove and a pan. Sergeant Graham and J. R. Davis and a couple of other paratroopers were with me and we were fixin' to have that chicken. I always regretted that we never got to eat it.

I had pulled some wood off a broken window frame to put on the fire we had going, I remember that much. And then the house just seemed to explode. I have no idea what hit it but it was powerful. It may have been a shell hitting close by or a hand grenade thrown through a window. In the flying debris and dirt, with some of the roof beginning to capsize, I dived under the table. About that time I looked toward the door and it had fallen in so there was only about half the opening there had been.

I saw a German soldier crawling through it and I had no weapon but the 44 revolver. As I rose on my elbow and turned to find it on my belt the German pointed a pistol of some sort at me and fired. He missed my head by only inches as the slug ticked the edge of my helmet, tore through my field jacket and burned along the front of my right shoulder. It went through my left foot and lodged just under the skin at the bottom of my foot. I can't remember for sure what happened next but there was lots of firing and confusion.

Somebody must have got the German soldier because he surely would have killed me if he had kept firing. Or maybe he just missed me except for that one shot. I just don't know. I don't remember how I got out of the building but I remember running and hobbling along as fast as I could, hurting so bad it was unbelievable. Whatever was going on around me, I couldn't tell you. All I was doing was running, I didn't know where.

I remember that I passed a motor pool just outside that little village and two American soldiers caught me hobbling along as fast as a man can go with a hole in his foot. An officer asked me how bad I was injured and I told him I was alert and had to find my outfit. He said they would get me to a field hospital and I forgot I was talking to an officer. I told him I wasn't going anywhere until I found my outfit and called him a few names buck privates aren't suppose to call officers. I do remember that he coolly pulled a pistol and put the barrel right in my stomach. He told me I would do as he ordered me to do and I said "Yes sir, I will, sir." Actually, I didn't much care if he shot me. It would have ended the awful pain in my foot and leg.

But my hard times weren't over. Two soldiers loaded me in a jeep and we headed somewhere at a pretty good clip. It seems as if there was another wounded soldier with us hurt worse than I was. We hadn't gone far until the jeep hit a hole in the road and was thrown into a ditch, rolling over on it's side and throwing us all out. The driver was hurt too and so now there were three of us injured. Shortly, an ambulance came along and took all three of us to the field hospital. I remember little about the trip but I can recall something about the hospital. It had board floors and walls, but a big canvas top, and lights strung up, blinking off an on, brighter and dimmer, charged by a gas generator.

They laid me on an operating table and started to remove the boot and I screamed bloody murder. The surgeon told me the foot looked pretty bad, and he wanted to get the bullet out and clean the wound. It was full of rabbit hair from the fur sleeves I had wrapped around my feet. They didn't have enough morphine and they strapped me down pretty good so they could keep my leg still enough to work on. But when they started probing in my foot, it was more than I could stand. I broke one of the straps and slung a nurse across the floor and they all jumped on me and gave me a shot.

I woke up some time later and my foot wasn't hurting. I looked down to be sure it was still there and realized I was completely secured to the bed I was in, my hands strapped down at my side. I made enough noise to attract a doctor or an orderly or someone. He told me that I was under suspicion of a self-inflicted wound. Apparently they had seen some of that, soldiers under so much strain and misery they had shot themselves in the foot to get out of the war. I didn't know that, and I didn't understand what they were talking about.

When he explained it to me I really went berserk, cussing and yelling and giving everybody hell. I wanted to get out of there and get back to my outfit. The guy was telling me I might be confined and court-martialed and I was so mad I wanted to kick the hell out of him with my good foot.

If there was ever a miracle over there in that God-forsaken war, and there were many of them, one took place that day. Sergeant Graham was in a bed not far away and I heard him telling me to calm down. He told me I was still a paratrooper, and I should act like one. "Take it easy Ridge-Runner," he said, "we'll get it straightened out." He called a doctor over and told him about the skirmish we had been involved in.

He told him he had been there with me and he had seen the enemy soldier, who was a German officer, and he had an American .45 caliber automatic. It took them some time but someone confirmed that the slug taken from my foot was from a .45 pistol and I had a .44 revolver strapped to my

The Last Skirmish

belt. If my pistol had been a .45, I don't know what I would have done.

Apparently the attack had been squelched and all the Germans killed. I should have stayed there, even though I had been wounded. But I had just gone off the deep end and took off and I'm still a little bit ashamed of that to this day. I think I was a little shell-shocked and addled from the explosion. All that, along with the foot wound, had aroused suspicion. But when they eventually looked harder at the flesh wound along the front of my shoulder they agreed that I couldn't have caused both. From my bed I thanked Sergeant Graham and he told me again to calm down and act like a paratrooper.

I took that as an order and it was the last one he gave I suppose. Sergeant Graham died a day or so later, from the wounds he had suffered there in that old house when we had lowered our guard because of a damn scraggly chicken I had killed.

I don't know how many days I spent in that hospital but it wasn't very long I don't think. My foot would get to hurting really bad and they'd give me a shot and I would sleep. When I woke up once, an officer was there beside the bed and he told me about Sergeant Graham and apologized for the suspicions about my wound. He told me why they were inclined to think the worst when they saw a foot wound. Before he left he gave me two purple hearts and the slug they had taken from my foot.

That same day they came and took a bunch of us out on stretchers to an ambulance and then to a train which headed out to a hospital at Marseilles France. I just remember these things in foggy sketches because every time I'd get to hurting they'd give me something. I woke up once on the train and there was a beautiful nurse there beside me. I talked to her awhile and she told me she was a movie star before the war. She said her name was Madeline Carroll. I don't know if that's who she was or not but she looked just like the Madeline Carroll I saw in movies later, except even prettier. Looking at her made me forget my foot. Hell, looking at her made me forget I had ANY feet. She looked at the tag around my neck and told me I was going home... .she said the tag was marked, "state-side". That meant I wouldn't be going back into battle. I found out why the next day or so when I got into the big hospital at Marseille.

A surgeon came by and tried to gently break the news that they couldn't save my foot. He said all the bones were broken up and there was lots of infection because they couldn't get that rabbit fur out. If they didn't amputate I could actually die from the wound.

I know you are getting tired of hearing me say I raised hell so I won't say that again. Let's just say I vigorously objected. I said I'd track down, on one leg if need be, any doctor who cut off my foot and personally cut off whatever I could get to for revenge! I explained how that same foot had weathered a copperhead bite and had looked much worse for just about as long and still it had recovered. There wasn't going to be any amputation. If my foot had to go I'd go with it.

They had it unbandaged and I got to see it that day, all red and blue and swollen and streaked, with a huge hole right in the middle. It was scary looking but I told them a second time I'd face the consequence of my decision with the foot intact. They cleaned it again and tried to get more of the rabbit hair out and then they put it in a cast. Despite medication, that was a day I'd like to forget. The pain was excruciating. It would be a lot of years before I'd learn words like "excruciating", but that's what it was if I understand the word. "A gosh-awful hurtin'" doesn't even come close to doing it justice.

There were women nurses there in Marseille and I talked one of them into buying me some cigars. She brought me several King Edwards and I don't know where they might have come from. They played lots of American music, most of it the big band stuff that came from the big cities. I complained to the nurses that there was no country music for us country boys, so bright and early one morning they started the day out with a country song and announced they were playing it for me. The name of it was 'The Prodigal Son', by Roy Acuff. Later they played 'The Wabash Cannonball' and 'San Antonio Rose'. Every wounded soldier in my ward made fun of that music I liked so much and good-naturedly cussed me every time any of it was played.

Looking back on it, I am amazed that I can so clearly remember the names of those songs and other little things which were of no consequence. I don't understand why the name of a song would stay with me when there's so much I can't recall, or so much that I seem to recall through a fog. Why can't I remember the names of many of the men I trained with and fought beside? I think maybe after you got into battle, you felt like having good close friends or even solid acquaintances was a bad idea because you figured many of them were going to be killed or taken away badly wounded. After what happened to Cassidy, I didn't want to go through that again.

I can't remember dates or passing days much. I don't know how long I lay in that hospital at Marseille but it seems like two or three weeks. I was getting lots of shots and being fed well. There was pie and cake to eat and I took advantage of that. I was starting to get up and hobble around on crutches and finally they came in and took the cast off. The foot looked awful, I couldn't stand to look at it. It was swollen badly and deformed looking, but healing.

I got up on my crutches and started to try to put some weight on it but it hurt bad when I did. I found out that I could tie that foot up behind me to my belt with my knee bent and it eased the pain, so I started doing that. Little by little it was healing and the swelling was subsiding. They told me one day that I would be going home the following morning and that afternoon the Red Cross people came around and told me I could have a free telephone call home. They found Jane's number somehow and that night I got to talk to my wife for the first time in months. But she wasn't

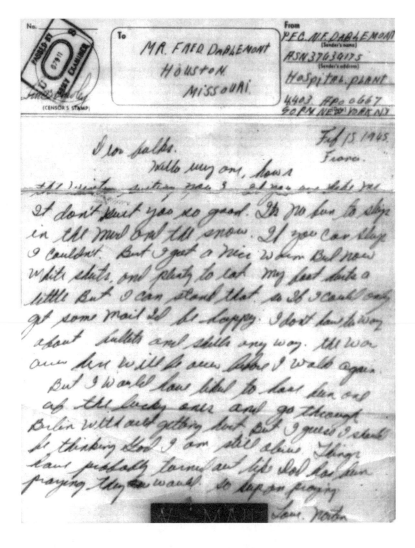

Mom kept this telegram I asked someone to write
and send home for me from a hospital in France.
I cannot remember sending it.

much interested in talking to me. Most of the time she put the baby on the phone and I couldn't understand anything she said. I only had a couple of minutes and by the time I got to talk to Jane I went over my allotted time. My free call wound up costing me several dollars.

The next morning an ambulance took me down to the harbor and attendants took me out on a stretcher to put me on a boat heading back to the U.S. Everywhere you looked there were wounded servicemen, men with arms and legs missing, men who were burned, some with head wounds..... It made me feel as if I wasn't hurt all that badly after all. We stayed there for hours and I got up and hobbled around on my crutches awhile and put a little weight on my foot. Much to my surprise. I could actually use it a little if I put the weight on the side of my foot. Anyway, we eventually went back to the hospital because the ship was full. A couple of days later we went through the same thing and there wasn't enough room again. The third time was the last straw. I didn't want to be taking up a place needed by someone wounded much worse than I and I was getting bored and impatient. I told the nurse to get me a pair of paratrooper boots and the left one a little bigger if possible.

For the first time in weeks I put on a pair of socks and boots and began to try to walk. For awhile it was really tough but I bit my lip and fought the pain and started to figure out how to get that foot on the ground and use it. In only a day or so I was walking on it, and then jogging a little and then running. True, I was running with a limp, but I was running. And then I requested to be sent back to my outfit and my request was granted.

I was attached to another airborne unit, I think, and sent out on a train headed back to the front. I remember going to sleep and waking up with a coat over me. There was a French lady sitting beside me when I awakened and she had felt sorry for me. That coat was so strong with perfume I could smell it for a week. But I thanked her... at least I think I did. I said "Mare see boo coo" or something like it. I never was sure whether or not the French words I had learned were really the words I thought they were.

At the end of the train ride I traveled by truck with a company of black troopers with the 82nd Airborne. They were the biggest paratroopers I had ever seen and they all had dyed their hair red and called themselves "The Red Devils". I spent a day and night traveling with them and they were a rough, rowdy bunch, with a language all their own. But they helped me in and out of the truck, picked me up like I was a stuffed toy and passed me around so I wouldn't hurt that foot. They couldn't believe paratroopers came in such small packages. I felt smaller around those Red Devils than I ever had before. But they were a spirited bunch and a joy to be around.

I can't remember how I got back to the 101st Airborne company I had been attached to, but I got there and they were dug in on a ridgetop somewhere just into Germany with the snow gone and the mud replacing it and signs of spring coming on. J.R. Davis was there, and he said he figured he would never see me again after that day on the river. Demeer had been badly wounded and was gone. I knew a few of the troopers there but not many. There were lots of new recruits. None of them jumped out of the foxhole and shook hands with me. They were a battle-weary bunch but the spirit and morale of the Screamin' Eagles was still there. The fighting was nearly over by then. J.R. said after I was wounded they had chased the Germans across the river and routed them, captured a lot and killed some, and were still getting a little artillery but not much.

What happened then was unbelievable. I hadn't spent more than a day back with my outfit before a First Lieutenant came by and called for Private First Class Norten Dablemont to leave the foxhole and come with him. I came out and told him I wasn't a p.f.c., I was just a buck private.

"I've been told they call you Ridge-Runner," he said. "How'd you come by a name like that?" I told him, and he told me he had good news for me. He said I had been promoted to private first class, and would be getting ten dollars a month increase in pay and a combat infantry badge. He said that a congressional act had dictated that after so many days in combat the promotion and increase was an automatic thing.

But then came the real surprise. He said I was being given a five day furlough with travel time added, and was to take some time for recreation and rehabilitation in England. I'm sure that Lieutenant expected me to really be happy about that but I wasn't. I was lost most of the time I was overseas, and I just wanted to stay with my outfit. The thing that scared me most was the thought of being lost or killed over there without the unit I had come over with. That company from the 327th Regiment was my home, my security, and I had just got it back and wanted to keep it. I told him I'd prefer to stay!

But the Lieutenant had been watching me walk. I wasn't flexing my foot, trying to keep my weight on the edge of my foot and my big toe, to keep the pain down. He said, "Trooper, you aren't combat ready. You aren't fit for combat physically and you aren't fit for combat mentally. . .and you are going to take a five-day leave and that's an order. When you come back your outfit will still be here or wherever you are sent. We aren't going to forget about you!"

And so just as I was beginning to feel good again they put me on a jeep to a train station where I was issued a dress uniform and a change of clothes, papers to show everyone at each stop, some cards to be used for meal tickets and twenty-five dollars in cash. We crossed the English channel again, the roughest water I have ever seen, and I got sick again. There was a big, beautiful new bus waiting, filled with injured and shell-shocked soldiers, and we were all taken to an old fancy hotel in the middle of London.

I had a room all to myself and a young blonde lady took me there and told me when I was ready she would show me around. That afternoon she took me to a big park nearby, a beautiful place with big trees and a lake and as quiet and peaceful as it would have been on the Big Piney. There were a lot of American and English soldiers there, and everywhere around there, but I never talked to any of them. I didn't want to know their problems and it looked like they had plenty. Some of them were limping around like me and some were just sitting and staring off into the distance. I hoped they didn't have to go back into combat. Rumors were that the Germans were about finished but all of us might wind up invading Japan. I remembered, just before we were shipped off in a hurry to Bastogne, the rumors about how the Germans were done. I believed nothing I heard and only part of what I saw. That evening, I told the young lady I wanted to see a movie, and she got a taxi and took me to a nearby theater. She left me there and went back to the hotel.

With some time to kill I went across the street to a pub and bought a cigar. They still were the most relaxing, enjoyable things I had ever happened across and I thought it was a great day for me when that parachute came floating down out of the overcast with those cigars inside. I was enjoying it so much that when I stepped back out into traffic to cross the street, I nearly stepped in front of a car. A woman behind me grabbed me and pulled me back and told me to wait until she crossed and she'd get me over to the theater safely. I couldn't believe my ears.. .she was American.

Chapter 18

A Reunion at the Eagle's Nest

It was great to be able to talk to an American woman and we had a long conversation there in front of the theater. She was several years older than me and she told me her father was a Colonel with an office there in London. Her husband had been a truck driver for the army, a Tech Sergeant who had just returned to the states. I didn't ask the details but apparently there were some problems between the two of them and they had decided to go their separate ways.

I asked her if she would like to go to the movie with me and she said that since I was an American soldier she felt it was her duty to go along and keep me company. I really enjoyed that movie... "Lassie Come Home". She was a nice looking lady with a gift for conversation, dressed really nice and educated and mannerly. You could tell she was confident and self assured and she made me feel comfortable. She was a little taller than me, with long dark hair and a nice figure. She wasn't beautiful or gorgeous but she was nice-looking and intelligent and made me forget my problems for awhile.

After the movie she took me back to the hotel in an army jeep and asked me if I'd like for her to come back and take me around London to show me the sights. Until then I hadn't been very excited about anything in England! The lady picked me up the next morning and told me that she had asked her father about allowing me to stay with them the rest of the week and if I'd like to do that, they had a room for me and I would be welcome. I left notification of where I would be and the next three days were wonderful.

She was a great cook but you know what I remember most... .there was white bread and strawberry preserves at her place and I never tasted anything better. She took me to lots of places and I remember spending most of one day at something called Piccadilly Circle or Circus or something like that. There were lots of pubs there and prostitutes everywhere, and an awful lot of American servicemen. We ate fish and chips and it had been so long since I had eaten fish I really liked it. I never thought that would ever happen. I don't know anyone who ate more fish in the first twenty years of life than I had.

I don't know if it would be entirely right to say we developed a romance during that week but something happened that was strong and lasting. I was young and longing for female companionship and she was an older woman trying to forget a bad marriage. Under different circumstances we would have never been a pair because our lives and backgrounds were so different. She was someone I confided in and who I could feel comfortable talking to about the awful things I had seen.

The army tried hard to keep American soldiers away from the European women, especially the hordes of prostitutes which were found in Paris and London. As I said before, they did a good job of impressing me as to the dangers of venereal disease. Pop had done an even better job when I was a kid, telling me about the awful things he had seen, most of which he probably made up or heard from someone else. But a lot of servicemen had come down with diseases and it was enough to keep me well away from any foreign women. Finally, there was a woman who was clean and dependable and intelligent and American and I fell for her hard.

But I knew, the day she took me to that ship to cross the English Channel that I would never see her again, and she knew it too, I think. It was one of the hardest things I ever did, saying good-bye while she cried and made me promise I would write her letters wherever I went. We still were both married and neither of us wanted to be. But I had a daughter and I wasn't going to abandon that responsibility no matter what.

And so as the ship left the harbor I watched her waving

goodbye until I could no longer see her through my watering eyes. I guess it was the salt from the sea or the London smog that irritated them so. But for months I got her letters, here and there right up until the time I left France long after the end of the war. J. R. Davis or Cassidy would read them to me and help me write an answer. J.R. would read those letters and tell me how bad he would like to meet her. When I told him I never intended to see her again he thought I was crazy.

I returned to my company and my old outfit so completely filled with new recruits it was like a new army. Thank goodness for J. R. Davis. He and I were about the only old veterans left even though most of the replacements were still older than me. I figure we were in Germany but I didn't know that for sure at the time. One of the odd things about my time overseas is the difficulty I have remembering where we went and when. It doesn't make sense. But I wasn't alone. Lots of the troopers didn't know where we were half the time and there were many who had that nagging worry about being separated from their outfits.

It was the only real security you had, there was that strength in numbers you felt even when the numbers seemed small. You developed something like a brotherhood, even with men you didn't know much about and with some whom you didn't know their names. Staying alive and staying warm was such an over-riding goal you didn't worry about names or backgrounds. You didn't want to get too close because there would be so much grief and sorrow in seeing your buddies killed and wounded. But still, we all knew that in the 101st Airborne any man would do what it took to save you if he could and we'd all fight the enemy with whatever we could muster, with whatever we had.

That was the pride and the morale of the Screamin' Eagles. You couldn't know about it unless you were there and a part of it. I wore a field jacket back to the front which had been given to me. It had a shoulder patch of the First Allied Airborne and it didn't take long for an officer to see it. He gave me hell for wearing it and told me to get me a field jacket with the Screamin' Eagle insignia of the 101st Airborne.

We were still in foxholes and it was still miserable and muddy but it wasn't cold anymore. It was finally spring and there was no shelling, no fighting, just sitting and holding and waiting. And then that day came that none of us would ever forget. A jeep came along the lines announcing that Germany had surrendered. We had been hearing that for days but no one wanted to get too optimistic. Before Bastogne, there had been similar rumors. But this was the real thing because there were high-ranking officers amongst us, bringing the word of the war's end. Everywhere, men were dancing and hugging one another and celebrating. But our C. 0. didn't let us forget that we still faced great danger.

There were German's who didn't know they were whipped and we could still face pockets of resistance or a lone sniper who just didn't give a damn. There was word of a paratrooper who had given a kid a piece of candy and then when he walked away the kid threw a potato-masher grenade at him and blew his leg off. We were still in a hostile land and there were still armed aggressors and booby traps and we would still fight if the situation presented itself. And there was still much to do.

In truck convoys we headed for a place in the Alpine mountains called Bertchesgaden. And again my memory isn't good about how long it took or where we went to get there. I know that I spent a day or so at some time or another in Bonn, Germany. It's not something I remember much of, just a boring stay in a bombed out town, and we were near a factory which had produced writing pens. The factory had been bombed and there were pens everywhere. Some of the paratroopers picked up some of them for souvenirs but I didn't. We had heard so much about German booby traps that I was afraid to pick up anything.

On that trip to Bertchesgaden we went through a concentration camp which had already been liberated. It was a stark ugly place and you heard through other troopers the rumors of what had happened there. I didn't know much about Hitler's hatred for Jewish people and it was hard to believe the stories others told me. But there was a huge mound of fresh dirt bulldozed over an area nearly as big as a baseball diamond and twice as long, where hundreds of people had been buried. Some of those camps held Polish and Russian people as well as Jews and I don't know which one it was that I saw, but I was glad to get past it. A cloud of evil and horror seemed to hang over that awful place.

Bertchesgaden was a little town and a resort area filled with storage buildings which had been used for military supplies for the German army. It was located in the Alpine mountains of Austria, surrounded by some unbelievable snow-covered peaks in one of the most beautiful settings you could imagine. There was a big restaurant and lodge partway up a mountain above the village and on up a winding road, at the top of the mountain, was Hitler's personal retreat known as the Eagles Nest.

There was an elevator there which led down into a lavish, giant underground bunker dug into the mountain for Hitler and his top people to retreat to. While we were there some of the Airborne troops were sent out to find and capture some of those very people and some real big-wigs in the German hierarchy were captured and held. I never got in on any of that. I was given a room by myself in the lodge and restaurant and assigned duty as a guard at the Eagles Nest itself.

I was puzzled as to why they gave me that room by myself until my new roommate arrived. I saw him coming down the porch of the hotel, and I couldn't believe my eyes... it was my old buddy, Glen Cassidy. That was some reunion. We were hugging each other like a couple of school kids but the first thing he said was, "Ridge-runner, you gotta see this scar!"

He took off his jacket and there was a big red welt half-

way around his body. It was the worst thing I ever saw
and I can't believe to this day he survived that. He said his
lung had actually been sliced by the shrapnel and it was a
miracle that he hadn't bled to death. Maybe the way I had
bound the wound and packed it in snow had saved him.
He said he had laid in a hospital bed in France for months,
taking medicine called "New-mo-thorax" (pneumothorax).
He could have gone home but he got a "Dear John" letter
from that red-headed girl friend of his and it made him de-
cide to stay with his outfit and see if I had survived.

"We're gonna have some fun now, Ridge-Runner," he
said. "The war's over and we survived it and we're still together." Cassidy knew all about how I had drug him back
on that makeshift travois and he kept telling me how I had
saved his life and how he'd never forget it. I told him I
knew he would have done the same for me. We spent the
next week catching up on all the things that had happened
to us. We worked at guarding the Eagles Nest for several
days and Cassidy got to riding a motorcycle from our barracks up to the peak.

The road up there was a series of rising hairpin curves
and I tried the motorcycle one time. It nearly scared me to
death so I didn't do it again. But Cassidy was a real motorcycle nut so he'd roar up there and back every day and risk
his life just for the thrill of it. I had risked my life enough.

While we were on guard duty we had two hours on and
four hours off and at night when we slept, we would sleep
in the back of trucks. I don't know why the place needed
guards but we guarded it and there was a constant stream
of important people coming and going. Some of them were
supposedly from Hollywood. There was a rumor that Dorothy Lamour was coming. If she did I never saw her. But
everyone was looking for souvenirs, even the soldiers, and
we did our best to see to it no one walked off with anything.

Cassidy and I got every other day off and it was hard
to find enough to do to fight the boredom. I went out on

the big lake below the lodge-turned- barracks and rowed around a little bit and then found some long storage-type buildings there at Bertchesgaden which were packed with thousands and thousands of skis. They said the Germans had stocked them for their storm troopers, who were adept at fighting on skis. I never saw any of them skiing around in the snow at Bastogne but I'm glad they didn't. If I'd have had to fight on skis I'd have killed myself. I took a pair up in the mountains and found some snow and tried it and it didn't work. One kept going a different direction than the other and I ran over a pretty good sized pine tree which, if it had been a little bigger, would have done some permanent damage!

About that time Cassidy found out about the horses. There were about 40 horses at a stable not far from the lodge and they were beautiful. Most of them were pure white with a few blacks and buckskins and they were something like I had never seen. No horse in the Ozarks ever looked like that. A few of them had been hurt and were being treated and nursed back to health. But the Lieutenant in charge let us ride the healthy ones around the field on our days free and I really got excited about that. Come to find out, they were about to send them back to where they came from.

I talked to my commanding officer the day I learned about that and he seemed interested. I don't know if I had a thing to do with it, but in about a week our entire company geared up to take those horses to someplace in Austria. They put together a convoy and I think some of the injured horses were taken in trucks but most of them would be driven as a herd, along a road which passed through a couple of villages which we were to disarm as we went. I remember that we traveled along a good-sized stream and there weren't many arms to confiscate.

I doubt there would have ever been a problem with any of those people. They weren't mean people, they were about half scared to death. Lots of the men wore short leather britches but there were no young men, mostly old people and a few children. The villagers had gotten wind of the confiscating operation and stashed their guns somewhere, if they ever had any. I found several thrown in a big pool of water and there were some beautiful engraved, double-barreled shotguns there. I fished some of them out and Cassidy got a couple of them. I kept two, a sixteen gauge and a twelve gauge. And I'll never figure out how it happened but I broke those two guns down, put them in an old barracks bag and tied it up as best as I could and tagged it with Pop's name and address and sent them back home.

Sometime during the summer Pop got them and that fall, well before I got home, he cut the barrels off both guns to make rabbit guns out of them! That was Pop for you. He didn't give a second thought to value, he just thought of practicality.

Our company traveled slowly into Austria and one day we had one heck of a storm, with wind and hail and heavy rain. The stream began to roll and the rain coming out of the mountains washed away our cook shack and a good portion of our rations. They sent a couple of trucks back to get more supplies but the roads were washed and in bad condition so we were hard pressed for food while we waited.

Cassidy and I got some trout out of one of the pools with a couple of hand grenades and the troopers went on and on about how good they were. But there weren't enough and while we were waiting to be resupplied, I volunteered to go find some deer to eat. The Captain gave me his own carbine, which I could shoot, because it had regular open sights, and Cassidy and I took two horses and rode them up into the mountains to find deer where we were told there would be some.

We were back up into the foothills when something spooked the horses and they bolted and headed back for the rest of the herd. I think it was a bear because I saw fresh tracks and whatever it was really made those horses wild-eyed. We couldn't hold them. When they got back to the company saddled and with reins dragging, everyone as-

240

sumed the worst, figuring somebody somewhere had bush-whacked us. But I intended to go on with the hunt and I kept on up into the hills thinking I might get a shot at a bear. Cassidy was no outdoorsman and he wasn't happy about any of it.

Finally though, after hours of hunting and not seeing anything but a scraggly herd of sheep, we came upon the first reindeer I had ever seen and I shot it several times. It didn't go down right away though, and I had to track it down into another little valley, where we finally killed it.

We set out to dress it and it was a job. I figured we'd quarter it and probably get it back that way but I'd have to walk all the way back to camp and get a horse again and it might be dark before I could get back.

But luck was with me and I came across an old farmer with a horse dragging logs out of a little patch he was clearing. I told him I needed to borrow his horse for a minute. He was a cantankerous old so and so and decided he would run me off. I quickly changed his mind by making it clear to him I'd just as soon shoot him as not.

Neither of us could speak the others language but it is surprising how well he conveyed what he was thinking and how well I got across to him that in that situation, the horse belonged to the one who had the gun. He changed his attitude and went stomping off down the little creek no less aggravated, but much less cantankerous.

We got the meat back just about dark and the troopers made a big deal over that fresh venison. When they cooked it that night it was absolutely awful but no one seemed to notice but me and Cassidy. Cassidy had never cleaned and butchered anything and the whole procedure made him about half convinced he didn't want to ever eat meat again. The next day we took a pair of horses and the old nag we had used to drag back that reindeer and returned it.

The old boy wasn't there to thank us so we left the horse in the field and headed back. That same day we were looking along another little stream to see if we could find trout and we came across two ladies at a big hole, fishing with poles. We rode up beside them and Cassidy turned to me and said, "Ridge-runner, I get the pretty one and you get the ugly one."

Neither of them were beauties but one was a little older and plainer than the other. Both were several years older than either of us. But one of the two looked up at Cassidy as if about half perplexed, and said, "Vich von of us is de pretty von." Cassidy wasn't expecting her to understand English and he was so embarrassed he just left. But I stayed. I knew that deep clear hole had plenty of trout in it or they wouldn't be fishing there.

The two girls were excited about the prospects of getting some fish so I told them to go down at the end of the pool and wait and I threw a hand grenade in it. It killed lots of fish but they don't float and you have to go into that icy water after them or wait 'til they drift into the shoals at the end of the hole with the current, to recover them. We got some dandies, there were some three- or four-pound trout in that hole. It took awhile but we came up with thirty or forty fish. I took about two-thirds of them and left them the rest and they were tickled to death.

I spent several hours there talking to them and they told me some awful things about the war and what had happened to them and other people living in the mountains during the war. It made me thankful that no invading armies or ruthless dictators had ever made it to our shores and it began to make me see just what I had been fighting for. I had always been proud to be a paratrooper but more and more I was becoming proud to be an American and proud to be part of a country where things were so different than what I had seen in Europe.

I can't remember who this guy was or where this photo was taken but it reminds me of how tall most paratroopers were.

They marched along beside me, the heroes of
World War II

Chapter 19
The Last Days of the 101st

The whole company pulled out a day or so later, after we had some trucks come in with new supplies to replace what was lost in the flood. From then on it was a pretty uneventful trip or I just can't remember what happened. I know the horses were turned over to a group of Austrians and I hated to see them go. I loved those animals, they were they best horses I have ever been around.

I didn't know that in that small herd was the nucleus and the ancestry of the heralded Lippizanner Stallions that would be known the world over and travel the world putting on shows until this very day. Every now and then I hear on T.V. that they are going to be in this place or that, somewhere in the U.S. and I realize they are descendants of some of those horses I rode at Birchesgaden. I'm proud to have been a part of saving them.

We traveled a lot faster from there and we headed for France again. In fact it seems as if we didn't really change direction much, we just continued on as we had been going. We arrived at a train station somewhere and took a train to Sans, France, about one hour from Paris. We got there in early July I think. There were thousands of paratroopers there and I think we were among the last to get there.

The 101st Airborne made up the smallest contingent of them. We lived in big tents set up in a big field with board floors and board walls halfway up. Paratroopers were jammed in there by the thousands, sleeping on cots, and it was pretty hot at times. But I loved the heat. Only a few months before I could never have imagined being warm again.

I didn't know it then, but we had been assembled there with the idea of getting us ready for an invasion of Japan and there was some more training going on. We made another jump there and it is one I'll always remember because the guy who jumped in front of me went all to pieces at the last minute and tried to come back in the plane. When I went out I hit my front teeth on his helmet and chipped them off. I've had them capped all my life because of that incident. It was the thirty-second jump I had made, I think, and it was the last jump I ever made. By then, after what we had been through, there wasn't much of anything which could scare me. Jumping out of a plane at 1500 feet was old hat and it was easy.

Just after we arrived there, we were all asleep in the middle of the night when one of the paratroopers nearby began dreaming he was still fighting, and he jumped up screaming and firing his pistol at the enemy in his dreams. Boy that woke us up in a hurry, and in a panic. No one knew what was happening. A couple of guys in bunks next to him wrestled him down and grabbed the gun, but he had already emptied it. Miraculously, with thousands of men sleeping all around there, the bullets found none of them and no one was hit. I guess he was firing up into the air above his cot, but I thought later how awful it would have been to have had one of your own comrades shoot you in your sleep after it was all over.

I didn't sleep as well for quite awhile after that. Doctors took the trooper away for treatment, but hell, we all were plagued with dreams like that. For most of my life, I have fought the war again at night in my dreams. It's often a nightmare about crawling through the snow toward that German sentry at Bastogne.

At Sans, France, plans had been made to merge the 101st Airborne with the 82nd Airborne. The 101st had been decimated and there were still good numbers of troopers in the 82nd so one day there was a big celebration and we all marched and lined up and listened to speeches as the 101st airborne was deactivated. I think General Eisenhower was there and that was one time I didn't have to stand on anything. A big-time French politician was to give us a French Liberation Medal and I got good conduct ribbons, a combat infantry badge, ETO operation ribbons, two oak leaf clusters and a presidential citation.

I also got two new purple hearts to replace the other two, which I had lost by then. I was given two rope braids of different colors to go around the shoulders of the dress uniforms, one known as a French fourragere and a Belgium fourragere. We were also given a shoulder patch of the 82nd Airborne, to wear on our right shoulder. On the left shoulder we still wore proudly the insignia of the screaming eagle, the 101st Airborne patch.

In early August there was news of the atom bomb dropped on Hiroshima. Of course most of us didn't know the magnitude of such a thing. If you couldn't comprehend that it was hard to imagine how one bomb would have any long term effect on the war. Then in a matter of days they dropped another one and the war was all over. It was just unbelievable and there was a celebration everywhere, even there amongst the troopers. It was about that time that plans began to be made for a big victory parade in New York City, and the 82nd and 101st Airborne combination was to be a big part of it.

With the war over thousands of paratroopers began arrangements to ship out and go home. You had to have thirty points to be eligible to go home. If you had a family and children you automatically had twelve points and six months of service gave you six points, combat time another six, and there were additional points for a purple heart and good conduct. I had a ton of points, enough to send me home twice except for one thing. I had enlisted!

Drafted troopers were eligible, enlisted men were not. So l went to the Captain and told him I'd just as soon go home anyway since I had been a paratrooper over a year and had been a big part in whipping the Germans and didn't give a damn about marching in New York anyway,-- so how about it, can I get on the next ship. The captain seemed amused by that. He told me that as an enlisted man I had time to serve and the folks in New York City would be awful upset if I wasn't marching with what was left of the 101st.

I didn't argue but I was awful mad when I left. I had decided I would do about anything to go home and one option was reenlistment. If you reenlisted, you were sent home for thirty days and drew extra pay to boot. It seemed like a good thing to do. I might become a career man, I got to thinking, might even work up to a Sergeant in time, maybe a Second Lieutenant someday. After all, look how quick I had went from buck private to private first class.

Back in the barracks, I told everyone what I had decided to do and J.R. Davis called me an idiot. He said I wasn't thinking straight and he wasn't going to let me re-up until I had thought about it awhile. I told him it would be a cold day in a hot summer before he'd keep me from doing anything and we got into a pretty heated discussion. And then it turned into a full-fledge fist-fight and in all my life I guess I never had a better one. I always had figured that I could whip J.R. pretty easily and that afternoon I learned that either I wasn't as tough as I thought I was or he was a heck of a lot tougher than I thought he was.

We really tore things up in that corner of the barracks, we broke some cots and broke some boards in the wall and put a rip in the side of the tent. Everyone gathered around and tried to keep the damage minimal and see who was going to come out on top. Eventually they got us separated and calmed down. Cassidy said he was pulling for me the whole time but he tried to remain neutral because he and J.R. were good friends too. The fight was intense but it was short, with bloodied noses and swollen lips and puffy eyes.

J. R. and I stood before the Captain the next morning first thing after breakfast and told him we had no idea what had torn up the barracks. He just smiled and said he understood that the two of us were good friends. We assured him that we were and that was the end of it. I thanked J.R. later for causing me to take a closer look at my options and then I found out I couldn't reenlist anyway because of my foot. It wasn't bad enough to get me sent home early but it was bad enough to keep me from ever getting back in.

In the nearby village of Sans, there were lots of taverns and probably twenty houses of prostitution. The army signified those places to be off-limits to all servicemen, and if a trooper got caught there by the military police he was in serious trouble. The problem was, some of the troopers just didn't give a darn. They had seen serious trouble and didn't mind taking a risk.

I guess the Airborne brass decided they had better do something to keep the troopers they wanted to march in that parade out of the brig with serious charges against them. And so they established an Airborne M.P. unit, not so much to throw troopers in the brig as to keep them from being caught by the regular Army M.P.'s.

They picked about 90 or 100 men, gave them specially marked helmets and a .45 automatic with a billy club and jeeps to travel in. Cassidy was chosen right off the bat and I wasn't. We both had clean records but he was six foot-two and I was five-foot-five. I'd go up and see him in the hotel rooms where they stayed in Sans and soon found out that several of the new M.P.s had been dropped for one reason or another. One of them was Cassidy's partner, and I got the idea that maybe I could do the same thing I had done with the horses. So I had Cassidy go to the commander of the M.P. unit and tell him I was the perfect person for a replacement.

I was one of a very few troopers who had an unmarred record and didn't drink. I went to that commander after Cassidy had talked to him and told him my Captain had said I was the only one left of the caliber required to be an M.P. Then I hot-footed it back to my Captain and received permission to talk to him about the replacement. I told him that the M.P. commander had wanted me and I'd sure like to have the job since Cassidy and I had been fox-hole partners for so long.

I suppose that kind of finagling could have gotten me in some trouble if it hadn't worked so well but I'm darned if I didn't get away with it. I was named as Cassidy's partner, moved into Sans and officially became an Airborne M.P. My captain had reason to be glad he chose me. One night several of us walked into one of those off-limits houses and an officer went out the window. Cassidy was outside waiting with some other M.P.'s and guess who they apprehended... Good guess, it was our company commander, the Captain who had helped me get to be an M.P.

He was in bad, bad trouble. For most troopers that apprehension wouldn't amount to much, they'd spend a night in the brig and have a mark on their record which wouldn't hurt much if it wasn't repeated. But for the Captain it would have cost him his rank and some severe disciplinary action. Cassidy and I took him into custody and took him back to his quarters and no report was ever filled out on it. He had got to drinking and got a little bit soused and wound up there because of it.

He thanked us later and said that we had been doing our jobs and he would have not expected special treatment and we should know that. But I think our Captain was a good commander and a tribute to the 101st airborne. Besides that, our job was to keep paratroopers in our division from the kind of problems they would have if the regular military police caught them in those off-limits places.

We'd work at night and sleep in the mornings, then practice marching in the afternoon. We may have set some kind of record for marching. That victory parade in New York City was to be perfect and we marched so much I think when the time come we could have done it in our sleep.

The M.P. work was fun, but nothing of much significance took place there. One day Cassidy and I went to Paris in a jeep to retrieve an 82nd airborne Second Lieutenant who had got thrown in the brig for something. We got there late in the evening and Cassidy met some woman and took off with her. Since he received that Dear John letter from that red-headed girlfriend of his he had chased every woman he came across who acted half interested in him.

I went into some little bar where he was suppose to meet me that night, and he wasn't there. I got into a little bit of an argument with a pair of black soldiers who were truck drivers and they picked me up and threw me through a screen door. I gathered myself and seriously considered going back in there with my billy club and giving those two guys a good whipping. But the two of them together made about three of me and that may be why I decided against it. Besides that, even as an Airborne M.P. I didn't have any authority there and so I walked away with the satisfaction of knowing they'd probably have to pay for that screen door.

A week before we were to ship out I was called before that Captain of ours and told that all Airborne personnel with perfect records were being given a special pass to Paris and I was the only one in our company who qualified. As I prepared take that furlough, troopers began to gather all the invasion money we had been given in the form of German marks, and I wound up with a whole barracks-bag full of it. I was to try to get it converted to American money or English pounds and make whatever arrangements I could and then bring it back to be split up amongst the whole company. No one really thought I could do it, but what the heck, the German money was of no good to anyone.

I went by train to Paris, and again had a room at a hotel already reserved. But there was a woman waiting for me at the train station who knew who I was and what I had with me. I have no idea how she knew but she walked up to me and asked me in English if I was the trooper with the invasion money. She was a hard-looking, tough-acting woman in her forties or fifties but she knew what she was doing. She took me to the hotel, helped me get settled and then took some of the money with her. She came back to say that she couldn't get it changed into American or English money but she could get it changed into French money. To do that she'd want a third.

So I wound up with a heck of a lot of French money, which wasn't really of any benefit to any of us heading back to the U.S. I asked the English lady if she'd see if we had enough to rent the entire hotel and provide rooms to any American servicemen who wanted one, then use the rest for meals. Within a day we had packed that hotel with soldiers and had some of the biggest feasts you can imagine. I tried about everything but the snails and the wine.

I took a subway train to see the Eifel Tower and spent much of one day there, then got lost going back and thought I'd never find that hotel again, especially with no one being able to speak English and tell me where I was. After that I decided to stay close to the hotel and I took in a couple more of those vulgar shows with some other soldiers, tried to find a theater and couldn't, and played cards and shot craps with French money for a couple of days. I still had a bunch of money when I was ready to leave and I had gotten to know an elderly couple who worked in the kitchen there and were apparently pretty poor. I gave them everything that I had left and they were so happy I thought they were going to hug me to death. I slept great that night...at 10 a.m. the next morning my outfit would be coming through Paris to pick me up and I'd be heading home. I would never again spend another night of my life outside the good old U.S.A.

But my outfit didn't show up when they were suppose to and I started worrying that they had forgotten me. Four hours later I was pacing the floor in front of that hotel trying to figure out what the heck I was going to do, when I heard the roar of truck motors. I have never seen such a convoy of trucks as there was coming down that street. It seemed that a hundred roared past me, all filled with paratroopers, and finally one pulled over in front of the hotel and Cassidy hopped out and greeted me. He said "Ridge-Runner, are you stayin' or goin'." I was in the back of that truck before he got the last of it out.

I don't know where we went nor how long it took but the ship we got on was called the Queen Mary and it was one of the fanciest ships you could ever imagine, with beautiful woodwork and fancy ballrooms and dining rooms and wooden decks. We packed it with troopers, there were bunks and hammocks in every available space. Late in the afternoon they pointed the bow west into the setting sun and headed toward America.

The trip was suppose to take five days but the ship hit a tremendous storm about three days out and they cut the motors down to half speed for several days as that storm raged. It took seven days to get to New York. Everyone was worried that the overloaded ship might break up in those waves and wind but somehow it made it through. I was so seasick I spent most of the time in my hammock unable to eat and just drinking a little water on occasion. Every now and then they went through a drill to practice putting on life jackets and getting to places on the ship where we were suppose to be in case it started to sink.

I don't think I would have cared much, I was just too sick to give a damn. The ship was a mess by then, troopers had vomited all over it and the smell was awful. Floors around the bathrooms were slick, you didn't want to get near one. And this time there was no medicine to help. It took seven days to get to New York and we must have arrived there about mid December, just about the same time we had arrived at Bastogne the year before. But I'm not sure about any of those times. I think the victory parade must have been about two weeks after we got back. I saw the Statue of Liberty in the distance and was surprised to see so few people waiting for us. I figured there would be a heck of a crowd, but the celebration for homecoming soldiers had been over for months.

They took us to barracks outside of New York City and we practiced marching for a week or so, as I remember. We'd have inspection every morning followed by hours of practicing. I started feeling better a day or so after settling in and found a big drugstore up there where I bought the first banana split I had seen since the night at Fort Benning when Jane and I had our last fight. I couldn't eat half of it but what I could eat was so good that words can't describe it.

I bought a box of Dutch Masters cigars too. I was hooked on them good by that time. Funny thing, I had stayed away from women and alcohol in Europe, the two things that caused soldiers the biggest problems. But I had become addicted to cigars just because a bundle of them had come drifting down out of gray skies to land out in front of that fox-hole on a foreign battlefield.

They came in and measured us for tailor-made uniforms and we got new boots. Isn't that something! They made new boots for us to march in that parade but at Bastogne thousands of troopers had suffered from frostbitten toes and feet, and some even lost their feet, because we couldn't get supplied with the proper winter boots at the Battle of the Bulge.

We were a spiffy looking bunch---the last of what was once the 101st Airborne. We had to have our stripes and hash marks and medals in place on our dress uniform and we practiced marching in it for several days until the big day came. Early in the morning we lined up and loaded into buses which took us to Fifth Avenue and about 10:00 a.m. it all began.

We were pretty close to the front of the parade and the reviewing stand was only about a half hour or so in front of us. If I remember right President Truman was there, with General Eisenhower and all kinds of military brass. There were thousands and thousands of people screaming and yelling and confetti coming down like snow. We had been told what to expect but I wasn't ready for that.

But brother, were we good. The lines of paratroopers in perfect step were unbelievable. You could barely hear the commands over the roar of the crowd, but somehow we did it all just as we had practiced it for so long. Just before we reached the reviewing stand something hit my rifle barrel over my shoulder and nearly knocked it out of my hand. And I know everyone who reads this is going to think I made it up but I swear it's the truth. A roll of toilet paper landed on my barrel and slid down over the end of it. I guess people had been throwing the toilet paper out of those big high buildings and one hadn't completely unrolled. And now that danged half a roll of toilet paper was going to march down Fifth Avenue with me in the victory parade.

I didn't know about it until we were in front of the review stand and we were given the 'port arms', command. I pushed the barrel out in front as we were suppose to do and there it was, blocking my view and sticking up like a white flag. Conscious about being the shortest paratrooper in the parade, I knew now that I would be twice as conspicuous. I tried to shake it off but the only way I could have done it would have been to break the formation and take it off with my hand. So I just let it go. I'll bet a dollar that Truman and Eisenhower noticed me when we passed the review stand.

We must have marched ten or fifteen miles that day and every step of it there were wildly cheering, screaming, crying people. Police on horseback lined the route and sometimes they'd turn those horses sideways to push the crowd back and I wondered if people were being stepped on by those horses. There were times I thought the crowd was just going to close in on us and stop the whole parade.

I thought about a lot of things as we marched down the middle of New York city. My foot hurt a little toward the end but I kept on like I didn't even notice it. A flood of memories came back, of those days in the snow outside Bastogne, the horrible cold nights and the terrible barrage of artillery. There were so many who had not survived and so many others marred and crippled for life. I was marching for those men too, a few that I knew and hundreds of thousands that I didn't.

I was marching with pride to let the world know that neither the Japanese nor the Germans nor any other country in the world could take our freedom. They couldn't break us, couldn't defeat us. We withstood their best and strongest attack and we held and pushed them back and finished them for good. I don't know how many "Screamin' Eagles" marched down that avenue that day but I know how many were there... the whole 11,000-and-some men that rushed to meet the Germans that December day in Belgium a year before. The whole damn division they referred to as "The Battered Bastards of Bastogne" marched along beside me.

I was one of the lucky ones... I came back. I know my mother's prayers helped but I also know there were mothers praying whose sons didn't come back and I'll never understand why there were so many men better than me who were amongst them. I have no answers, I only know they can't be forgotten. They were the greatest heroes of World War II, just ordinary, common men who walked the Bataan Death March, who landed at Iwo Jima, who walked from North Africa through Italy, who landed on the beaches at Normandy.

There were heroes in those planes who bombed and strafed the enemy, some who returned and many who did not. There were heroes on the ships sunk at sea and at Pearl Harbor. There were heroes by the hundreds of thousands and they all marched in that parade that day. No, they weren't ordinary and common...they were America's very best. I felt them beside me and I have never forgotten. I pray to God that no one ever will.

All dressed up for the parade

In the Spring of '46, Cassidy came all the way to
St. Louis on his motorcycle to visit me.

Chapter 20

Civilian Life

When it was over, it was over. Cassidy's folks came down from Maybrook to pick him up and J. R. Davis disappeared without ever saying good bye. In some ways, it was better to just go and not look around for last words and last farewells. Paratroopers didn't go well with hugs and tears and that kind of thing. There wasn't apt to be any get-togethers in years to come and we didn't need to be remembering an awful lot of what we saw and did together. We trained together, we fought together and we did our job. Germany fell and Hitler died. It was done and over.

I stayed for a day or so for some special duty the army assigned me and then got a pass to go visit Cassidy and his folks. I paid a taxi ten bucks to take me to the highway that went to Maybrook, only 60 or 70 miles away, and I stood there in my uniform and tried to hitch a ride. I stood there longer than I thought I would have, only two days after those screaming thousands of people had cheered us as we marched down Fifth Avenue. One guy even slowed down to holler at me out his window as he went past.. .he called me a dogface. I said to myself that if he had stopped and got out to call me that, he'd have learned something about paratroopers.

An old farmer finally stopped and picked me up and took me to Maybrook, right to Cassidy's house. He said he was going back in two days and he'd give me a ride back to the city when he went. I was ready to go. I was beginning to learn that life outside the 101st Airborne wasn't going to be easy. I was jumpy and edgy and wanted to be doing something. Sitting around and talking to Cassidy's folks got boring in a hurry. They spoke broken English, and for the first time I realized that my fox-hole partner was the son of immigrants. They treated me like a hero because they thought I had saved their son's life but I didn't do anything any trooper wouldn't have done for any of the rest of us, and I told them that.

A few months later Glen Cassidy came to see me in St. Louis and he and I and my wife went out on the town a couple of nights. I remember going into some bar and he ordered a strong drink, trying to act western like he always did. It was so strong and so awful-tasting he just took a sip of it and poured the rest out under the table all over Jane's foot. Even with a cowboy hat, Ol' Cassidy just wasn't a cowboy. He never got over those motorcycles though, after riding that one up and down the mountain at Birchesgaden. A year or so after the end of the war, he got his own motorcycle and rode it off into the sunset. A motorcycle crash ended his life before I ever got to see him again. When I think of him I can see the snow and feel the cold and hear the artillery shells. And I can hear him say in that cowboy-style New York dialect, "Ridge-runner, you reckon we're gonna cash?"

I headed for home on a train about a week after the big parade. Thank goodness it was a faster train than I had been on before. I called and told my sister Zodie, who was living in St. Louis, when they said I would arrive, and when I got off at Jefferson Barracks I didn't even go through the administration process like I was suppose to. I just walked out of there and headed for the streets of St. Louis with two barracks bags over my shoulder and everything I owned inside them. I was going to find a taxi but I found Pop instead. He was walking up the sidewalk and I have never been so happy to see anyone. The first thing he said was "Well, you old son-of-a-____, you made it home." I threw my arms around him and we stood there with tears streaming down our faces.... the first time I ever saw both of us crying at the same time.

Zodie must have been there too but my memories of the next few days are very foggy. My sister took us home and Mom and Jane and Carolyn were there. The baby was walking and talking, I just couldn't believe how much she had grown. She was a little bit afraid of me for awhile but I

Civilian Life

won her over in a hurry. Jane looked great, she had gained a little weight and it seemed she was completely recovered from her illness. Still, she seemed like a stranger to me, it was like we were trying to start all over.

Mom broke down and cried and cried and then recovered her composure for awhile and then cried some more. I hadn't known what she had gone through because when I had left that foxhole in Bastogne half delirious with fever from the shrapnel wound, my unit didn't know where I was, and until I showed up in the field hospital the commanding officer received a report that I was missing in action. Mom and Dad received a letter to that effect, that I was missing in action. Of course, they had feared the worse and didn't find out that I was all-right for more than a week. No one can know what Mom went through.

I received word from the army that I had to go back to Jefferson Barracks to be discharged and receive my papers. I found out that I was to get 300 dollars in 'mustering out' pay. I had 1500 dollars coming when I was discharged because I had signed a supplementary payroll slip where my pay was kept in an account except for ten dollars per month. And they evaluated my wounds and told me I had been judged to be twenty percent disabled and therefore would receive twenty-three dollars per month.

That first week home, I bought my first car, a 1937 Studebaker Dictator four-door sedan. We were evicted from the apartment on McRay avenue because we had a child. As long as I had been in the army Jane and Carolyn couldn't be evicted but as soon as I got back and the war was over they could kick us out, and did. That happened to servicemen everywhere, returning from the war to a wife and child. Landlords didn't want kids and they could ask more money from new tenants. Most of them didn't know what we had gone through and didn't care.

I didn't want to stay in St. Louis anyway so we headed for Houston in that old Studebaker and visited Mom and Pop. It was too early in the year to catch any fish but I head-

261

ed for the Big Piney and washed my face in it's cold flowing waters. I could feel spring on the way and I could hardly wait to float the river again. Finally, I really felt as if I was home and I thanked God for bringing me back to the river as I had asked Him to do a year and a half before.

Pop said he had taken a fellow from St. Louis on some float-fishing trips the past summer and he was really anxious to meet me and have me guide him. He said his name was Carl Adolph Emmick. I told him I wasn't guiding anybody with the name of Adolph. I hated Germans, where ever they were. I didn't know it then but I would change my mind about that soon. Carl Adolph Emmick, German or not, was a wonderful man who would someday become like a second father to me, even more of an influence than Uncle Jabe. And it would be Mr. Emmick who got me to continuing my life's work as a fishing guide.

While I was home Pop said I just had to see the new lake down south on the Missouri-Arkansas border. I left Jane and Carolyn with Mom and we fixed some racks up on top of the Studebaker. Then we loaded one of Pop's old john-boats on it and headed for the new lake they called Norfork.

It was something to behold, water was backing up into the vegetation and the fishing was great. I bought an old Pflueger Supreme casting reel filled with that braided black line and fished with a Heddon River Runt if I remember right. It must have been some time in March because there wasn't any greenery yet and the white bass were tearing it up. I had never seen a white bass before but they fought like tigers and I was catching some that were better than three pounds. And there were crappie up to two pounds and largemouth bass I couldn't land. It was fishing I had never seen the equal to. We didn't stay long but I knew I would be back.

There were no jobs in Houston, lots of young men were home from the war and everyone was looking for work. I didn't want to go back to St. Louis but it seemed there was no choice. We found a one-room furnished apartment and I went to the Veteran's Administration for help. They decided to give me some aptitude tests and I didn't do very well. I had been teaching myself to read and write and was making progress but I wasn't far enough along to be taking tests. For some reason the VA decided I would make a good automotive electrician. They would get me a job with on-site training and pay me 125 dollars per month. The people I'd be working for would pay me fifty cents per hour in addition to that.

They took me to my new employer in downtown St. Louis, a place at the juncture of Kingshighway and Gravois avenues known as Briggs Brothers Auto Service. The owner was Harold Briggs. He ran the place, his son Harold Jr. did all the accounting and office work. His next son, Charlie, was a good mechanic and body man, and then there was Joe, also a mechanic, and the youngest boy Tommy, who was just sort of there to help. Harold Jr. and Joe had both been in the service, during the war, but neither had been in combat. Anyway, the VA sent Mr. Briggs a complete set of tools for my automotive electric work and explained how I was to learn as I worked and all that.

As soon as they were gone Harold Briggs Sr. told me to get the broom and keep the place clean. I never touched one of those tools the government provided nor did I do a minutes worth of electrical work. Instead I ran errands, cleaned cars for Charlie to work on and did general work around the shop. But I didn't care, I liked all of them and I took home a paycheck every week.

In a couple of months the V.A. came around to see how I was doing and Harold Briggs told them I just was too dumb for automotive electrical work. He didn't tell them he had kept all the tools and never gave me one minute of training or instruction. They asked what he thought I was best suited for and old man Briggs told them he thought I'd do better at paint and body work. I guess he needed some new tools for that. And he got them. The VA had all kinds of paint guns and sanders and tools delivered, and sure enough, they put them away and told me to keep cleaning and sweeping.

Still and all they treated me good so I stayed at it. Then the V.A. contacted Briggs again and he told them I just wasn't making any progress at all and would have to have a lot more training. Again, he didn't tell them that they were using the new tools and that I hadn't yet touched a one of them or received any on-the-job-training whatsoever.

I guess the whole thing is typical of what happens with so many government programs. There's good intentions behind them and in a perfect world those programs would probably do a great deal of good. But the world is far from perfect and the program depends on everyday people doing what they should do to make it all work. That plan assumes that everyone is going to do what they are suppose to do and do it with honesty and effort. Welfare and government assistance programs end up being wasteful and corrupt sometimes because what starts out as a good idea and a good program, falls into the hands of less-than-honest people.

Many of the people in the Ozarks were too proud to take the assistance, because they looked upon it as charity. At the same time, some of the most worthless, lazy undeserving people, who could have worked but just wouldn't, figured out ways to use the system to get their share and more. It has gone on that way ever since and there doesn't seem to be a thing anyone can do about it.

Finally the Veteran's Administration decided that I was a lost cause and they told Mr. Briggs they would no longer pay the 120 dollars per month to keep me working. Briggs moaned and groaned about that. He was getting a lot of work out of me for his contribution of fifty cents per hour. And even though I knew what was happening I couldn't do much about it. Besides that, they treated me good and I never minded a little hard work. I wasn't all that crazy about the old man, but I really had come to like all of his sons. Best of all, the Briggs brothers liked to fish, and about every weekend that summer they had me take them to the Piney or to Norfork lake and they'd rent one of Pop's boats

and pay me fifty cents an hour plus all the expenses to paddle for them while they fished.

When the VA money ended that year I told the Briggs brothers I was quitting and Mr. Briggs decided I had learned enough to be worth keeping on. So he offered me two dollars an hour and told me he'd teach me to do body work and paint cars. Finally, we were getting somewhere. I learned quick and the first car I painted was a 1939 Chevrolet four-door sedan. I even remember the color, it was a ruby maroon metallic lacquer which had to be thinned with banana oil. I spent three days on that car, sanding and masking and carefully painting it and and hand buffing it when I was done. Old man Briggs looked at that car and told me I had a real future painting cars. I didn't tell him, but my future would be somewhere back in the Ozarks as soon as I could get back there, guiding fishermen like I had done as a boy.

One day they sent me across the street to the American Exchange National Bank to get some checks cashed and a policeman was waiting on the other side to write me a ticket for jay-walking. He was a belligerent kind of guy and all he wanted was to give some unfortunate person a ticket to fill some kind of quota. In order to go to the bank without jay-walking I would have to walk a half block one direction, wait for the light, cross and walk back a half block back. Usually there was very little traffic and I could walk straight across the street without the slightest danger.

I was so mad about that ticket that I went in front of a judge to protest it. I explained that I worked at Briggs and we all walked across the street to the bank without going so far out of the way and I felt I didn't deserve to be ticketed for doing what caused no problem for anyone. The judge sat up there on his high bench and looked down on me and told me that he was fining me ten dollars for my own good. He said, "Young man, we are simply trying to protect you."

I felt like what they were trying to do was get as much of the ordinary worker's money as they could get and I said as much. I was really steamed and I didn't let it go at that.

"Your honor", I said, "where were all of you when I was sitting over there in the cold and snow fighting for my country? I could have used some of your protection there."

You could see right off he wasn't impressed. "That will

be another ten dollars." he told me. "Do you have anything else to say?"

"I sure do," I told him. "Why is it when I was over there at Bastogne and didn't have enough clothes or the right boots to stay warm, you weren't over there worrying about my welfare enough to fine me for being there?"

"That will be another ten dollars Mr. Dablemont," he said, and you could see he was more angry than he was judicial. "Do you have anything more to add?"

I didn't. But that court appearance had a lasting effect on me. All I was to that court was an opportunity to make money. I had fought for the freedom to speak up and have my say and I thought I had that right. The judge felt I should pay for that right again.

It may have been a turning point in my life! There I was struggling to make a living for a wife and baby and I had been evicted from a decent place to live. I had watched Briggs take those tools and hand me a broom and now I had been told that if I didn't bow my head and pay a fine and keep my mouth shut I would have to pay more. Nothing around me seemed to be right anymore. I began to think that going by the rules was for fools. And I started thinking about getting even.

I spent very little time being a husband and father. I had to make money and I could make more of it by going back to the Piney or Norfork on weekends and guiding fishermen. In the midst of the turmoil in my life, there was one float trip on the Piney that just added to it. Pop had lined up a day-long trip on the Big Piney for about fifteen dollars guiding a local store owner who was a neighbor of his. This was a guy who was tight as the bark on a tree and Mom had been working at his store for the smallest of salaries. He had once given Dad a half bag of popcorn left over from the day before and told him it was something he wanted to do to show him how much he appreciated what he and Mom had done for him over the years.

The fellow's name is not of importance, he is long since

dead and gone and the life he lived in pursuit of his own gain amounted to little in the great scheme of things. That morning I was guiding him, we were approaching mid-day, having fished for several hours, and the fishing had been good. Just after a hard fight with a bass he began to get ill. He said he had already had a heart attack and he was afraid he was having another. I took him to the bank, laid him out as comfortable as I could get him and told him I would get help. It wasn't far from the old mud-daubers nest where I had spent much of my boyhood, and I knew the old trails and roads.

I could get help down to him if he didn't die before I could get it there. So I ran the entire distance up to the top of those ridges and ran the tops of them almost all the way back to Houston. They got an old truck down to the river and the guy was apparently going to make it. I went into the doctors office to see him, where he seemed to be doing just fine, and he thanked me for such an effort to save him. Then he told me that since he hadn't had an opportunity to finish the fishing trip, he felt he didn't owe me anything and that perhaps the next time he'd throw in a little extra. There wasn't going to be a next time. I had a court fine to pay which I didn't deserve and now I had been cheated out of enough money to pay half of it.

It was about that same time that the Missouri Conservation Commission decided to hire a man to work on the Big Piney river as a person to travel the river and check fishermen for an accurate account of what was being taken from the river, by species and size. There would be no enforcement involved. I was approached by one of their employees, a man named Pritchard, who asked if I would be interested. I told him I was learning to read and write, but didn't have it mastered yet, and he said I could do all that was necessary.

I was really excited about that until my Uncle Thurman Harris, who owned a restaurant on main street, told me not to get my hopes up. The fellow who owned the variety store where Mom had been working and the owner of a service station and the owner of a local pharmacy had gotten together and presented a petition of some sort to the Conservation Commission asking that I not be given the job because my presence on the river would be a threat to the fish.

They said that people who floated with me had verified that Pop and I could catch fish so well because of our years on the river that I would be ruining the resource they were wanting to protect. As a result, an elderly man who was related to one of the three was given the job. He couldn't paddle a boat much, he'd just pick a place and sit there and talk to whoever floated by.

For me, it was sort of the stick that broke the axle on the wagon. I vowed revenge and I decided I wouldn't worry again about rules and laws. They weren't made to help everyone, I was convinced of that. And I had been a paratrooper...I didn't need anybody. I could help myself just fine!

Joe Weis with a stringer of fish from Norfork Lake in the early '50's. Joe was the first friend I made after returning from the war and the two of us were inseparable fishing buddies for 20 years.

Chapter 21

Outlaw Days

Back in St. Louis, I acquired a good friend who was working in the accounting department of the bank. His name was Joe Weis and he was only about nineteen years old at the time. He had been too young to go to war and in the war years he had worked as a cleaning boy at the bank. They liked the kid and he was working his way up. In thirty years Joe would become the President of that bank but at that time he was just a poor kid like me trying to make ends meet. The people at the bank were sending him to school several nights a week to learn all about banking. And he loved to hunt and fish more than anyone I ever met except me.

We began fishing and hunting together and I found out he was a great shot and a superb outdoorsman. We'd go to St. James and hunt rabbits and quail, and we fished the Piney and the Meramec and the Bourbeuse every chance we got. But it cost money to make those trips and we didn't have much of it. We could pay for our trips by selling catfish... everyone wanted fresh fish, and though it was against the law by that time, we felt like Robin Hood when we gave poor people some fish they could easily afford. We weren't out to make much money, we just wanted to pay the costs of our trips. Nobody was any poorer than Joe and I. But Mr. Briggs gave me a little bit of a raise and traded me a 41 DeSoto for that old car I had and some extra work so I felt like I was at least doing a little better. And you can't feel too poor when the fishing is good.

That spring, we went to Norfork and set trotlines and caught catfish like you can't imagine. My younger brother Bryce had gone with us once and we bought him a fishing license. When we made the next trip, my brother Vaughn wanted to go, so to save money, we just gave him Bryce's license and told him he was to tell any wardens he was Bryce. Back in that day no one expected any identification on a kid his age anyway.

We were camped out on Norfork Lake just on the Missouri side of the border near Tecumseh, and having a great time. We had too many trotlines and too many hooks and too many catfish, and game wardens had been watching. They came into our camp while I was visiting the willow thicket and I saw them before they saw me. I got down to the lake and turned over a pair of live boxes we had filled with fish and therefore escaped the greater charges we might have faced. But we were still in trouble. I got there just as one of the wardens looked at Vaughn's license. He was scared to death and when the agent looked at him and said, "What's your name son?" Vaughn forgot everything.

"I'm Vaughn," he said. Then he stammered a minute and said, "I mean, no, I'm Bryce." Then it was all more than he could handle and he threw his hands in the air and said, "Oh hell, I'm guilty."

They confiscated our trotlines and took us in to the jail at Gainesville MO. It was the only time before or since that I have ever been in jail. They got a judge out of bed about 2:00 a.m. to come in and try us. To this day, I don't know why they did things that way, but they did, and I was glad to get out of that jail. The judge wasn't thrilled about being there at that time of the night and he made short work of it. We paid him twenty-eight dollars in fines and court costs but he let us keep five dollars to buy gas to get home on and he told us we could keep Pop's boat since it wasn't ours. He said if we ever got caught again it would mean a jail sentence.

Like always, Joe and I began thinking of ways to recuperate that money we had lost and there were ways to do it. A restaurant in St. Louis said they would buy all the bullfrogs we could bring them. They knew it was illegal but they bought them anyway for fifty cents apiece, a lot cheaper than they could get them from the seafood companies.

I was becoming an outlaw, a habitual lawbreaker, and dragging Joe along with me. And he was just a kid so he might be excused for that. But I wasn't a kid any more and I

In the late 1940's, Joe and I looked like a couple of kids, but we were far from it. We were on the verge of geting into serious trouble.

knew what I was doing. I had a family, times were hard and I really needed the money, but it was more than that. What I was doing was a way to strike against authority, to rebel against a system that didn't seem to care anymore about what we had gone through for our country. It seemed as if there was no freedom anymore compared to what I had known as a kid. And too, it was adventure and craved that. When I was going against the law, I was at the peak of my senses like it had been in combat. There as excitement and challenge to it and I couldn't get enough of it.

We got the best of them one weekend on the Big Piney when Joe and I went to get another sackful of bullfrogs. We made a bad mistake in the preparations, how-ever, by stopping by McCaskill's feed mill in Houston and getting some burlap sacks. Somebody figured out what we were doing and they alerted the game wardens.

It wasn't hard to figure out where we were, I left that old Desoto sitting alongside the highway there a ways down from the bridge a couple of miles north of Cabool. Joe and I headed upriver just after dark with carbide lamps on miner's caps, picking up bullfrogs as we went. It was pretty reckless of us, bullfrog season wasn't open yet and anyone who might have seen us would have known immediately what we were doing. It was the upper end of the river, the Big Piney headwaters where the stream was too small to float but perfect for wading. No one spent much time along that section, and it was full of bullfrogs. I might add that today that beautiful headwaters stretch is a stagnant, nearly dried-up cesspool which you wouldn't want to put a finger in, filled with slime and scum where nothing can live. No one would ever believe that once it flowed clean water filled with fish and frogs.

In two or three hours we had two sacks full, maybe fifty or sixty frogs, and about all we could carry. So we headed back to the old car, figuring to leave the frogs at Pop's and go after some more somewhere else.

My night vision was very good back then and when we got close to the bridge I saw two tall radio aerials sticking up against the dark sky. I knew we had problems. I whispered to Joe that we had to stash the frogs and told him to keep his light on. I extinguished mine and made a big deal out of how much trouble I was having keeping my carbide lamp from clogging up.

While I was doing that, I dragged both bags back in under some willows away from the river and covered them with gravel and leaves and brush as best I could. Then I relit my lamp and we waded on up to the bridge talking and laughing about the good places we had found to seine bait for a trip to Norfork. There were a couple of game wardens and a couple of deputies there if I remember right. Old timer Bland Wilson was one of them and he didn't buy our alibi.

"Norten", he told me, "you know every hole and riffle in the Piney river, you don't need to be looking for seining spots in the middle of the night. We know what you are doing and we'll find those frogs when it comes daylight.. why don't you just cooperate?"

I tried to act innocent but we knew and they knew that when they found those frogs, our goose was cooked, or our frogs were fried, however you might want to look at it. Wilson wanted to know where we were staying and I told him we were at Pop's. He told us to stay there and they'd be by to see us the following morning.

Back in Houston I went straight to my brother Farrel and told him I needed his help. I explained what had happened and told him I had to get to those bullfrogs before the game wardens did and asked him to take me back there. Farrel wasn't too pleased with me but I knew he'd help. After midnight, he drove me toward the Big Piney bridge where the agents still waited. A mile before we got there, I got out and lay on the running board of his old Chevrolet, and as we neared the bridge he slowed down as I had instructed him to do. When he did I rolled off the side of the road and down into the gully which led to the river.

The adrenaline was pumping and I felt a little like I had felt in combat. But this time it was a rush of excitement and I was enjoying it. In the water, I swam and crawled upstream as quietly and slowly as possible, found the frogs and released them, then intentionally threw both bags out on the gravel bar where they would be in plain sight. I could hear people on the bridge talking and laughing and I even saw one of them light a cigar. An hour later Farrel drove back through, heading toward Houston, and I was on the highway below them, waiting.

Joe and I were off the hook. But we hadn't come out ahead. We weren't going to pay for the trip or make back any money we had lost to the wardens on Norfork. Pop really got a kick out of the whole thing and he just couldn't keep quiet about it. He told most of his friends and of course he had to brag to Bland Wilson, his old adversary, about how his son had foiled them. In doing so he made it really tough on me, because I never arrived in that county again that I wasn't being watched like a hawk.

But I was still bent on revenge and they couldn't stay ahead of me. I found out that one of those merchants who had cost me the opportunity for a job on the Piney had bought a johnboat from Pop. He had the money to pay him what Pop needed for the boat but he went out there and made a big deal of being Pop's old buddy and going on about how he admired what we could do with those johnboats and of course Pop gave him a real deal. I think he sold him a boat and two paddles for about twenty dollars.

I despised that so and so, and when I found out about how it had flim-flammed Pop, it really made me hot. So I borrowed an old trailer and pulled it down to a crossing on the Big Piney just downstream from his place. The old S.O.B. had some land on the river and had that boat chained and locked there. I had asked him once if we could use his road to put in or take out on fishing trips and he told me he'd better never catch me on his property. I assured him he wouldn't. And he didn't. It was in the middle of the night when I snuck down the river and used a pair of bolt cutters to snap the chain, and in the middle of the night, I paddled it down to that crossing three or four miles down river where Joe was waiting. We loaded it and headed up Route 66, stopping at Sullivan, where I sold the boat to a Meramec river resort for thirty-five dollars. I sent ten or fifteen dollars of it to Pop and kept the rest. And it felt great.

In the fall of that year we began to find people who would buy rabbits and quail and so one day I asked a few of them if they'd be interested in buying some venison. Of course there weren't enough deer back then to ever hope of getting venison to sell but I had a plan. I told Joe I intended to get what that variety store owner owed me for the float trip which he had never paid me for. I wanted the revenge as much as I wanted the money. On our next trip to the Piney, I'd drive my old car down to the river across from land he owned, we'd paddle across the river and kill and butcher one of his young steers and sell it in the city for venison.

Joe didn't much like the idea but it was an adventure and he agreed the guy owed me something so he said he'd go along with my plan. We got to Pop's one afternoon in the early fall, put one of his smaller johnboats on top of the car and headed for the river with .22 caliber bolt action rifles. Thinking back on it, I'm not proud of what I did that night but it is typical of the way I began to think and act in those first few years after the war.

We paddled across the river, picked out a young steer and killed and butchered it as darkness came on, then quartered it and took across the river in three trips. We lost some of it on the third trip, the boat was small and we swamped it in the current because we had too much weight.

But I fished one ham out of the river and we filled the trunk, wrapping the meat in paper. There was just about more than we could get in there. It was a cold night and we were so wet we about froze to death getting the boat out of the river and getting it loaded, but we finally got it all done and headed for Pop's to unload his boat and get some sleep before setting out for St. Louis the next morning. As luck would have it, my younger brother Farrel was there waiting for us. He helped unload the boat, took note that Joe and I were soaking wet, and he saw the bloody water dripping out of the trunk of my car. Farrel had been too young to go to war, but at the end of the war he had joined the merchant marines at the age of seventeen and he had seen a lot of the world. He had become a man in a hurry. He was only nineteen years old at the time, had married a young woman from Houston and had a new baby. He stood six inches taller than me and when he said something, he had a way of making you listen.

He said he wanted to talk to me and so while Pop and Joe went off to do something, Farrel and I leaned up against the car and talked. "I don't know what you have in that car Norten" he said, "but if it's what I think it is, they use to hang people for that."

I didn't say anything, there wasn't any use in trying to

fool him.

"When we were kids, Vaughn and Bryce and I looked up to you," he went on. "You didn't steal and you didn't cheat. Pop taught us what was right and we all tried to live by it. You did too. You're a decorated war veteran and people look up to you. What would they think if they knew what you are becoming, someone who has no respect for the laws of the nation he fought for?"

I broke in to argue that I hadn't been treated with much respect since I got back but Farrel wouldn't hear it. "Times are hard for everyone," he said, "I'm working at a factory right now to try to pay the bills. But a man doesn't have to be a crook to make it Norten. Especially you... you can do so much. Hell, you can guide fishermen and make a living doing what you love. Everyone talks about how good you are with that boat paddle and what a gift you have for catching fish."

I didn't say anything but I was a little aggravated at my little brother trying to give me advice. I figured what I was doing was none of his business. But then he started to get down to brass tacks.

"Vaughn and Bryce are still just kids and you've had both of them in trouble already. They worship the ground you walk on.... all they talk about is Norten. When they know you're coming home, they both start counting the days 'til you get here. They want to be just like Norten."

He took out his pipe and began to fill it and went on. "Pop has a pretty good idea what's going on and he'd back you if you were robbing banks, but Mom doesn't know anything about what you are becoming. They've both got the respect of the community, even as poor as we've always been. Mom is proud and she's honest, and it would kill her if she heard the stuff that's going around. And maybe Pop isn't looked on as a saint but folks know he'd never steal. The name 'Dablemont' means something around here, even though we ain't got much and we ain't big shots. None of us have ever been in trouble and none of us have ever brought shame to

Mom and Pop. I don't think you want that Norten and you ain't so far along with this you can't turn around your life and go the right direction."

He stopped a minute and I didn't say anything. Farrel must have figured he had me where he wanted me, cause it wasn't often I didn't have anything to say. And that's when he really got to me.

"What you've got in there isn't something they'll fine you for," he said in a low solemn voice. "They send you to prison for that. Have you ever thought about prison...or not ever seeing Mom again? 'Cause you wouldn't! Having a son in prison would kill her just as sure as putting a gun to her head!"

Not much has affected me like that little speech from my younger brother. He was talking about the only things that really did make a difference anymore, my brothers and sister and Mom and Pop. We didn't risk spending the night at Pop's, I told Joe I wanted to take off that night. We got into some dry clothes and pointed the old DeSoto toward St. Louis and while Joe slept, I thought and thought and thought.

And I can truthfully say that from that night on my outlaw days were over. Oh I'm not saying I didn't break a few game laws now and then but there was no more stealing and no more revenge. What Farrel had said was just the snowball that started the avalanche. I thought about what my frame of mind had been down there on the river at dusk, about halfway back overseas again in enemy territory, my mind foggy at best. I don't know what I would have done if someone had come along and caught us, somebody like that no account landowner or one of the Abney boys who I had always seen as a mortal enemy. I know it wouldn't have been hard to kill someone in a situation like that. I had killed the enemy before and I was thinking along those lines. Or maybe I shouldn't call it thinking. Maybe that night on the way back to St. Louis, I did the only thinking I had done in a long long time.

Mr. Emmick and I with a string of fish sometime
in late '50's or early '60's. He became my number
one client and one of my closest friends.

Chapter 22
Mr. Emmick

In the summer of 1948, Joe and I caught fish like no-body's business. He got himself a Pflueger Supreme casting reel and a glass rod and a lure called a Hawaiian Wiggler and we slayed 'em. We fished the Piney and the Meramec and Bourbeuse because it was economical, but every now and then we'd spend a weekend on Norfork Lake. Harold Briggs agreed to let me work twelve hours a day Monday through Thursday so I could have three days to guide fish-ermen, and I was beginning to get some business through Joe's bank connections.

And finally I went to see Carl Adolph Emmick, the old German who had been taking occasional trips with Pop and my brother Farrel. Actually, he wasn't that old. He was in his mid-fifties, and he sure wasn't much of an outdoors-man. When I first met him I didn't like him all that much because he was a little bit like an old woman and so particu-lar in everything. But for someone like me who was trying to turn his life around, Carl Emmick was the perfect fishing partner. He had some kind of high position at Carr-Adams Sash and Door company in St. Louis, and had quite a bit of money. He was a man of high morals and convictions and he took it upon himself to teach me the things I didn't know about getting along in the world.

Over the years I learned more from him than any other man I ever knew...things about personal hygiene and ordi-nary etiquette, how to dress and how to deal with people, and how to speak properly. I used awful language back then, it was something I had come by in the service and I didn't really know how bad it was. Mr. Emmick let me know that when I was guiding for him, I would refrain from vulgarity. Every time I used incorrect English he would tell me what I should have said. You may not think that would have a strong impact but you can't imagine the hours we spent together fishing and how that constant teaching and

Mr. Emmick

tutoring had an effect.

Carl Emmick was a great man and I was privileged to know him. He was constantly worried about my health and welfare and what kind of life I was making for myself and my family. Over the years I guided a tremendous number of fisherman but Mr. Emmick had no peers. He was a gentleman and a sportsman like no other. From the first, he seldom called me by my name. He would refer to me as "my boy".

"Paddle me over a little closer, my boy," he would say, or "slow down just a little, my boy, " or "what lure do you think would be best today, my boy." And in time I began looking at him as a second father, as much an influence upon my life and the way I lived it as Uncle Jabe had been.

At first Mr. Emmick was paying me twelve dollars a day and all my expenses. And there was always a little extra so in two days of fishing I would make twenty-five or thirty dollars, which was all profit. I made a boat trailer at the Briggs Brothers shop and took it down to Pop's place on Brushy Creek just east of Houston. We put a trailer hitch on Mr. Emmick's new Plymouth, and traveled back and forth in style. He gave me all kinds of fishing lures and helped me buy my first really good rod and reel, a Langley Sportscast reel with a Heddon rod like the ones he used.

And talk about picky, he'd jump all over me for laying a reel down somewhere without covering it. He protected his reels from any dirt and took care of his equipment as if everything was gold plated. He always had a towel tied to his belt to keep his hands clean when he handled fish. The man was a great caster and he caught fish like no one because he knew where to put that lure and how to make it act.

On our first trip on the Piney, he caught a three and one-half pound smallmouth in about the first half dozen casts and it was an omen of things to come. I learned that he couldn't see very well with those thick glasses he had on so I began to help him by telling him where the limbs were hanging down and where the logs were underwater. Mr.

282

Emmick didn't much care for Joe, whom he often referred to as a "shyster" but we all three fished together on occasion and even Joe began to be influenced by the old man. We didn't often disagree with him. He paid for everything and when you paid for everything you were the boss. Besides that, Joe and I were experiencing some great fishing and having the times of our lives.

About that time, there was a new development in fishing. Mr. Emmick bought a new reel known as a Cox casting reel, which was made to hold the first monofilament line. We called it 'catgut' back then. We had used it before in short lengths attached to the end of the braided nylon as a leader. It was strong and it would stretch, and though it wasn't anything close to what we have today, it was a big improvement.

When we floated the Piney, Mr. Emmick would stay at the Piney Inn in Houston and I'd stay with Mom and Pop, so some-times Jane and Carolyn could go along and see Mom and be with me a little more. But we were drifting apart and I knew it. Jane wanted a home and the things women wanted and I was just trying to make enough money to get by, hoping to save a little eventually. And I was born to be outdoors and Jane never understood that. I lived to see that river or the lake, to hunt and to fish, or set in the back of a johnboat and paddle for someone who loved it as much as I did. I hated the city more and more each day.

Looking back, I realize I wasn't much of a provider and even less of a mate to her. If there were occasional weekends in the summer when I didn't go fishing, I took her and Carolyn to some city park and played ball with Uncle Jabe. I just didn't think much about what she might want. But there never was enough money. About that time, President Truman or Congress or someone decided to try to get some of the war veterans off disability to reduce the budget. I was called in to have my wounds checked to see if they could cut my twenty-three dollars per month. It looked as if eventually they would take it away and I started wondering how we would make it. There certainly was no future painting cars for Briggs Brothers, but at least the guiding was going well.

Mr. Emmick had hired lots of guides in his life, because he loved to fish. He told me he had never seen anyone handle a boat like I did, to be able to paddle from one side all day and back a boat up against the current. He said that from that first day forward I was his personal guide and he'd never hire another one. But he didn't much like driving those brand new Plymouths (and he had a new one about every year) down those gravel roads to the river. So he went out and bought me a 1938 Oldsmobile with a trailer and a hitch and fixed it up and put good tires on it. When we floated the rivers we used it but if we went to Norfork

we still took his new car and instead of taking a johnboat of Pop's, we would stay at a little resort and use the metal V-bottom Lone-Star boats which they provided free to their customers.

Those V-bottom metal boats were harder to paddle but we managed, and Mr. Emmick caught fish hand over fist. In fact, my reputation as a guide began to grow because of all the luck he had on Norfork and I began to get to know more fishermen who were willing to pay good money to catch some fish.

One of Mr. Emmick's fishing friends was a fellow by the name of Harry Reel, who was the head of the Better Business Bureau. He often went along with us and I really liked him because he smoked cigars he got from Havana, and they were good. He'd tip me with a supply of those Cuban cigars.

I'll never forget one trip on the Big Piney in the early 1950's when we stopped to cook some bass and eat a hot dinner. Harry Reel opened up a can of corn, made by a big company still producing canned vegetable's even today. When he dumped the can out into a small pan to heat it, there was the end of a woman's little finger in it, about an inch long and perfectly preserved. He put everything back in the can and took it back to the city with him. He said he was going to make that company give him a whole year's supply of canned corn for that. As for me, I still have a hard time eating corn.

I played some good tricks on Mr. Emmick and his friends over the years. Harry Reel always wanted to have coffee at lunchtime in the spring or fall when the weather was cool. Mr. Emmick didn't drink coffee and on one trip he forgot to bring any. That morning we passed a backwater slough where the water was so black it looked like coffee and I dipped up a canteen full of it. When we stopped for lunch I put it in a coffee pot and boiled it really good so I figured it wouldn't make him sick. Harry took a sip of it and said, "Damn Norten, your coffee just keeps getting worse and worse." And then he started to drink some more of it.

In the early 1950's, Joe Weis lined me up with one of my best customers and when I met him he didn't even fish. Joe had bought a motorcycle and was awfully reckless with it. I hated those darn things. I had already lost one friend because of a motorcycle and I figured the way Joe was going I was about to lose another.

One day on his way to work he took a short cut across a vacant lot which he had used several times before. But that last time there was a fallen tree limb in his way and he wrecked his motorcycle. He shattered the bones in his left leg between the knee and the ankle. Everyone said he would lose his leg but a bone surgeon at a St. Louis hospital by the name of Schmemier said he could save it. He removed part of the leg bone which was so badly damaged and replaced it with a steel rod.

Dr. Roy Schmeimier

Gradually, little by little, Joe began to heal... and with therapy, regained the use of his leg. He would always walk with little bit of a limp but he could walk again. And it was Joe who lined me up with Dr. Schmeimier, a man who had never fished before, had worthless gear, couldn't cast and was about half obnoxious. But you had to get to know him because underneath it all was a great guy. Over the years he performed surgery on each my parents and never charged them a penny because he knew how poor they were. And he also paid the hospital bills out of his own pocket. He told me to repay him, I had to take him fishing. Over the years, we made a lot of fishing trips.

In 1952 or '53 we began to fish the brand new lake just west of Norfork, known as Bull Shoals. If you think there was ever a better lake in the Midwest than Bull Shoals, you'd get a big argument from me. It has always been my favorite. I took Dr. Schmeimier there often and the bass fishing was spectacular. We took him down to a local sporting goods store and helped him buy new gear, a Shakespeare President casting reel, handmade rods and a tackle box full of lures. Thursday was his day off, so I started putting in only three days at Briggs Brothers and guiding the rest of the week. They didn't like it much but I was doing a good job of painting cars and Mr. Briggs didn't want to lose me.

About that time, Joe and Dr. Schmeimier bought an outboard motor, the first one I ever used. It was a Martin Sixty. I don't know what the "Sixty" meant, it was only five horsepower. We used it to go to different spots on the lake and then, as usual, I would paddle.

You can't believe what fishing was like back then, how easy it was to catch big bass from six to nine pounds. Bull Shoals had bass like that in only its third or fourth year and Norfork had them the first time I fished it. No one ever released a big bass, because the limits were high and there were no length limits at all. You turned back anything that wasn't two or three pounds, and some fishermen wouldn't keep anything under four pounds.

Mr. Emmick

Vaughn had gone off to the Korean War and Bryce came to live with Jane and I looking for work in St. Louis.

He and Joe and I found an old shack down on Norfork just above Hand Cove, one of the better places to fish. It wasn't much, just an old shed with stove. There were some cracks in the wall we had to cover with cardboard. We paid the guy who owned it a dollar per weekend to sleep there. In the spring of 1953, it was one of those trips to Norfork which changed my way of fishing forever.

My brother, Bryce, (right) came to live with us when he was just a kid. He fished with me and Joe Weis one spring and we caught some impressive strings of fish. Note the big small mouth on the far right.

You have to remember that the lures we had to choose from back then were limited in number. Joe was a big fan of that Hawaiian wiggler and I used Heddon lures like the River Runt, a wobbling minnow imitator called the Cisco Kid, and Lazy Ikes and Flatfish. The best topwater lures were the Jitterbug, the Lucky 13, the Hula-Popper and the Bass-A-Reno. Those lures didn't go very deep and when the bass were deep you had to go to a jig of some type with a strip of Uncle Josh pork-rind.

But that day early in the spring, we were having trouble getting down to the depths we needed to fish and so Joe pulled out a box with something really strange looking. It was called a Hauser Hell-Diver. Paul Hauser, the man who made the lure, had a sporting goods shop over on Kingshighway in St. Louis, and Joe had made his acquaintance. Hauser had given him the lure, which they were making a few at a time in the back of his shop.

I decided I was going to try it and Joe basically laughed at it. He said I could have the thing, he wouldn't use it on a bet. It was a big silver spinner blade with yellow plastic skirt, the first true spinner bait I had actually seen. I decided to make it look more appealing by adding a strip of the pork rind and I added a trailer hook beneath it. The first cast or two I made with it caused a heck of a backlash because it was so much heavier than the other lures we had been using.

We were working back into the end of Woods cove and I cast the lure in beside some flooded willow trees and let it sink. When it got down deep, I'd pull it up and feel that big spinner vibrating on the retrieve, then let it sag again. I hadn't cast it a half dozen times until I got a savage strike and I set the hook into a really heavy fish. Everything stopped while I fought that big bass around the boat, my rod arcing down into the water every time he made a hard run for the depths. And then finally he came up to try to throw the hook and we got a good look at him. The hook and trailer hook were both secure in the side of his mouth and I finally landed him. He was better than seven pounds.

Then the discussion began over who owned the lure. True, Joe had owned it and still had the box, but then he had told me I could have it. We finally decided that to be perfectly fair, we would declare joint ownership of the lure and take turns using it. Joe tied it on that morning and had a bass nearly as big as mine within twenty minutes of the time he started fishing it.

Mr. Emmick

We shouldn't have let Bryce have his turn. After all he hadn't never owned it, like Joe had, nor had it given to him like I had. But we gave him a shot at it and another big bass nailed it and got it around a tree somehow in ten feet of water. That was the last of the Hauser Hell-Diver. We put those two big bass on ice and took them in to show Paul Hauser and he gave us a dozen more. He said the publicity that I could give him was worth the cost of the lures. And he hired me to take him to Bull Shoals the following week.

I think I only guided him on a couple of trips but he fished differently than anyone else. He wanted me to keep the boat in close to the bank so he could cast parallel to the shoreline and work his spinner bait back while always being close to the cover. And it worked, he caught some eye-popping strings of bass on those spinner-baits, and with the pictures began to sell them to fishermen who came into his store. And of course, he began to send fishermen my way. It was getting to be more than I could handle, trying to get everyone fishing who wanted to go fishing. Fishing with Paul Hauser, hugging the bank and casting parallel to it, made me think about wading and walking the banks to fish for big bass rather than doing it all from a boat. It was to become a way to catch more and bigger bass and almost no one else ever did it but me.

I took Roy Schmeimier to Bull Shoals one weekend in June and went to sleep on the way back to the city one Sunday night. I ran the car off the road and through a fence into a farmers field. That one event also played a big part in the next few years of my life. It was a turning point that very nearly destroyed me. Schmeimier said he wasn't going to take any chances riding with me when I was sleepy and he said he would fix me up a prescription for a kind of medicine which would keep me awake on weekends when I fished. He said it was a pill I could take once a day and never even think of sleeping.... something called dexadrine.

At first those dexadrine capsules seemed to be the best thing that ever happened for a fisherman. No one talked

291

about drugs back in those days, there was nothing taboo about it and I never heard about or thought about any type of addiction or adverse effects. The first one I took made me happier than I had ever been, gave me boundless energy and turned me into a fishing machine. We'd start in the afternoon and still be going strong at daylight. I didn't need much food, didn't need any sleep. A pill on Friday and Saturday carried me through to Sunday night, when I'd crash and sleep for hours, waking up with an awful headache and very little ambition. So then I'd take a pill on Monday and paint cars all night for Briggs Brothers.

People who knew me thought I was going crazy. On dexadrine I was wild-eyed and rowdy, loud and obnoxious, filled with devil-may-care energy. Coming off of it I was morose and moody and irritable and it made life hard for Jane and Carolyn.

But I was becoming a big-time guide, everyone wanted to hire me and I was turning away more people than I had time to take.

At the end of the summer in 1953, I had a big Labor Day weekend planned with enough clients lined up wanting to fish Norfork to make me almost one hundred dollars. Mr. Briggs fired my helper, a man who was a com-

I didn't do much with my little girl but she got to go fishing a lot.

bat veteran of World War II, because he wanted the holiday off. He had been working with me and we had a car which the owner wanted ready the following Monday. This was a guy who had part of his face gone from a wound suffered overseas and he was a fine decent person who seldom asked for anything. And because he wanted a holiday off, Briggs fired him. That was enough for me.

I went in and told Mr. Briggs I would sand, mask and paint that car over the weekend but I needed forty dollars to hire someone to help me, since he had just fired my helper. He gave it to me in cash and on Thursday night I took a dexadrine capsule and went to work. I painted the car red, white and blue, without sanding it. I painted the wheels and tires and bumpers and windshields.. the whole works, red white and blue. Then in the middle of the night I headed for Norfork with that forty dollars and a weekend of guiding fishermen at a place called Schmidt's resort.

I didn't go back to Briggs Brothers of course. Janie packed everything and when I got back to St. Louis we loaded up and headed for California where her mother lived. That tells you a little bit about how far I had come since returning from the war. Everything we owned we loaded in the back of a 1941 Desoto.

Some of the happiest days of my life were those
spent on the Piney after moving back home.

Chapter 23
A Full Time Fishing Guide

I don't have much good to say about California. Joe Weis contacted me to let me know that Mr. Briggs was trying to have me arrested and brought back. Joe was becoming a very influential person by then, rising quickly in the bank. He had a friend who was a lawyer who promised I wouldn't have to worry about being arrested but he suggested I stay out of Missouri for awhile. I got a good job right off the bat in Oxnard, California, making unbelievable money painting cars, so it wasn't hard to stay there. Through the winter all I did was work and save money.

Jane was enjoying herself, being there with her mother and sister, and the climate was great. But there wasn't much there I liked... no fishing, no hunting, and people who looked much differently at life than we did in the Ozarks. If you lived for money and the things it could buy I guess you couldn't beat California. But I knew I didn't want to spend my life living like they did. And I didn't want my daughter growing up like California kids I saw around me. And so that spring we came back to the the place where I really always wanted to be... the Big Piney.

We moved into an old house in the country and Jane got a job at that variety store where Mom had worked, for the old tightwad who had the heart attack on the float trip. I let everyone in St. Louis know I was guiding and kept burning up the road to Norfork and Bull Shoals. Best of all Pop and I were close again. He'd go with me on some of those trips, especially when there were large groups and they wanted to catch catfish.

And we spent a lot of time that year guiding float fishermen on the Piney and a tributary, the Little Piney. Sometimes Pop and I would spend a night or two on the river and set trotlines and catch bullfrogs. And Bryce and Vaughn and Farrel were all living there around Houston too. We had the chance to do things together again. It was a great life.

Mr. Emmick and Doc Schmeimier came down often. One weekend, Doc brought his wife to the Big Piney and decided he'd go on a float trip on his own. I was off somewhere on the lakes and Pop told him he'd send Bryce or Vaughn along to paddle for him, but Schmeimier decided he had watched me paddle a boat long enough to do it for himself. He always referred to a boat paddle as an idiot stick and he figured anyone could make a johnboat go down the river.

We had been catching some nice smallmouth out of the Little Piney so he wanted to float that smaller and rougher stream. It was up about a foot after a rain and he should never have tackled it, but he did. He swamped the boat on rough shoals three times and lost some tackle and other things. And his wife got caught between the boat and some willows and nearly drowned. She had a big bruise on her side and down one leg and was pretty upset with her husband. I think it was her first and last float trip. Doctor Schmeimier said he'd never again call a boat paddle an idiot stick.

In the fall of 1954 I began to guide clients at Schmidt's resort across the Arkansas line at Norfork Lake. It just sort of snowballed. As more and more people began to catch bass they spread the word and eventually there were more fishermen asking for me at the resort than I had time to guide. Jim Schmidt finally offered me a full-time job and his best cabin for us to live in. It seemed like the opportunity of a life-time. So early in 1955 we packed up again and moved to Norfork Lake in Arkansas.

I liked Jim Schmidt, he was an easy-going, shy type of fellow who made lots of friends. He and his wife had moved from St. Louis several years before, where he had been a top-of-the-line builder and contractor. On Norfork, he built a dozen cabins, an office and a small restaurant and a boat dock. He supplied the docks with rental motors and boats and couldn't keep up with it all. Jim wasn't real ambitious. Sometimes he didn't get up until 8:00 a.m. I was always up an hour before first light if I went to sleep at all and I'd take care of all the customers who had rented boats and motors, seeing to it all the tanks were filled with gas and mixed with oil and that everyone was happy and enjoying themselves. Jim never paid me for any of that but I got ten dollars for every guided trip I took and when an acceptable limit of bass was caught the trip was over.

Sometimes I'd go out with a couple at daylight and be back by 10:00 a.m., ready to take out another pair of fishermen. Sometimes on weekends in May and June I'd have three different parties out during the day and then another party out at night. When you added tips to that, I was making money like I never had. And I was selling Paul Hauser's Hell-Divers like hot-dogs at the ball game and making a little bit on that too. It seemed that Jane and Carolyn were happy at first, we finally were able to save some money and buy the things we needed. Carolyn was going to school in Viola, Arkansas, a small town school where they still taught some values that I agreed with even if I didn't always live up to them as well as I should.

Jim's wife was an accountant and bookkeeper who kept all the records and reservations and financial matters. She wasn't the easiest person to get along with and was always watching me to be sure I wasn't stealing gas or something. She had been a lawyer in St. Louis and probably should have stayed with it. The woman smoked more cigarettes in one day than anyone I've ever seen and if she was ever real happy, she hid it well.

Jane cleaned cabins and helped in the restaurant and even began to guide some fishermen herself. She was finally completely well and healthy and strong and I had taught her how to paddle a boat and where the fish were. Jane could take fishermen out and get them into bass or crappie as well as I could. She was very pretty and very outgoing and there were plenty of fishermen who would much rather go fishing with her than me.

But those serious anglers who wanted big bass knew I

was the best there was for that. To get the big ones, you fished at night. And to guide fishermen day and night all week-end, I had to go without sleep. The dexadrine was still the answer. Sometimes I'd take a pill on Friday and Saturday and Sunday and not go to sleep until sometime on Monday. When I did, I slept for twelve or fifteen hours and would wake up with a terrible headache. But I'd be over it by mid-week and ready to go again. Jim Schmidt learned to tell fishermen not to count on me on Mondays and part of Tuesday because I had to have time to come off that dexadrine.

As I said before, I wasn't the easiest guy in the world to live with on that stuff. I would be so wired up I couldn't sit still and so happy I couldn't quit singing. And then I'd go from that to terrible headaches and depression and being mad at the world. I lost weight because I never ate much of anything. I'd eat a little bit once or twice a day and drink lots of black coffee. At one time after returning from the war I weighed 160 pounds. During that first summer on Norfork I got down to 125 pounds. But there were so many people wanting to fish and so little time. Doc Schmeimeir told me it wouldn't hurt me if I had the heart to take the strain and he said he'd never seen a man stronger than me.

What I really enjoyed, and when I really relaxed, was those times when Joe Weis and Mr. Emmick could come down, or when Pop could come down and fish. My dad was getting old. He turned sixty in 1956 but he was still as strong as most men are at forty. And he still loved to set trotlines for catfish, and on Norfork in the fifties, we really caught them. Norfork wasn't far from the Piney so I still took a day or so every now and then to go float the river I had grown up on and spend some time with Pop.

Even then, every now and then he'd get mad about something I had done and call me a blankety-blank Harris. Pop was still hot-headed and eccentric and he could rant and rave with the best of them when things didn't go to suit him. It was about that time that I left a bogus note on

Pop loved Norfork Lake but he wasn't impressed much by big bass. To him the only fish was a catfish.

his door as a joke on his birthday. I signed it from the Klu-Klux-Klan, saying they were tired of him catching all the catfish out of the river and intended to tar and feather him and run him out of town. I figured he'd know it was me and laugh about it but he didn't. He loaded his shotgun and went to town looking for whoever the Klu-Klux-Klan was. The local sheriff took him home and later I had to go in and tell them it was all a joke. The prosecuting attorney didn't laugh and he told me that my little joke had nearly landed me and Pop both in jail. I had finally learned to write and that's what it got me!

About that time, a local bass fisherman by the name of Shorty Evans hired Pop and I to go to Wisconsin with him and a friend of his to fish a lake up close to the Canadian border for muskies. We took along an aerated tank of some sort with live suckers from the Big Piney river. Shorty Evans was a great fisherman, he was about ten years older than me and had started out in the funeral home business, then later got to producing trolling motor propellers and some other outdoor products and he had the money and time to fish a great deal.

Shorty spent a lot of time at Bull Shoals when it was new, then fished Greers Ferry after it filled. He did some tournament fishing later on when the tournament craze was just beginning. And I learned a lot from him, especially about how to fish a jig and eel, which back in the early days was just a lead-head and hook with a hairy body and a long pork strip of six or eight inches in length. Nothing will catch more big bass even today, but you have to learn how to fish it and there's a knack to it. I learned it from Shorty.

Pop and I were going to paddle the boats for Shorty and his fishing partner in Wisconsin and that would have been just fine if it hadn't been for the trip. Shorty Evans didn't drive, he flew. If I hadn't been on dexadrine most of the trip I think I would have had a nervous breakdown. Shorty didn't intend to waste any time, he wanted to get there and fish and that's what we did. Thank goodness he was also a good driver, he had spent years driving an ambulance which his funeral home operated. The hospital was in Springfield, ninety miles away and Shorty had a lot of emergency trips when he put it on the floor and kept it there. He looked at that muskie trip to Wisconsin as another emergency. Pop and I were so happy to get there alive we enjoyed the paddling. The two fishermen did catch some nice muskie, up to twenty pounds or so... and then we went back home about like we went up there. I fished with Shorty a few time in years to come but I never rode with him, I always took my own car. But if I had ever needed to go to the hospital I would have wanted him for a driver!

Mr. Emmick and I took a trip in the winter of 1955 down to Florida to fish for bass in the St. John's river, where there were some real monsters being caught. We fished there for one day with spinnerbaits and various lures and hardly caught anything. A fellow back at the bait shop told us if we wanted to catch bass, we'd need to fish with the big shiner minnows that everyone used and he gave us ideas about where to catch the really big ones. Those shiner minnows were great big things about six or eight inches long as I remember, and cost about a dollar apiece. Back then, that was unheard of, paying that kind of money for bait. I remembered back home on the Piney when we sold a whole bucketful of minnows for a nickel to fishermen at the Lone Star Mill.

But we bought some anyway, and Mr. Emmick caught several nice bass that day and I caught one. Using the biggest minnow we had, I fished it along a grassy bank beneath a float and hooked a tremendous largemouth. I figured I had a nine or ten pound bass but he wasn't fighting like one. There was five minutes or so of hard lunges down deep and then an attempt to get back under the boat and I got a net under him. When I did, I couldn't believe my eyes. It was the biggest bass I had ever caught or ever would catch. We weighed him several hours later at the bait shop and the bass tipped the scales several ounces over twelve pounds.

It was a strange looking bass, with tremendous girth and a huge head. The tail seemed tapered and small and it wasn't colored anything like an Ozark bass, much darker without much spotting or marking. As big as it was, the guy at the bait shop said he had seen a dozen bigger ones that winter. He said the real lunkers there on that river were the ones above fourteen pounds. I figured the guy was lying at the time but I've learned since that he wasn't.

We left for Louisiana the next day and I gave all our bass to some people who wanted to eat them. There wasn't any use in trying to get them back home, we had too many days yet to be gone. Mr. Emmick had some relatives he wanted to see in Louisiana so we went there and fished a couple of days in a lake beginning to fill in the Atchafalaya River basin. It was a mess at that time, with lots of mud to deal with just getting into a place to fish, and the wind was strong and the waves high. But the place was full of bass and they liked the spinnerbaits and crankbaits we used back home, unlike the Florida bass. I never got any big ones though, about four pounds was tops. When we headed back home I had already decided that I had the best fishing in the world right there in the Ozarks

It was about 1956 when I began to guide on Bull Shoals out of Al Cooperman's Resort and also on the White River and Crooked Creek while working out of Schmidt's resort. I bought a new Pontiac station wagon and I'd take one of Pop's wooden johnboats to those rivers. We would just slide the boat in the back of that station wagon with the back seat folded down, and head for the river with it. Of course on the White River it was all trout fishing and nothing but rainbow trout back then. The water was cold and clear and to catch fish you had to use very small clear line. It wasn't my type of fishing but there were lots of people who wanted to try it, especially when it got hot in July and August. That cold water in the White made it a little more tolerable when the temperature reached 95 or 100 degrees.

I learned from other trout fishermen how it was done

and it was nothing like the kind of fishing trips we took on the unaltered Ozark rivers. On the White you had different water situations to contend with and sometimes you just drifted sideways with the current, letting a nightcrawler drift along behind you. On other occasions, when there wasn't much current, you could fish small jigs or natural bait in deeper pools. I never looked at it as fishing. I never considered trout as real fish, just something they brought in from somewhere to live in water where real fish couldn't survive. How those people could be so happy about catching something twelve-inches long was beyond me.

Occasionally though, someone would catch a four or five pound rainbow and there were a few even bigger than that. One of the most memorable trips I ever took was the day that an Indianapolis woman caught a rainbow trout nearly twenty pounds in weight. I would have bet anything she'd never land it but we kept at it and the current was just about right for her. We drifted a mile or better and she fought it for twenty or thirty minutes. Finally she had it worn down and I got in near a gravel bar and jumped out waist deep in that icy water and pushed it up on the bar. It was too big for the net we had. And in all these years, no one I have guided for ever landed a bigger fish or anything close.

I caught my first ten-pound largemouth that year out of Norfork, fishing with Mr. Emmick. We had just had one heck of a big rain and the lake was coming up, all the tributaries muddy. I got back in the end of a cove and one of the little creeks that came in was really rolling. Fishing that muddy water coming in, using a yellow-skirted Hell-Diver, I hooked him and landed him and knew I had finally reached a level as a bass fisherman that few people would reach. I had taken several bass from Norfork and Bull Shoals which weighed from eight and one-half to nine and one-half pounds and I had seen people catching fish that size and putting lead weights in the gullet to get them over nine pounds. One of the guides on Norfork was notorious for that. He claimed to already have three or four ten pounders but none of them really were. Several people who fished with him a lot said that ten-pound, two-ounce bass I brought in that day was the first one they had seen that really did exceed ten pounds without any help.

In February of 1957, Bryce and Joe and I were fishing back up that same creek after a late winter warm spell and I caught a smallmouth bass on a red Hauser Hell-Diver which was perhaps the most impressive bass I'll ever catch. It weighed seven pounds and three ounces and fought like a tiger. We took it up to Smitty's taxidermy in Mountain Home, Arkansas and because I couldn't afford to have it mounted, I just gave it to him. It was there in that shop for a lot of years. That was a spectacular fish, and in looking back on it, I think it was more of an accomplishment than catching a fifteen pound largemouth.

Smallmouth exceeding seven pounds are occasionally taken in some of the reservoirs in the south but almost never in the Ozarks. In all my years of fishing, I never caught another small-mouth above six pounds. But back then there were so many big fish and it was so easy to catch them, I always expected to catch something bigger any day. I never even got a picture of that big smallmouth. Jim Schmidt did. He took a picture of the fish which hung on the picture board at the resort for a long time. A sign under it said it was the biggest smallmouth ever taken out of Norfork Lake and for a while I guess it was. But several years later a smallmouth a couple of ounces larger was taken and then an even bigger one was taken from Bull Shoals.

I think it was the spring of that same year that we took our first float trip on Crooked Creek, which flowed into the White River below Bull Shoals. Crooked Creek was a wild little Ozark stream which started over near Harrison, Arkansas and flowed eastward past Yellville. There was about 30 miles of great fishing between those two towns and as good as fishing was on the Big Piney and the Meramec when I was a kid, nothing ever equaled Crooked Creek as a smallmouth stream. Mr. Emmick made that first trip with me and we caught more smallmouth than I had ever seen before, lots of them from two pounds to three pounds and maybe a half-dozen fish between three and four pounds. It was a stream with lots of drop and some of the shoals were really wicked, but it was fun to run them and the swift water was filled with bass. When Crooked Creek was low, it could get so clear the bigger bass were hard to catch, but after a rain when it was dinghy colored or even a little muddy and rising, you could fish a big spinner bait and catch some whoppers... deep-sided, dark-bodied smallmouth which knew how to use the current to their advantage.

From sometime in late February, when the weather broke and we began to get some spring type temperatures, all the way through most of June, I was busier than a wind-mill in a hurricane. But in July and August and part of September, fishing was more difficult and I had lots of time, because no one wanted to pay a guide to go swimming and in the heat it was more fun to swim than to fish. During those late summer months the night fishing was still very good and I could catch big bass on jigs with eels and the Hell-divers. And some fishermen liked the night fishing so there was some business but there were too many who were afraid of the lake at night and they wanted to fish during the day. I knew I had to figure out ways to catch fish during the summer so that I could take clients fishing during the day and still catch some nice fish.

Jim Schmidt had a big spotlight which operated off a twelve-volt battery and I took that out one dark July night and began to look down into the water to see where the bass were. I tried to learn as much as I could about where bass stayed at various seasons of the year and it became obvious to me that they were very deep in July and August, off points and along ledges near the channels. Some would move into shallower water late and early and feed for a short time but then they would end up back in deep water most of the day. Northern fishermen were catching fish trolling and I got the idea that it would work on Norfork and Bull Shoals.

A Full Time Fishing Guide

I talked to other fishermen who were having some success that way and I bought some Hellbenders, Bombers and Martin Lizards, and started trolling. At first I wasn't getting very good results. I had to get a new reel to make it work. I bought a Shakespeare Glass-Kid which would hold much more line than my Langley casting reel and I filled it with 100 yards of ten pound line. Finally, after I began to troll seventy yards behind the boat, I began to catch bass. And I also began to catch lots of white bass and an occasional crappie. When you hooked a crappie back then trolling those big lures, you had a dandy fish. And I found out that ten pound line was too light, so I went to fifteen pound test.

It was a balancing act because the heavier the line, the higher the lure would ride in the water. If you got too heavy with the line you couldn't get down as deep as you needed to get. And to have luck trolling in July and August and early September, you needed to get down around thirty-five or forty feet deep. Today you won't catch fish that deep in those lakes and I think maybe it's because the quality of the water is much less today. Pollution was something we didn't know about in the fifties, but we know about it now.

One of my first trolling customers may have been the richest one I ever had as well. His name was Dave Anderson and he was a wealthy farmer with more land back in Illinois than all of the land Norfork Lake covered. He had some other things going, some different businesses besides farming, and obviously money didn't mean much to him. He flew into Mt. Home and always stayed several days each year that I guided at Schmidts. I got to know him very well and I liked him.

Anderson had enjoyed some great fishing trips with me but he had never caught a really big bass over seven pounds, and that was unusual, because most fishermen who worked at it would get one that size in a couple or three days of fishing. He was also something of a sporting man. He came down in September of 1959 and wanted to take back a real

306

lunker. He said he wasn't interested in catching a lot of fish, he wanted to catch some big ones.

He challenged me to help him catch that once-in-a-lifetime lunker by proposing to pay me one hundred dollars for every bass above seven pounds which he landed. On the other hand, if he didn't catch any bass above seven pounds, he would owe me nothing. One hundred dollars was about all I would make out of any three day period so I figured I would come out ahead regardless. I took him up on that challenge and told him I hoped he had several hundred dollar bills with him.

As luck would have it, that was the week that my daughter Carolyn was in a beauty pageant or something of that sort at school. I had pulled my old silk parachute out of a trunk, the one I kept from my very last jump in France, and had a local seamstress make her a gown out of it. It made a beautiful dress and everyone said Carolyn was just gorgeous in it. She was sixteen years old and growing up in a hurry. But she wasn't too thrilled with a dress made out of a parachute. She was her mother's daughter and more and more they were both growing tired of the life I had made for them on Norfork. It was understandable. For three years we had lived in a fishing cabin, doing without much of the things other families enjoyed. And the lake and fishing was my whole life, I didn't know much about anything else.

Where I had grown up that little fishing cabin would have been a mansion. Jane and Carolyn weren't satisfied with that life and if I had been a better husband and father I would have known it. But I was consumed with what I was doing and putting money in a bank account for the first time in my life. On top of that I was living much of my life on dexadrine. The Friday night that Carolyn was in the beauty pageant at school was the night I was to take Dave Anderson fishing for a lunker bass and I couldn't change those plans because he had been looking forward to this one trip all year. Jane was awfully mad and we had a big fight about it. Jim Schmidt finally said he would take them in to school that night and I took Dave Anderson fishing.

We were out most all night and then back out on the water again at dawn. Trolling a Martin Lizard about 10:00 that morning he hooked and landed his third bass of the fishing trip over seven pounds, and this one was the biggest, better than nine pounds. I had made 300 dollars. When Anderson and I came in that morning, jubilant with our success, Jane was gone. She and Jim Schmidt had gone to Mountain Home to file for a divorce.

It didn't take me completely by surprise. There hadn't been any love in our marriage for some time and I suspected that something had been going on between the two of them. But I didn't really care anymore. Carolyn was old enough to make up her mind where she wanted to go and what she wanted to do. We had at least made it that far,

to give our daughter a foundation of some kind and the chance at a good life. But our marriage had been a mistake, the kind of mistake dumb kids make when they are too young to think straight and too passionate to care.

I slept off the dexadrine and early the next week, signed the papers which gave Jane everything we owned and our bank account. It had grown to a few thousand dollars and I told her if she wouldn't ask for alimony or child support she could have it all. I had my station wagon, my fishing gear and the 300 dollars which Dave Anderson had given me. Jim and Jane and Carolyn headed to California where her mother still lived and Georgia Schmidt took over the resort. I took another dexadrine and headed for Bull Shoals where a new client waited for a week-end of fishing. Right then, all that was left in life was the quest for one more big bass.

Mr. Emmick and I caught this string of bass
during a storm on Norfork in the '50's.

Chapter 24

A New Life

I never did like Georgia Schmidt much and she liked me even less. I stayed on at the resort until the middle of November and when a real bad cold spell hit, she closed it for the winter. I drove back to St. Louis to see my sister Zodie and while I was there I really did a stupid thing. I stopped by Briggs Brothers to see how everyone was doing. Heck, except for old man Briggs, I liked those guys, and they liked me.

When you are down and out, you go looking for old friends. Joe Weis was a bank officer by then and he told me they had been coming in the bank asking about me. So I just strolled in there about Thanksgiving like nothing had ever happened. It was quite a reunion until Harold Briggs Sr. came down to see what all the ruckus was about.

He stood there looking at me for awhile as if he couldn't believe his eyes. Then he stuck out his hand and told me it was good to see me and commented that I had lost a lot of weight. "Guess you're back here looking for a job," he said.

"Nope," I told him, "I'm a fishing guide now, wouldn't work here for a million dollars.

"Good," he said, "'cause we ain't got no work and if we did I wouldn't hire you... unless you wanted to paint cars."

"What's it pay and when do I start?" I asked.

Mr. Briggs offered me a pretty good hourly wage and he threw in an apartment above the shop. It was nothing fancy, just a place to sleep with a kitchen where I could cook my own meals. And he said I could set up my own hours during the winter so I could be free to hunt and fish when I needed to. He just wanted to be sure I wouldn't paint any more cars like I had that last one. I promised that wouldn't happen again.

It wasn't a bad life, on my own again and free from all obligations. I bought a new 1960 Buick and went in debt for that. I went back to the Big Piney before Christmas and hunted ducks with Pop, made a fishing trip to Tablerock with Mr. Emmick and didn't save a penny. I just lived from day to day and enjoyed it.

Joe was recovering well from that leg operation and he and I hunted every chance we got that winter. He was single too and lined me up with quite a few ladies that he thought would be perfect for me. Most of them liked to party and drink and so I didn't date anyone more than once or twice. I liked to do the simple things in life, like go to ball games, float the river and fish for bass. Parties weren't for me and neither was alcohol. I had enough problems with cigars and dexadrine. I had also decided I would never make the mistake of getting married again. But I didn't know about Velma.

There was a restaurant just down the street where she worked and a couple of the guys who worked with me told me about her. She was blonde but smart, built like a brick backhouse and all business, with no flirting. They said you

couldn't get her to pay attention to you at all, she just didn't like men like us. I told them all that she hadn't seen me yet, I could have her all starry-eyed in ten minutes with my new Buick and my Stetson hat.

After I met Velma I had my first studio picture taken. Couldn't understand how she could resist me. Somehow she did.

And so eventually I wound up betting everyone of them five dollars that I could get a date with this waitress in only one week. When I met her I thought maybe I had lost a good days wages. This lady was a knockout all right but cold as sleet. She didn't smile at all and you could see she was very unhappy. I didn't know it then but she had just recently gone through a divorce herself, from a man she had adored but who had become abusive and a heavy drinker. For two or three days I did everything I could do to get her to pay attention to me. Finally I got her to talking a little and I took it from there, telling her all about my history and fighting in the war and my love of the outdoors. It was fishing that finally won her over just a little. She had grown up near the confluence of the Bourbeuse and the Meramec and had fished there on occasion and she loved it.

Velma told me she had often sat there on the bank, fishing for drum and catfish with bait, watching people float by and wondering what it would be like to go floating. Little did she know her time was gonna come. I wonder, looking back at all the times I floated through that area working for Alton Benson as a kid, just how many times we were only a stones throw apart. I told her about those days and convinced her that her best chance to finally take that float trip was me, the best float-fishing guide in all the state and maybe even the whole world.

Finally just before the weekend I went in for coffee and told Velma I was so lonely and bored I just didn't know what to do with myself. I knew I'd never get her to go out with me alone but I had a plan. I told her that if she'd go to a movie with me on Friday night I would take her and any friend she wanted to take, just to show how innocent my intentions were. All I wanted was an enjoyable evening, I said, and that was the truth. Of course I also wanted to win that bet.

Brother I did some talking that morning. I think Velma finally agreed to go just to get me to shut up, as everyone in the cafe was beginning to pay attention. She said she'd go if she could take her cousin along and I said we'd not only take her cousin, I'd pick that lady up at her own doorstep in my new Buick. And then came the difficult part. I told Velma I'd like to pick her up at the drugstore across from Briggs Brothers shop. She agreed and I could have turned handsprings. The guys at the shop wouldn't know a thing about the cousin, they'd all think I was a real ladies man. But the best thing was, they'd owe me five bucks apiece.

When I met her at Herrings Drug Store that evening at 5:00 o'clock, all the guys at the shop were watching and I felt like a million bucks. This little waitress who had always dressed so modestly had on a beautiful dress and high heels and her hair was fixed really nice and my jaw nearly fell open. We picked up her cousin and went to dinner somewhere and I found myself really enjoying talking to Velma. I was having a great time in spite of her cousin, who was about half goofy. Then I had an awful thought. What if we went to the movie and I had to sit by her cousin!

It was a MarIon Brando movie, a western called "One-Eyed Jacks". I got to sit by Velma. I used my head and let them sit down first while I got some popcorn. Then I got the good seat. Not that it mattered that much. All I got to do was hold her hand and we were most of the way through the movie before I could do that. I remember telling myself that Velma could have been a school teacher; she was so wary of me.

Hot dang, was it a great evening. I found myself enjoying everything far more than I had ever supposed I would. But it was over too soon. Velma and her cousin both had to work the next morning and Velma's apartment was closer to the theater so I got to take her cousin home last. I never heard a word the girl said all the way home and she said a lot of them. I was thinking about Velma.

Back at the shop on Monday I collected a pretty good chunk of money from the Briggs brothers and a couple of the other employees. Then disaster struck! One of those idiots who didn't know what was going on went into the restaurant and told one of the waitresses that I had to buy coffee that day because of the big bet I had won. It got back to her in short order and for a week she wouldn't even speak to me. I kept going back in and drinking coffee, buying one cigar at a time, doing anything to get a chance to apologize. But it was like I didn't exist. Sleet never got that cold!

It was really beginning to get to me because I really liked this lady and I had broken the ice only to wind up in cold water... cold, deep water. So I told her that if that stupid bet was standing between us I'd give everyone back the money

I had won and just to show her I was really interested in
her and nothing else, I'd go ahead and pay everyone just
as though I had lost. I only asked that she go to the movies
with me again and give me a chance to show her how sorry
I was. Thank goodness I never had to give back the money.
Finally she gave in just to get me out of her hair.

My real break came when she decided to move in with
her cousin and I spent the weekend helping her move. She

was beginning to see that I was sincere. We went out to the movies several times and I think she made me dinner once. So I decided I'd take her home to meet my parents and take her on a float trip on the Piney. You never really know a lady until you take her float-fishing. And Velma was finally going to go on a float trip, like she had -always dreamed of doing.

My brother Bryce had married some girl named Betty, from over in the Southeast Missouri swamp country and I think the first time I met his new wife was on that float trip. Velma stayed with them and I stayed at Pop's place and we floated the Piney the next day with Bryce and Betty. I paddled the whole way and Velma learned to cast a push-button Zebco reel and fish with lures for the first time in her life. She caught some nice fish and it was a beautiful spring day and I think from that point on, I had her hooked. A good boat paddler is hard for a woman to resist!

We fished a lot that summer and when I proposed it was just a formality. I figured I'd better do it quick before she beat me to it. As the summer ended we made wedding plans and were married in September of 1961. That would make a pretty good place to end a book like this, but for me, it was the beginning of everything. Velma's parents had left her a little place out in the country near Pacific, about thirty miles southwest of St. Louis.

I built on to a small garage behind the house and had my own shop for the first time in my life. Slowly but surely the resentment and hatred that had developed in me since the war began to wane. I was beginning to think about the future instead of the past, beginning to forget about revenge and retaliation and taking what was mine regardless of the consequences. There were two people in my life responsible that, Velma and my old friend Carl Emmick.

Velma and Mr. Emmick really hit it off well and the three of us fished a lot together. I began to guide less and less for others because I was enjoying fishing with those few old reliable clients and spending as much time as I could with

A New Life

my wife. The dexadrine use ended with Velma. She saved my life with the ultimatum that I never take another one and I complied. Those pills had cost me one marriage and they had made me about half crazy. I threw out the last bottle on our first fishing trip together and never took another one. I figured out ways to fish at night and sleep during the day or take turns driving back when I was tired. And it was about that time that Dr. Schmeimier had a devastating stroke while on dexadrine. He was in his early fifties at the time. I knew I could live without the drugs and I wasn't sure I would live if I didn't do without them. Velma said it was pretty certain that I wouldn't live long if I kept taking them. She said if I ever took another one she'd kill me!

During those first few years I bought her a shotgun and a deer rifle and we did everything together. She killed a nice eight-point buck on the Big Piney in the early sixties and I took her mule-deer hunting in Colorado where she got a mule-deer. Joe Weis had been going out west hunting about every year since I had been divorced. When he saw how happy I was with Velma he decided he'd get married too. He chose the right girl, a red-head by the name of Mary Lou. They are still together and happily married today.

The sixties were great times for me, going back and floating the river with Pop every now and then and fishing Bull Shoals and Tablerock. I came to know a St. Louis lawyer by the name of Robert Burns who became a regular client. He and his son fished with me often. We made a couple of trips to Texas lakes and to Greers Ferry in North-Central Arkansas. I'll never forget one of those trips in March when Burn's son Randy decided he didn't like the lake in Texas and wanted to go back to Greers Ferry. Randy was soon to go to Viet Nam and it was an emotional trip. His dad wanted him to enjoy himself so we picked up and left Texas and headed for a resort on Greers Ferry.

That evening after we got there I walked down to the lake behind our cabin and began to fish a red Hauser Hell-Diver along the bank. There was a tangle of submerged briars and brush about a hundred yards down the bank and I decided I'd fish that good. It was blustery and raining a little and cold, like March usually is when you want to fish. I worked that spinnerbait around the edge of that flooded brush and a huge bass just engulfed it. I saw the flash of her side and I knew she was a dandy. And usually I'm going to win a fight like that because I have a trailer hook on those spinners, I have strong rods with lots of backbone and I have heavy line, back then about sixteen pound test. But on occasion you knick or fray the line on something and it is weakened, and when I tried to turn that big bass the line snapped. I could tell she was really something from the resistance she gave me before the line broke and I really moaned about it all night.

At first light the next morning it was cold and still and before Randy Burns and his dad got up and around, I went back down to that submerged rabbit thicket and started casting around it with a black Hell-Diver and a white pork rind, wondering if there might be another bass like the one the night before. And I know no one will believe this but you know what I'm about to tell you. I had never seen it happen before or since and if I hadn't seen it, I wouldn't have believed it either. That same bass, almost in the same place she had been, came up and took that spinner, just about like she had the evening before. This time my line was undamaged, but she was a handful. I got out in the water up to my crotch and put everything I had into it.

The bass gave it her best too but this time I would come out on top as I fought her to a complete surrender. When I pulled her into the shallows and lifted the bulging bass from the water, there was that red Hauser Hell-diver embedded in her jaw, the one she had broken off the night before. As I said, in all my years of fishing, I never saw that happen but that once. And that bass was my second ten-pound bass from the Ozarks, weighing a couple of ounces over.

A year later I took a St. Louis real estate man to Greers Ferry, a man by the name of Herman Mullenhoff. Fishing with him in the spring, I caught another bass a few ounces above ten pounds, this time on a jig and eel. Mullenhoff was so impressed with that bass he took it back and had it mounted and for many, many years it hung on the wall in his office on Gravois avenue in St. Louis.

In the mid-sixties Carl Emmick and I began to fish the Long Creek Arm of Tablerock and it was a real hotspot. That arm backed up across the Missouri border into Arkansas and in that time it was beautiful fishing water. The development which chokes the lake today hadn't begun yet and in that time there was only one boat on the lake for every 100 or 200 you'll see today. One of the greatest coves I ever fished in any lake was Clevenger Cove, back up in big part of that Long Creek arm on the east side. In the mid 60's you just couldn't fish it without catching several big bass.

It was brushy and filled with flooded timber and they really were in there. There was an old abandoned house there at the time and we took shelter there on occasion when a storm would pass through. I even slept in it a few hours or so when I was there by myself. Today there are lots of homes and cottages and it doesn't even look like the cove I once knew. Well heck, it's been more than forty years, I guess that's to be expected. But Mr. Emmick and I fished it a lot back then and I saw it when it was a fisherman's paradise. We would stay at Three Oaks Resort not far away, and catch boatloads of bass.

In 1965 I caught a bass out of Clevenger Cove which weighed eleven pounds and two ounces, my biggest Ozark bass to this point. It was in April and it was raining pretty steady so Carl stayed in the resort while I went back up in the end of Clevenger cove, wading around in a flooded thicket, casting a Hell-Diver with a pork rind and trailer hook. That lure looked two feet long because it was the biggest one I had and I put a ten or twelve-inch black pork eel on it. The rain was steady and it was fairly cold but I had on my waders and a good rain coat. My cigar had been out a long time and I was about to give it up. I had caught some bass but nothing to brag about.

When I cast into a flooded jungle of briars and small brush and lifted that big spinner bait up over the top of it, that whopper of a bass engulfed it and took it down into her hideaway. I had twenty pound line that day and good gear for a hard fight. The bass gave it all she had and I just leaned back on her and gave it all I had too. Since I had better footing than she had, I thought I would win out. With the rain pelting down and the lake rising with murky water I pulled that giant bass out of the water and couldn't believe my eyes. It was full of eggs, with tremendous girth and a huge mouth.

But what I saw then was even more unbelievable. The hook which I know had been well set into her jaw just after the strike, had come loose somehow and the pork rind eel was securely wrapped around the bony structure below the gills, where the rough, sharp protuberances of that part of the throat had made it impossible to dislodge. I'll never know how far I pulled that big fish without a hook in her but it wasn't a hook which brought her in, it was a long, tough pork eel.

A New Life

The people at Three Oaks Resort kept that bass to be mounted and the next spring they were all excited about a fishing contest Sports Afield magazine had going. If I could catch another big bass close to the size of that last one it would bring a great deal of publicity to their area. They had always been good to Mr. Emmick and me so I told them I would give it a try.

On Easter Sunday of 1966, I went farther up Long Creek than I had ever fished, way past Clevenger Cove to a place where an old roadbed went across the lake. The lake was rising and fairly muddy because a big rain had come before a cold front and we had arrived at the tail end of it. It was cold that day and it would snow awhile, then rain awhile, then sleet awhile and then the clouds would break for awhile. Carl Emmick was catching some crappie from the boat and so I got out and began to wade out onto that old road bed where some logs and rootwads had floated up. I got up on top of a log to make a cast and a big bass picked up the jig and eel I was using and moved away with it. I set the hook hard, lost my footing and came off the log as the bass headed for deeper water. That time, the bass had the better footing!

I got ahold of myself and finally got a good breath or two after the shock of the cold water. My bass was still on and she fought like a champion. I worked her around the logs and back toward the bank, finally pulling her out onto that old roadbed. The folks back at Three Oaks were really excited and they went about getting the bass officially weighed and flouroscoped to be sure it had no lead added to it. I got into some dry clothes and got warmed up and signed all the papers and affidavits as to how and where it had been caught.

It tipped the scales at ten pounds, four ounces, and I'll be darned if it didn't wind up being the biggest largemouth registered in Missouri in 1966, winning first place. The results were published in Sports Afield at the end of the year. I got a pin of some kind from the magazine and a new rod

322

and reel with a lot of lures and other fishing equipment. And the resort gave me a weeks stay free of charge the following spring. Velma and I started fishing there every time we had a few days free and she caught her biggest bass in Clevenger cove in 1967. It weighed eight pounds, six ounces.

In the summer of 1968, Mr. Emmick and I went on a float fishing trip on Crooked Creek which will always be one of the most unforgettable trips of my life. My old friend was growing old, nearly eighty at that time, and he didn't fish much that spring because he hadn't felt well. His heart was failing him and he knew it. A big rain had raised Crooked Creek in late July of that year and I told him we might get some big smallmouth bass if we caught it right. I wonder if I should have taken him but I remember how his eyes lit up and the prospect of a float trip and he was awfully happy as we headed down the big new highway out of St. Louis toward North-Central Arkansas.

It's a funny thing about smallmouth bass in an Ozark river. The big ones are tough to catch when the water is low and clear in the summer. They lay low under cover during the day and come out to feed at night. If you want to catch big smallmouth out of Crooked Creek or any other reasonably clear Ozark stream when it's low in the heat of the summer, go after them at night with jitterbugs and you'll get your arm pulled out of its socket. But they are going to be tough to catch when the sun is high and hot and the water is clear, unless you use small line and small lures. I don't use small line and small lures.

That all changes when a summer storm raises the stream a foot or two and the water goes from clear to murky. When that happens you can fish a big spinner bait or a large crankbait of some kind and just murder the bass. The bigger the lure, the bigger the bass, it seems.

That July of 1968 we had those conditions and Crooked Creek was wild and wooly. I fixed Mr. Emmick up with a comfortable seat and told him to enjoy the ride and just cast a lure when he wanted to. He wasn't at his strongest but he'd hook a bass on that big red Hell-Diver I tied on for him and fight it 'til both of them were wore out.

We stopped for lunch on a gravel bar and he took a long nap after we ate. As we loaded up to continue, I helped him into the old johnboat and he admired a couple of nice bass on the stringer. One was nearly four pounds.

"You know my boy," he said to me, "I've caught some nice bass in my life fishing with you but I fell short of one goal. I always wanted to catch a five-pound smallmouth and I never did."

I told him we were still going to have opportunities to get a lot more fish in years to come but he and I both knew better. And I would have just about given anything to have seen him catch one that size, but five-pound smallmouth are hard to come by. In all my years of guiding on rivers of the Ozarks I had seen less than ten caught and half of them came from Norfork and Bull Shoals Lakes rather than the rivers.

But I think maybe God intervenes from time to time when good people get his attention. Mr. Emmick was one of those good people and God was watching and listening that day on Crooked Creek. An hour later, in a swirling, bubbling pothole beneath a shoal, Mr. Emmick made a short cast and watched the line leave his reel against the drag. The water was swift and high and there was no stopping to fight that smallmouth in a gentle spot. We just rode the river and my old friend fought the fish for all he was worth. A quarter-mile or so downstream I got us out of the current and into some slack water and I netted a true five-pound smallmouth if I ever saw one.

The smile on Mr. Emmicks face was one of the greatest rewards I've ever experienced as a guide but he was done in. I helped him out of the boat in a nice grassy place and he lay back against the bank and admired that big brownie. He asked if I thought it was really a five-pound fish.

"You don't have to ask me that," I told him. "You've

seen enough big fish to know a five-pounder... and this one will beat that by several ounces."

We rested there and I could see he was very sick. "I think that's my last fish, my boy," he said to me, his voice weak and his face pale. I told him there'd be more trips and he'd feel better soon. He shook his head and asked me to turn the big bass back to the stream. I thought he must be out of his head and I argued against it. But I could see it was something he wanted...he was serious about it. And so I took it to the waters edge and watched it disappear into the murky water with a mighty swirl. Mr. Emmick nodded his approval.

I carried him over and laid him in the boat and made him as comfortable as I could and quickly ran the rest of the river to the take-out point. He slept most of the way back to St. Louis and I could see he was in awfully bad shape. Velma went with me to the hospital in the city and they admitted him that evening. I talked to him briefly and he said he was in no pain, just very, very tired. He passed away the next day as he slept, peacefully and without pain. It was about the greatest loss I had ever felt.

Doctors told me that his heart was so diseased that he had very little time left anyway. It wasn't just the fishing trip that was to blame, they said. Still, I felt as if I had made a mistake taking him on that float trip. And then I remembered how much he had enjoyed that last fish and how satisfied it had made him to release it when it was over. And I figure right then he was in heaven telling his family and old friends about that lunker smallmouth and all the others we had caught together. Even today, I can hear him saying, "We had some great times, my boy....we had some great, great times."

Pop was still strong at 70; still running the river in his johnboats, hunting and fishing and occasionally guiding someone else.

Chapter 25

A Tribute to Mom and Pop

The seventies began with tragedy. Pop turned 74 that year and had seemed to be as strong and healthy as ever. In fact he was still doing some trotlining on the Piney in the late 60's and catching some nice flathead catfish. But as the decade came to a close he began to feel tired and sick.

He was diagnosed shortly afterward with Lymph Gland cancer. He and Mom moved from his little cabin on Brushy Creek, where he had lived for the past twenty-five years without electricity or running water, to a senior citizens housing project in Houston. But on most days he would go back out to his place and sit on the back porch overlooking the creek, rocking in the old rocking chair which he had made, sometimes making a boat paddle or two for old friends.

I'd drive down and pick him up and take him to the veteran's hospital in St. Louis for treatment but nothing did much good. He passed away just before Christmas of 1970 and before he died he asked me to take his traps and destroy them so that no creature would ever have to suffer in one of them. He had known suffering and wanted no part in causing more of it.

I came to realize that as much as Dad enjoyed the outdoor life he had lived, he hated the idea of anything suffering. He had always taught us to never clean a fish until we had killed it quickly and he never liked the idea of a furbearer waiting in a leg hold trap through the night. Pop had trapped the river and used drown sets which brought a quick death to whatever he caught, or deadfalls which were even quicker. He had no choice in those early days but to trap. He was a riverman and he knew no other way to provide for a family. But I don't think trapping was something that brought him much pleasure. The outdoors did... he loved that river and the hills around it as only he and I can understand.

327

A Tribute to Mom and Pop

And it killed him to see it all being destroyed, to see all the freedoms he had as a boy come to end because there were such ever-increasing numbers of people. The people who destroyed the land did a greater harm to the wild creatures than the man who trapped them or hunted them. Was it less cruel to cut the den trees and poison the water than to set a trap to take a fur? Pop knew that a muskrat or a beaver or a raccoon or mink would never die peacefully. He had seen the struggle of predator and prey, he had witness the mink killing and eating a muskrat, the raccoon dying of distemper, the hawk eating the quail even before it was dead.

Pop knew that nature was harsh and that there was suffering every day. He showed us that struggle and helped us to understand it. He taught us a reverence for life. We learned to try to recover anything we hunted and utilize it to the fullest. If dad would have seen one of us kids treating an animal cruelly, we would have been in bad trouble. And he taught us that nature might not be as city people would like it to be but that God's hand had created perfection even in it's harshness. I think Pop expected heaven to be a great deal more like the world he knew, with tall trees and clean water and fish and wild ducks and furbearers, than with cities paved with streets of gold.

Pop didn't care anything about gold! Gravel bars and granite bluffs were his treasure. He knew God's greatness from a life spent seeing what He had created and watching Him continue to create. He sang no hymns from the front pew at the country church but he sang them as he paddled his johnboat down the river in a cathedral as magnificent as any ever made. He read the Bible, argued with it, took comfort from it, preached his version of it, and eventually accepted it when he got older and wiser and got tired of wrestling with it.

Pop wasn't a simple man, he was complicated, with periods of depression and mood swings that made him the hardest man in the world to get along with at times. He was eccentric and fiery on occasion and there were people who saw only that side of him and thought he was about half-crazy. I saw it all but I understood him. He was my hero, the greatest man I ever knew or ever will know. Pop didn't have to be perfect for me, I knew him and I saw a lot more good than bad. The good was all that mattered... what I remember.

Like all men, there were those who adored him and those who had no use for him at all. But if you went fishing with Pop you had a friend for life, because before you came back you understood who he was and his faults weren't so hard to overlook. If Pop liked you, you had no faults he could see. If you got on his wrong side when he was young, it was hard for Pop to get over it but he learned forgiveness as he grew old. He loved his family and loved to do things for the people he liked.

I watched him peacefully slip away to whatever reward his Creator may have arranged for him. I have to think it looks an awful lot like the Big Piney he knew as a boy, but without the hardship. Mom is there with him now. She died in 1999 at the age of 98, only thirteen months before her 100th birthday. As complicated as Pop was, Mom was steady and calm and solid. She was the rock of our family, the light that shined from the highest point. Truthfully, what most of us kids came to be in life was due to that angel of a woman whose faith and values never wavered. Pop preached his message, but Mom lived hers.

I'll make no pretense that life was as she might have wanted it.. it was rough. But she kept that smile and forged on and loved her family and others around her through the most difficult of times, a testimony to the belief she had in Jesus Christ and a better day to come through Him. I'll always remember how Pop would get carried away with his fish stories and embellish them a little and he would turn to Mom and say, "Ain't that right Tollie?"

Mom would always straighten him out with something like, "I don't think it was quite that big Fred." or "Well maybe we didn't catch quite that many."

Above: 1938 - Zodie, Norten, Farrel, Vaughn and Bryce
Below: 1998 - Farrel, Zodie, Vaughn, Bryce and Norten

Then Pop would have a fit! What could be worse than a fisherman and hunter winding up married to an honest woman? He loved her, I know that, and they did something right. All five of us kids are still doing great. Our lives have been blessed. Zodie and Bryce and Vaughn all live in Northwest Arkansas, and Bryce still operates a business in Springdale, still married to Betty, the web-footed girl who came from that swamp-east Missouri country. Vaughn, who went to Korea during that war, spent 30 years in Alaska, and he and his wife Elinor are now retired and still fishing with me quite often. Zodie recently wrote her own book about life in the depression years. She spent much of her life as a nurse and is retired and healthy. Farrel stayed in the Big Piney country all his life and kept building the wooden johnboats just like Pop made until just a year or so back. He and his wife Jessie have been married for 60 years now and never had an argument that lasted more than a week or two. They raised the nephew who is compiling this book for me and keeping all the exaggerations to a minimum.

It is a tribute to our parents that the five of us are still close and each of us has always been there for the others and always will be. We've had our squabbles from time to

Pop and Mom, 1968

1939

time but we've learned to respect one another and accept each other despite the differences we have. But we are a family, brothers and sisters today as we have always been and always will be. At a Dablemont family reunion a few years ago, we posed for the photo you see on the bottom of page 330. I think Pop and Mom were watching, and proud. Amongst their grandchildren and great grandchildren today there are teachers, ministers, nurses, doctors, counselors, bankers, lawmen, writers, business men and women. But not one lawyer, not one politician and not one game warden.

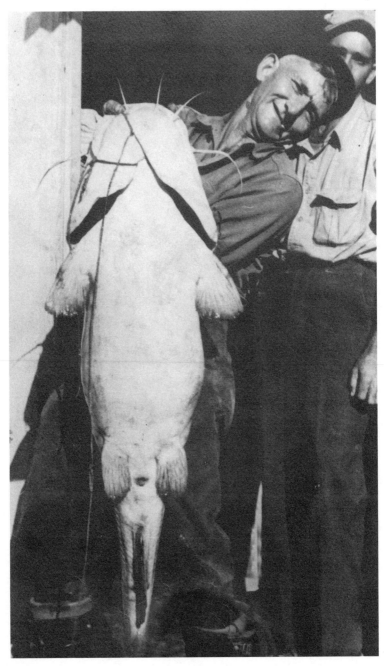

Northwest Arkansas in the late 60's and 70's was a fisherman's paradise. It was there that I became interested in catching big catfish again.

Chapter 26

To Arkansas and Back

Velma and I discovered Arkansas' Beaver Lake in the early 1970's. It was fairly new and another hot lake for bass. But there was something else there which drew me like a magnet, two rivers which had once flowed into the White River just to the east of Rogers in North Arkansas just south of the Missouri border. They were, in that day, a couple of the best float streams I have ever seen, rivaling the Big Piney in it's heyday, and right up there with Crooked Creek. They were the Kings River, flowing into upper Tablerock Lake, and the War Eagle river, flowing into Beaver Lake.... pearls of the Arkansas Ozarks.

I went down there often to float them with my brother Bryce who was living in Springdale and operating his own body shop. When I learned a little about them I started taking Robert Burns and his son Randy to float them. The Kings was a beauty, with clear clean water and high bluffs and timbered watersheds. It was primarily a smallmouth stream with a few Kentuckies and largemouth. The War Eagle, flowing in the same general northerly direction only thirty miles to the west, was different. It was full of rock bass and had plenty of smallmouth too, but more large-mouth than any Ozark stream I had ever seen. It was a bit murkier and slower and the bluffs weren't as high.

We fished those streams and fished Beaver Lake as well. In 1972, Velma caught the second biggest bass of her life out of Beaver Lake, a little better than eight pounds. I found out more and more about the area and liked what I learned at least as far as the fishing was concerned. I'd go visit Bryce and we'd set some trotlines on occasion, and that's what really got me excited. Not only did I land some hefty flat-head catfish, Beaver had a strain of catfish which were near-ly white in color. Most folks called them white catfish and others said they were just a pale version of the blue cat but to me they looked entirely different than most blues I had

335

caught. And they were huge, it didn't take much effort to catch thirty or forty pound whites back then. Occasionally you'd get one fifty pounds. or better.

This big white cat came from Beaver Lake in the early '80's and weighed better than 50 lbs.

One morning in the fall of 1973 I woke up and found myself fifty years old.   I told Velma I wanted to go to Arkansas and retire and she said she was all for it. We sold all the property she had owned and bought a place east of Rogers, on Beaver Lake. For a year I did little but fish, trying to learn all I could about the big lake and the rivers around it. But the float-fishing and lake-fishing was slow to develop then. It was the new day of tournaments and bass boats and 150 horsepower motors. Suddenly the past-time of sport fishing was becoming a big money racket and the kind of people involved in fishing were in it for different reasons than the people who had been my clients in the past. Fishing would suffer because of this new trend.

I had a sixteen-foot Mon-Ark lake boat and a 9.9 horsepower motor. I'd take fishermen back into heavy cover and paddle that boat most of the time with my clients in front, casting to the most likely spots. Lake fishermen began to want to fish with guides who ran the big outfits, even though they might fish all day from the back of the boat and never cast to a spot the guide hadn't already hit. I'll never understand why a fisherman would tolerate that and still pay for it. I knew that I could get people into fish like no one could, but still, I took my fishermen to small areas and they couldn't go fast.

The day of the wooden johnboats ended sometime around the time Pop passed away. But in the sixties a company in Lebanon, Missouri, known as Lowe Boat Company, began making johnboats which were styled after Pop's wooden boats. In fact, the patriarch of that company, John Appleby, had come to pop in the early 1960's and ask if he could design a boat from aluminum with Pop's measurements and shape. The result was one of the best float-fishing boats ever made, called a Lowe Paddle-Jon. I have used one ever since and on most float trips I conduct with two people fishing with me, I use that boat.

But Robert Burns gave me another floating craft which I have depended upon heavily and that is a 19-foot square-sterned Grumman canoe. Made from airplane aluminum in Marathon, New York, that canoe is about the only one I would ever use for serious floating. I'd never even consider taking someone on a serious float trip in one of those seventeen foot capsize-and-chaos double-enders. Any canoe you want to paddle efficiently needs a squared stern and some stability. For thirty years now we have used those two boats, the Lowe johnboat and the Grumman, and nothing comes close to the things they will do if you learn to use a paddle efficiently and from one side.

In Arkansas I depended on a few people who had fished with me before and those who liked to float the rivers. One of them was a man by the name of Harry Beerman. He was an unusual story. When Harry was a kid of sixteen he banged up a car his dad had bought him and was really upset. I was working for Briggs then and he came in and asked me if I could fix it. It wasn't any big job, just a bent fender. I told him I'd take care of it for him and I worked way up into the night and made it look as good as new. He was always in there after that, talking to me about fishing. The kid went away to college and finally graduated and got a good job and wanted to learn to fish. I'd take him to places like Tablerock and Greers Ferry for very little money, but I liked him and he was becoming a good fisherman. In the late '60's he became a buyer for a major grocery company and shortly afterward bought his own company.

By the early 1970's Harry Beerman had become a grown man and he was rich. He started coming to Beaver Lake and he knew I was having a hard time getting my guide business off the ground, so he'd leave tips much greater than what I would charge him and bring Velma and I expensive gifts. Harry came often and I would have enjoyed fishing with him even if he hadn't paid me. He was just a great young man. About 1980 he bought his daughter a new bass boat and took her and her boyfriend out on the lake to demonstrate it for them. A bigger boat came by, throwing a high wake, and Harry was thrown out. His boat circled and ran over him and killed him instantly. Once again I had lost a great friend in a tragedy.

I made some more great friends there in Northwest Arkansas. During those first few years I was really into catching big catfish and people around the area began noticing that I was catching lots of impressive fish. In 1975, I caught a ten pound bass out of Beaver Lake, and a year or so later a forty-three pound striper. Sometime in there, I landed a seventy pound flathead catfish and some others better than fifty. Local newspapers carried some of the pictures and that kind of thing gets you business in a hurry.

But I made one friend and client in an unusual way. I began to go back up to the Big Piney and dig nightcrawlers which I couldn't find in the Beaver Lake area. Those earthworms they had on the Big Piney were great big things, twelve to fourteen inches long and so strong they often grabbed my potato fork and threw it back at me. There aren't many of them today, for some reason they too are nearly gone from places you once could find thousands and I think the chemicals and pollution in the river has something to do with that.

But at any rate, several local fishermen started buying some from me, and I used that money to pay for the trips back to Missouri. One of the anglers who liked to use them was a fellow by the name of Gene Paryzek, who had moved to Beaver from Chicago and retired. His wife was a buyer for Wal-Mart and they had bought stock in that company years before, so Gene could live comfortably and afford to hire the best guide in the country. I told him that was me! He became a regular client and a very good friend.

About that time I was fishing over on the Illinois river, west of Beaver Lake and close to the Oklahoma border, when I ran into a fellow by the name of Phil Mammel, who wanted to know if I ever guided for fishermen. He too was retired and he and his wife went on a float trip with me shortly afterward, also to become regular clients and good friends. Phil has floated rivers with me each and every year since, for more than twenty-five years, and I enjoy having him with me so much I should be paying him.

I picked up one of my best clients and best friends just by going to the dentist. He was a fisherman as well, or wanted to be. Doctor John Robert Bland fixed those teeth that were chipped on my last jump in France back during the war, and I told him I'd take him fishing. He went on one float trip with me and told me to hold all my Thursdays open for him, that was his day off. He was the first float fisherman I took to the Fourche Ia Fave River down in the west Arkansas Ouachita mountains. On the lower Fourche Ia Fave just above Nimrod lake, Dr. Bland hooked a bass in the spring of 1979 which was the biggest largemouth I've ever seen in a river. I believe it would have been a ten pound bass or close. He fought it well and I started to net the fish and knocked it off the hook with the edge of the dipnet.

Dr. John R. Bland on The Fourche River

If that would have happened to me, I think I might have choked the culprit, but Doc Bland wasn't upset. He said he'd catch a bigger one, and the fight was worth it all anyway, even without the fish. Heck, people like that make any fishing trip a great day to be alive.

In the early '70's, my nephew Larry Dablemont, moved to Harrison, Arkansas, about an hour east of me, near Bull Shoals, Tablerock and Crooked Creek. He had guided float-fishermen on the Big Piney as a boy in the early '60's, and together in the '70's and early '80's we combined to guide fishermen on one or two-day float trips on the Ozark rivers of north Arkansas, the War Eagle, Kings, Buffalo and Crooked Creek.

In the late nineties, the two of us, both back in Missouri by then, started taking parties of fifteen or twenty floaters at a time down Missouri's Niangua river on interpretive float trips like nothing I ever imagined. Those folks never even fished and they still liked it! We still do that, even today, two or three times a year, usually in the fall, and we have a big fish fry. We have several other guides on those trips now and sometimes the group numbers thirty or forty.

Sometime in the late '70's Larry and I took a party of fishermen which included country music entertainer Grandpa Jones on a float trip on the Kings River. He was pretty distraught about then, he had lost his best friend only weeks before, the Grand Ol' Opry Comedian known as "Stringbean" to everyone familiar with country entertainment. Grandpa and Stringbean were regulars then on the T.V. show "Hee-Haw" which was very popular back at that time. Stringbean and his wife had been shot and killed by intruders in their home when they returned late one evening from a performance.

To Arkansas and Back

One of the fishermen caught a big bass that day but Grandpa didn't catch anything spectacular. He went back to the Grand Ol' Opry and told them that he had fished with me and caught a 'whole jar-full' of fish. He got to hear me sing some so that had to be worth something. He said that I had a good voice and if I had got started singing a little earlier in life I probably would have still been a good fishing guide.

I stayed in Northwest Arkansas until 1997, quite a while after the fishing began to decline. Beaver Lake became heavily developed and overfished and began to become polluted by a variety of problems. The Fayetteville area boomed and everything from there went into Beaver Lake or the Illinois river. The Kings became a real estate developer's dream on the lower end and big homes began to appear on the high ground above the river. The War Eagle declined overnight as the poultry industry smothered the Ozark hills and the watershed above it. Huge poultry operations sprang up, with very little concern for what it was doing to the water quality of the area. The man behind it was a close friend of the Governor at that time and nothing could stop him from doing whatever he wanted to do.

Hundreds of rural people in Northwest Arkansas came up with polluted wells and when the rural people wouldn't work in the conditions of those chicken plants for the kind of wages being paid, thousands of people from Mexico were brought in to do the jobs.

The poultry company of course, became the biggest in the world and the Governor became President. I remember hearing him talk of his concern for water pollution and the environment and wonder why no one ever mentioned the War Eagle and the Kings. He never gave the water of Northwest Arkansas a second thought.

But maybe it doesn't make any difference. Maybe it's all a hopeless cause anyway. With the kind of numbers we have today, is there really any hope to keep water clean, and streams and lakes pristine? When there are twice as many people even than we have today, how are we going to have any resources left? Survival of the masses may claim our timber and wildlife just because we have to produce huge numbers of cows and chickens and hogs to feed everyone. I was born in a day and time when there were only a fraction of the people we have today in this nation. We didn't have traffic jams or illegal immigrants. Life was hard but the land was bountiful and clean. I think I would have chosen that because I loved the outdoors so much, but realistically will future generations make that kind of choice? Of course not. Those of us who thought about saving the rivers and the forests in a natural setting once talked of future generations but I look at the generations coming on and the things they value and I realize that they probably could not care less if there are smallmouth in the rivers or giant oaks on Ozark ridgetops. This is a generation buying it's clean water in bottles from stores. Do you know how unbelievable that would have been to someone 50 years ago? Buying water!!!!!!

I'm too old to give a new generation advice but I will say that I have seen nature work and I know what happens when any species grows to levels greater than the land will hold. Get ready! A day of reckoning will come if and when we overpopulate the earth and begin to destroy it. Nature will retaliate and win in the end, and in a time when this book is long gone and forgotten, I believe there will be oak trees growing where there is concrete and pavement today and rivers running where giant dams now stand.

You and I may not see it happen but I also believe our nation may have hard times ahead just because of the way we now see things and the kind of heroes we have and the kind of leaders we saw come about in the recent decades. I have noticed that much of our nation believes that what was once right is now wrong and what was wrong is now right. What we fear nowadays is a prayer in a school, or the ten commandments posted where someone might see them.

We accept things called alternate lifestyles and individual choices regardless of what those choices and lifestyles are. Television sets teach us what is normal and good, and Hollywood dictates that we accept anything and everything. Stand for nothing... allow anything!

But there is much good yet about our country. We have made such great advances in relieving suffering and everywhere I go I see good people of all ages clinging to those values and traditions which made our country great. Mostly, these gentle, loving and good people are found in rural areas and small cities and towns in the Midwest. Don't look for them in the major cities of the east and west. Good people exist there too but they are being swallowed up by a new attitude of prospering with no thought to how it is done and ignoring basic beliefs which our forefathers thought were so important when our nation was young.

We have a cancer in places like New York and Los Angeles and Chicago and San Francisco and Boston and Washington, and cancer has a way of spreading. Sometimes though I can be out on a river or lake in the Ozarks or deep in the woods somewhere, and I can see that the Creator still has a plan for things that isn't one bit different than it was 200 years ago. There, it is still as He made it to be... unchanging and perfect. And I am thankful that at 82 years of age, I can still find it.

Velma and I live now in the Ozarks of southern Missouri near Pittsburg, only a stones throw from the Pomme de Terre Lake. And I still guide float-fishermen on the Niangua and the Gasconade. No, they aren't the rivers they once were but they still have some smallmouth and the bluffs and sycamores still stand guard over flowing water. And I caught a nine-pound and eight-pound large-mouth bass only a couple of years past from Truman lake, just north of me. I know there's a few ten-pounders there and I figure to get one that size or bigger in the next year or so. Truman is my kind of lake, undeveloped and uncrowded and with so much flooded timber it's tough on big boats.

I still guide bass fishermen there in my small boat, back away from the bass-masters and lunker-busters in the small coves which they don't often find or can't get to in their big boats. If you leave the lakes to those people on weekends and get out in the middle of the week, you can still fish with some solitude.

I go back and trotline for white catfish on Beaver Lake every now and then. The bass fishing there is really poor, as it on as is Tablerock...too much pollution and too much pressure and too many people for the resource. But my favorite lake is still Bull Shoals. It has somehow escaped the overwhelming pressure the other two have and I think its because it has never had the development. Much of Bull Shoals is still a timbered watershed without a lakeside home in sight. It won't stay that way, I don't suppose.

It still has better than average bass fishing, some big walleye and catfish as well. I get there as often as possible, especially in the spring. Pomme de Terre itself is over-developed and too crowded for me, and the water quality is going downhill, but it has some of the biggest channel catfish I have ever seen. While trotline fishing I've caught a dozen or so above 15 pounds and one 25 pounder back in the spring a few years ago. That's the biggest channel cat I have ever taken and I think there are bigger ones yet.

My nephew and I caught some nice flathead the past few years too. There have been several in the was a 40 pound class and one weighing 52. I figure we'll we'll beat that this year or next. Of course I may have to cut back on my garden a little. Those 500 tomato plants last year were just too many for a man who has serious fishing to do in the spring. I may only plant 400 this spring, and maybe increase the beans and cucumbers.

I guess that's always been my problem, so much to do and only 24 hours in the day. I get started early out of bed every morning about 4:30 or 5:00 , and always in bed by midnight if I'm not fishing. People ask me the secret of my good health and longevity, and that's part of it...four or five hours of sleep every night unless I'm fishing or catching frogs. Nothing else is worth staying up for. I don't drink and I have cut back on my cigars to about one or two a week. I can't afford the darn things. Maybe I am so healthy because I keep my weight down to around 130 to 140 pounds, just like when I was a paratrooper. I don't eat much, and I eat healthy, lots of pie and cake and fish. And I don't argue much with Velma, another key to staying healthy!

Really, I don't feel very old. I can do anything now that I could do 40 years ago. I can paddle a boat all day, load it and unload it on top of my pick-up rack, seine minnows and set trotlines and still outrun all these young women who are after me. I look forward to the coming of each new season and I figure on catching bigger fish tomorrow than I caught yesterday. That's important because I know lots of people who like to eat fish and I have to get enough for all of them.

God has blessed me with a great life. He has blessed me with a wonderful wife and good health and lots of friends to give fish to. Someone once said that you could count your true friends on the fingers of one hand. Not me. I have so many I can't count them all and I figure on making more friends...lots more! It's going to take lots of fish. But I keep my trotlines set and baited and I go float-fishing just about as much as I ever did. You oughta come and go with me sometime.

Epilogue

In September of 2002, just before the outbreak of the war in Iraq, Norten Dablemont was invited to Ft. Campbell, Kentucky to meet with officers of the 101st Airborne Division, and receive a distinguished service medal in a ceremony honoring him and his service to his country in World War II. He and his wife Velma spent two days there, as guests of the 101st Airborne, and Norten had no idea whom he was to meet.

The Commander of the entire Division, Major General, David Petraeus, invited Norten and his wife into his office for more than one hour, where he and his aides talked with him about his experiences during training at Fort Benning Georgia and in Europe. General Petraeus had Norten sign one of his "Ridge-Runner" books for him, and in turn signed a book for Norten to take back home. He wrote..."With admiration and the utmost respect for all that you did, to a great paratrooper from an awesome Screaming Eagle Unit and the greatest generation."

The awards ceremony took place later that afternoon, and as Norten was greeted with about three dozen officers who stood and saluted him as he entered. Later that day he was given a tour of the complex, and met and talked with young soldiers who were in training and many who would soon be deployed to Iraq.

He also toured the museum at Ft. Campbell, and got to see again close up and personal one of the big transport airplanes that carried World War II paratroopers in training and in combat. His picture was placed on the "Wall of Fame" at the Division headquarters, where he was the 79th 101st Airborne paratrooper so honored.

Norten and Velma with
Major General David Petraeus

Photos from the Past

Newlyweds 1962

Norten & Velma 1996

- Bronze star, top left;
- Purple heart, top center
- French Liberation medal, top right
- Paratrooper wings, center
- Combat Infantry Badge, bottom center

Photos from the Past

Table Rock Largemouth 1970

Greers Ferry Bass 1964

Truman Largemouth 1999

Bull Shoals Bass 1958

Photos from the Past

52 lb.
Flathead Cat
Pomme de Terre
Lake 1999

25 lb.
Channel Cat
Pomme de Terre
Lake Spring of
2000